Laura

THE LOVES AND HEROINES OF THE POETS.

EDITED BY

RICHARD HENRY STODDARD.

NEW YORK:
DERBY & JACKSON, 498 BROADWAY,
MDCCCLXI.

W. H. Tinson, Stereotyper.

Geo. Russell & Co., Printers.

PREFACE.

My object in this volume is to present specimens of English love-poetry, especially that which is, or seems to be, addressed to particular women—"the Loves and Heroines of the Poets," and to give, as concisely as possible, all that is known concerning them. I begin with the three great Italian poets, because I conceive their love-sonnets—above all, Petrarch's—to have been the models after which our early poets shaped their amorous fancies. Wyatt and Surrey, even when most original, are little better than imitators of Petrarch. Indeed, so notorious was this fact in the generation immediately succeeding them, that they were said to have travelled in Italy, and to have brought their art from thence. I trace the course of love-poetry in English Literature from Wyatt to the poets of the present day. I have gone over the ground carefully, and have selected what seemed to me the best specimens for a volume of this kind. The poetic literature of the age of Elizabeth and the times of Charles the First and Second, is largely represented. I have arranged my materials chronologically, giving the dates at which the different poems were written, wherever they were known, or at least the dates and names of the volumes in which, as far as I could ascertain, they were first printed: where there was nothing positive to guide me, I have arranged them conjecturally. When I could consult the early editions, I have done so, although I have not always followed their readings, when a later one seemed better. I have chosen authenticated portraits, when I could obtain them, in preference to ideal heads, greatly, I think, to the permanent value of the work. For some of the best of these illustrations I am indebted to my friend Barry, who has copied from their scarce originals the portraits of Laura, Beatrice, and Geraldine, and drawn from his imagination the ideal heads of Shakespeare's Mistress, Burns's Highland Mary, and Coleridge's Genevieve.

R. H. S.

CONTENTS.

DANTE ALIGHIERI.

	PAGE		PAGE
BEATRICE	1	"So noble and so modest"	4
"To every captive soul"	2	"He the perfection sees"	5
"Young, tender, noble maiden"	2	"A lady piteous, and of tender age"	5
"O Love! since while I gazed"	3	"Say, pilgrims, ye who go"	7
"Tell me, kind ladies"	3	"Remembrance had brought back"	8
"All thoughts that meet"	3	"Farewell, alas! farewell"	8
"Many the times"	4		

FRANCESCO PETRARCH.

LAURA	10	He envies every spot that she frequents	18
He confesses the vanity of his passion	12	To the sun	18
He blames love for wounding him	13	To love, on Laura walking abroad	19
On the portrait of Laura	13	He leaves Vaucluse	19
Recollections of love	14	Hearing no tidings of her	20
He is bewildered	14	He desires to die	20
Could he but see the house of Laura	15	He prays that she will be near him	21
Though he is unhappy	15	He would die of grief	21
To the fountain of Vaucluse	16	Since her death, he has ceased to live	22

TORQUATO TASSO.

LEONORA	23	"Ah me! it is a cruel destiny"	30
"If love his captive bind"	28	"One day my lady at a balcony"	31
"I see the anchored bark"	28	"Three high-born dames it was my lot"	31
"Thou, in thy unripe years"	29	"She, who a maiden, taught me, love"	32
"Till Laura comes, who now"	29	"Anger a champion bold"	32
"I saw two ladies once"	29	"Wandering Ulysses"	32
"'Twas night and underneath"	30	"A hell of torment"	33

SIR THOMAS WYATT.

NOTE	34	The lover curseth the time	37
The lover prayeth his offered heart	35	An earnest suit to his unkind mistress	38
The lover forsaketh his unkind love	35	The forsaken lover consoleth himself	38
The lover despairing to attain	36	The lover laments the death of his love	39
The deserted lover consoleth himself	36		

HENRY HOWARD.

EARL OF SURREY.

GERALDINE	41	Request to his love	44
Description and praise of his love	43	A praise of his lady	44
Complaint	43		

JOHN HARRINGTON.

	PAGE		PAGE
Isabella Markham	46	A sonnet	48
To Isabella Markham	46		

THOMAS WATSON.

Sonnet	49	Sonnet	50
Sonnet	50		

THOMAS LODGE.

Rosador's sonneto	52	"Now I find thy looks were feignéd"	54
The shepherd's sorrow	53		

JOHN LILY.

"Cupid and my Campaspe played"	56	"O yes, O yes, if any maid"	56

SIR PHILIP SYDNEY.

Stella	58	"Because I breathe not love"	62
"In truth, O love"	59	"Dear! why make you"	62
"You that do search"	60	"Highway, since you"	63
"Because I oft"	60	"Stella! think not that"	63
"Come Sleep, O Sleep!"	61	"O happy Thames! that did'st"	63
"Having this day my horse"	61	"Unhappy sight, and hath she"	64
"In martial sports I had"	61		

ROBERT GREENE.

Doron's description of Samela	65	The praise of Fawnia	66

SAMUEL DANIEL.

Delia	67	"When men shall find"	69
"Unto the boundless ocean"	67	"Read in my face"	70
"Fair is my love, and cruel"	68	"Beauty, sweet love"	70
"Restore thy tresses"	68	"I must not grieve my love"	70
"Look, Delia, how w' esteem"	68	"And whither, poor forsaken"	71
"But love whilst that thou may'st"	69		

MICHAEL DRAYTON.

Note	72	"Why should your fair eyes"	74
"Bright star of beauty"	72	"Clear Ankor"	74
"'Mongst all the creatures"	72	"You, best discerned"	75
"I hear some say"	73	"Since there's no help"	75
"Dear, why should you command"	73	An hymn	75

CHRISTOPHER MARLOW.

The passionate shepherd to his love . . . 78

EDWARD VERE.

EARL OF OXFORD.

The shepherd's commendation of his nymph . . . 80

EDMUND SPENSER.

	PAGE		PAGE
NOTE	82	"The glorious image"	86
"New Year, forth looking"	83	"Like as an huntsman"	86
"The merry cuckoo"	83	"The famous warriours"	86
"This holy season"	84	"Fresh Spring, the herald"	87
"While guile is this"	84	"Being myself captivéd"	87
"Mark when she smiles"	85	"Since I did leave"	88
"When my abode's"	85	"Like as the culver"	88

B. GRIFFIN.

"Fair is my love"	89	"Sweet stroke, (so might I thrive)"	90
"I have not spent"	89	"Weep now no more, mine eyes"	90

WILLIAM SHAKESPEARE.

NOTE	91	"The forward violet"	96
"So is it not with me"	93	"My mistress' eyes"	97
"My glass shall not persuade me"	94	"How oft, when thou, my music"	97
"Weary with toil I haste"	94	"Thine eyes I love"	97
"How careful was I"	95	"When my love swears"	98
"That time of year"	95	"O call me not to justify"	98
"How like a winter"	95	"O me! what eyes hath love"	99
"From you have I been absent"	96	"Canst thou, O cruel"	99

SIR WALTER RALEIGH.

The silent lover	100	His love admits no rival	101

SIR EDWARD DYER.

To Phillis, the fair shepherdess 103

NICHOLAS BRETON.

A pastoral of Phillis and Coridon	104	Coridon's supplication to Phillis	105

FULKE GREVILE.

LORD BROOKE.

Of his Cynthia	107	Myra's inconstancy	108

FRANCIS DAVISON.

Of his lady's weeping	110	His farewell	111
His sighs and tears are bootless	110		

BEN JONSON.

Song	112	To Celia	114
Song	113	A celebration of Charis	115
To Celia	113	His discourse with Cupid	116
To the same	114	Claiming a second kiss by desert	117

WILLIAM ALEXANDER.

EARL OF STIRLING.

	PAGE		PAGE
Aurora	119	"Now when the Siren sings"	120
"I swear, Aurora"	119	"I dreamed, the nymph"	121
"If that so many brave men"	120	"Ah, thou (my love) wilt lose"	121

SIR ROBERT AYTON.

On love	122	Song	124
On a woman's inconstancy	123	Song	125

THOMAS HEYWOOD.

Song	126	"Ye little birds that sit and sing"	127

WILLIAM BROWNE.

"Shall I tell you whom I love"	128	"Welcome, welcome do I sing"	129

WILLIAM DRUMMOND.

Note	131	"Are these the flowery banks"	133
"In my first years"	131	"Alexis here she stayed"	134
"O sacred blush"	132	"How many times"	134
"Trust not, sweet soul"	132	"Sweet soul, which in"	135
"Slide soft, fair Forth"	132	"Sweet spring, thou turn'st"	135
"She whose fair flowers"	133		

JOHN DONNE.

Note	136	The relic	141
Song	138	The anniversary	142
The sun-rising	140		

FRANCIS BEAUMONT.

The indifferent	143	Secrecy protested	144

JOHN FLETCHER.

"Go, happy heart"	145	To the blest Evanthe	146
Song	146	Ode	147

GEORGE WITHER.

A love song	148	"Shall I, wasting in despair"	151

SIR HENRY WOTTON.

The Queen of Bohemia	153	To his mistress, the Queen of Bohemia	155

THOMAS RANDOLPH.

PAGE
To one admiring herself in a looking-glass . . . 156

WILLIAM HABINGTON.

CASTARA . . . 158
To Castara . . . 159
To Castara . . . 159
To the spring . . . 160
To Castara . . . 160
To Seymors . . . 161
To Castara . . . 161
To Castara . . . 162
Love's anniversary . . . 162
To Castara . . . 163
To roses . . . 163
Upon Castara's departure . . . 164

SIR WILLIAM DAVENANT.

Song . . . 165
Song . . . 166

JOHN MILTON.

NOTE . . . 167
"Fair lady! whose harmonious name" 168
"As on a hill-top rude" . . . 168
To Charles Deodati . . . 168
"Lady! it cannot be" . . . 169
"Enamoured, artless, young" . . . 169
On his deceased wife . . . 170

THOMAS CAREW.

CELIA . . . 171
Song . . . 171
Song . . . 172
To his jealous mistress . . . 173
Ungrateful beauty threatened . . . 173
Parting, Celia weeps . . . 174
A prayer to the wind . . . 174
Song . . . 175

JAMES GRAHAME.

MARQUIS OF MONTROSE.

My dear and only love, I pray . . . 177

EDMUND WALLER.

SACCHARISSA . . . 182
At Penshurst . . . 184
Song . . . 185
To Amoret . . . 186

SIR JOHN SUCKLING.

NOTE . . . 188
"'Tis now, since I sat down before" . 188
Song . . . 190
Sonnet I. . . . 190
Sonnet II. . . . 191
Song . . . 192

SIR FRANCIS KINASTON.

To Cynthia, on her changing . . . 193

SYDNEY GODOLPHIN.

PAGE
Song 195

WILLIAM CARTWRIGHT.

A sigh sent to his absent love 197
To Chloe 198
A valediction 199

JAMES SHIRLEY.

To Odelia 200
Taking leave 201
The kiss 202

RICHARD CRASHAW.

Out of the Italian 203
The dew no more shall weep 205

ABRAHAM COWLEY.

Note 206
The spring 206
Clad all in white 208
The chronicle 209

ROBERT HERRICK.

Cherry ripe 212
The rock of rubies 212
The captived bee 213
To daisies 214
The night-piece 214
Upon Julia's hair 215
To Anthea 215
To Anthea 215
Being once blind 216
To the western wind 216
To his maid Prue 216
Upon Prue, his maid 217
To Electra 217
To Myrrha, hard-hearted 217
Upon the loss of his mistresses 218

RICHARD LOVELACE.

Lucasta 219
To Lucasta 220
To Lucasta 221
To Althea 222
Song 223
The scrutiny 224
Elinda's glove 225

JOHN CLEVELAND.

Upon Phillis, walking in a morning before sun-rising 226

PATRICK CAREY.

"Fair beauties! if I do confess" 228

THOMAS STANLEY.

The deposition 230
The tomb 231
The exequies 232

SIR EDWARD SHERBURNE.

Change defended 233
Love once, love ever 234

HENRY KING.

The surrender 235
The legacy 236
The exequy 238
Song 241

SIR ROBERT HOWARD.

To the inconstant Cynthia 242

CHARLES SACKVILLE.

EARL OF DORSET.

Song 243

SIR CHARLES SEDLEY.

Song 246
Song 247
Song 248
To Chloris 248
Song 249
Song 250

ANDREW MARVELL.

The gallery 251
The picture of T. C. 253
The mower to the glow-worms . . . 254

JOHN WILMOT.

EARL OF ROCHESTER.

Song 255
Song 256

CHARLES COTTON.

To Chloris 257
Estrennes 258

JOHN DRYDEN.

Song 260
Song to a fair young lady 261

JOHN NORRIS.

Superstition 262

THOMAS PARNELL.

	PAGE		PAGE
Note	264	Song	265
Song	264		

MATTHEW PRIOR.

Note	266	A song	267
An ode	266	Song	268
To Chloe weeping	267		

ALEXANDER POPE.

Note	269	Epistle to Mrs. Martha Blount	273
Epistle to Mrs. Teresa Blount	271		

JOHN BYROM.

Note	274	A pastoral	274

NICHOLAS ROWE.

Note	277	Colin's complaint	277

JONATHAN SWIFT.

Note	280	To Stella	287
Stella's birth-day	285	Stella's birth-day	288
Stella's birth-day	286		

ALLAN RAMSAY.

The lass of Patie's mill	291	"Gi'e me a lass with a lump of land"	293
O'er the moor to Maggie	292		

JAMES THOMSON.

To Fortune	294	To her I love	295

HENRY CAREY.

Note	296	Sally in our alley	296

CHARLES HAMILTON.

LORD BINNING.

The shepherd's complaint 299

WILLIAM SHENSTONE.

	PAGE		PAGE
NOTE	301	A pastoral ballad: III. Solicitude	305
A pastoral ballad: I. Absence	301	" " IV. Disappointment	307
" " II. Hope	303		

LORD LYTTLETON.

NOTE	309	An irregular ode	309

MARK AKENSIDE.

Song 311

NATHANIEL COTTON.

The fireside 313

ROBERT BURNS.

NOTE	316	O, were I on Parnassus' hill	325
My Nanie, O	320	To Mary in heaven	326
Mary Morrison	321	Song	327
Rigs o' barley	322	Bonnie Lesley	328
Song	323	Highland Mary	329
I love my Jean	324		

WILLIAM LISLE BOWLES.

NOTE	331	Approach of summer	332
In memoriam	331	Absence	332

WILLIAM COWPER.

NOTE	333	To Mary	335

THOMAS CAMPBELL.

NOTE	337	Caroline, Part II.	339
Caroline, Part I.	337	Song	340

CHARLES LAMB.

NOTE	341	"Was it some sweet device"	342
"Methinks how dainty sweet"	341	"When last I roved"	342

WILLIAM GIFFORD.

The grave of Anna 343

SAMUEL TAYLOR COLERIDGE.

	PAGE		PAGE
Love	345	Something childish, but very natural	348

WILLIAM WORDSWORTH.

"Strange fits of passion"	349	"She was a phantom of delight"	351
"She dwelt among"	350	A complaint	352
"I travelled among"	350		

JAMES MONTGOMERY.

Hannah . . . 353

ROBERT BLOOMFIELD.

Rosy Hannah	356	To his wife	357

ALLAN CUNNINGHAM.

Bonnie Lady Ann	359	The poet's bridal-day song	360

JAMES HOGG.

Gang to the brakens wi' me . . . 363

PERCY BYSSHE SHELLEY.

NOTE	365	To ——	371
To Harriet	366	Lines to an Indian air	371
To Mary	366	To ——	372
Love's philosophy	370		

LORD BYRON.

MARY CHAWORTH	373	To Thyrza	379
LADY BYRON	374	Fare thee well	381
THE COUNTESS GUICCIOLI	376	The dream	383
Maid of Athens	378	Stanzas to the Po	389

LORD THURLOW.

"Since all I see"	392	"I think you are the prophet"	393
"Thy love is to my heart"	392	"I called you, and too well"	393

THOMAS MOORE.

Believe me, if all	394	Lesbia hath a beaming eye	395
I saw thy form	394		

SIR WALTER SCOTT.

	PAGE		PAGE
Nora's vow	397	Song	398

LEIGH HUNT.

To my wife	399	"Jenny kissed me"	399

JOHN KEATS.

Note	400	"I cry you mercy"	403
"As Hermes once"	402	To ——	404
"The day is gone"	403		

JOHN CLARE.

The first of May 406

CHARLES WOLFE.

Song 408

REGINALD HEBER.

Lines 410

WILLIAM CULLEN BRYANT.

"O fairest of the rural maids"	412	The future life	413

EDWARD COATES PINKNEY.

A health 415

GEORGE DARLEY.

"Sweet in her green dell" 417

ALFRED TENNYSON.

Lady Clara Vere de Vere	418	"Come into the garden, Maud"	420

BRYAN WALLER PROCTOR.

"BARRY CORNWALL."

	PAGE		PAGE
The poet's song to his wife	423	Hermione	425
Golden-tressed Adelaide	424	Marian	425

WILLIAM MOTHERWELL.

JEANIE MORRISON	426	Jeanie Morrison	427

THOMAS HOOD.

Fair Ines	430	Lines	431

NATHANIEL PARKER WILLIS.

To her who has hopes for me 432

PHILIP PENDLETON COOKE.

Florence Vane 434

OLIVER WENDELL HOLMES.

La grisette 436

WINTHROP MACKWORTH PRAED.

Josephine 438

JAMES RUSSELL LOWELL.

"My Love, I have no fear"	440	In absence	441
"I can not think that thou"	440	"I thought our love at full"	441

ROBERT BROWNING.

The lost mistress	442	Evelyn Hope	443

WALTER SAVAGE LANDOR.

"One year ago my path"	445	"Little it interests me how"	446
"I love to hear that men"	445	"The maid I love ne'er thought of me"	447
"Have I this moment"	446	"Often I have heard it said"	447
"Here, ever since you went abroad"	446		

RICHARD MONCKTON MILNES.

PAGE

" The words that trembled " 448

EDGAR ALLAN POE.

To Helen . . . . 450 | To one in paradise 452

GEORGE MEREDITH.

Love in the valley 453

THOMAS BUCHANAN READ.

A glimpse of love 456

MATTHEW ARNOLD.

Excuse 457

ROBERT LYTTON BULWER.

"OWEN MEREDITH."

Song 459

WILLIAM ALLINGHAM.

Lovely Mary Donnelly 461

HENRY WADSWORTH LONGFELLOW.

Hiawatha's wooing 463

BAYARD TAYLOR.

The mystery 467

GEORGE HENRY BOKER.

" Nay, not to thee " . . . . . 469 | " I do assure thee, love " 470
" Where lags my mistress " . . . 469 | " I will not blazon forth " 471
" Your love to me appears " . . . 470 | " All the world's malice " 471

JOHN GREENLEAF WHITTIER.

PAGE
Maud Muller 472

COVENTRY PATMORE.

By the sea 477

THOMAS BAILEY ALDRICH.

Palabras Cariñosas 480

LOVES AND HEROINES.

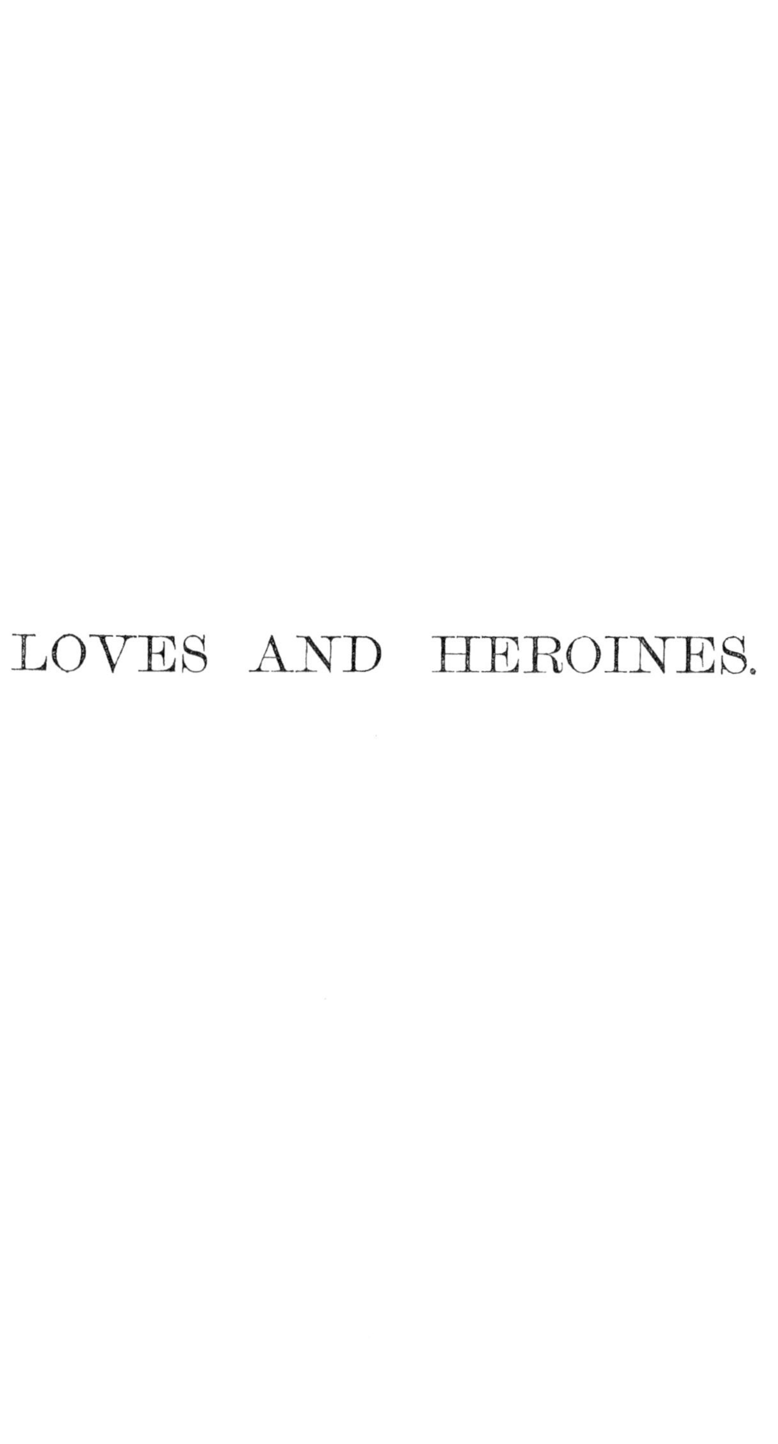

DANTE ALIGHIERI.

1265—1321.

BEATRICE.

All that is known of Beatrice may be summed up in a few words. She was the daughter of Folco Portinari, a wealthy citizen of Florence, in which city she was born in 1266. Dante saw her for the first time in 1274, at a banquet in her father's house. It was a May-day festival, and she appeared in a blood-red dress. They were mere children, both being in their ninth year, still they were old enough to love: at least Dante was, for at the sight of Beatrice he was seized with a sudden passion for her. At the end of nine years they met again. She was walking in the street at the time, between two ladies, and was clothed in white. Dante trembled at her approach, and would have shrank away, but she saw him, and he was rooted to the ground. She saluted him graciously, and he was in the seventh heaven of love. The next time that he saw her was at church. She sat at a distance from him, on a line with another lady, who intercepted his loving looks. He was accused of loving this lady, and for the sake of Beatrice, whose rank seems to have been superior to his own, he favored the mistake, and pretended to be enamoured of her. He wrote a poem on sixty of the loveliest women in the city, and do what he would to the contrary, the name of Beatrice always came the ninth in the list. She made a journey to a distant part of the country, and during her absence he feigned to be in love with another, which offended her so when she heard of it, that she would not salute him on her return. The next thing we learn is that she is married. The date of her marriage is not given, but it must have been before the 15th of January, 1287, for on that day her father drew up a will, in which she and her husband, Simone dei Bardi, were mentioned. The death of her father two years later, and her excessive grief on that occasion, closed the book of her life. She died on the 9th of June, 1290.

This is a meagre account certainly, but it is all that Dante's commentators, for five hundred years, have been able to wring from the Past, and much of this would, doubtless, have escaped them but for Dante himself, so stormy were the times in which he lived. A few years after her death he collected the poems that he had written upon her, and published them with a biographical and critical commentary. This work, which he called "THE NEW LIFE" (*Vita Nuova*), was followed by another called "THE BANQUET" (*Convito*), and at length by the celebrated "*Divina Commedia*," in both of which she is introduced, or rather her name is, for the Beatrice of the "*Divina Commedia*" and "THE BANQUET" is an embodiment of Philosophy and Religion, and not the Beatrice Portinari, whom Dante loved in his youth, and remembered with fondness in his age. The following extracts are from "THE NEW LIFE." The version used is that of Lyell. (London, 1845.)

To every captive soul and gentle heart,
  Into whose sight the present song shall come,
  Praying their thoughts on what it may portend,
  Health in the name of Love, their sovereign lord.
A third part of the hours had almost past
  Which show in brightest lustre every star,
  When suddenly before me Love appeared,
  Whose essence to remember gives me horror.
Joyful Love seemed, holding within his hand
  My heart, and in his arms enfolded lay
  Madonna sleeping, in a mantle wrapt.
Then waking her, he with this burning heart
  Courteously fed her, and in fear she ate.
  That done, I saw him go his way in tears.

Young, tender, noble maiden, since you see
  That Love, with your consent, has made me yours,
  And that for you I burn, and waste, and pine,
  O let me not expire without reward.
O Love! dear lord, haply thou disbelievest
  How hard she is, and cruel is my pain;
  For in thy generous heart there must exist
  The will to succor my fidelity.
And, lady, every pain would be removed
  If hope were realized, and I were blest
  With joy which Love solicits you to grant.
O help me, then, Madonna, ere I die;
  I live for that alone, and if denied,
  A corse you soon will see me at your feet.

O Love! since while I gazed, you struck this heart
 A blow so dire, that every nerve is pained,
 In pity, lord, afford it some relief,
 So that the sorrowing spirit may revive.
For see you not these mournful eyes consume
 In weeping, through extremity of woe,
 Which brings me to the verge of death so near,
 That my escape is barred on every side.
See, lady, what a load of grief I bear;
 And hearken to my voice, how weak it is
 With calling still for pity, and your love:
Yet if it be your pleasure, gentle lady,
 That by this grief my heart should waste away,
 Behold your servant humble and resigned.

Tell me, kind ladies, have you seen, of late,
 That gentle creature who my life consumes?
 To you I own, that if she do but smile,
 My thoughts dissolve as snow before the sun.
Hence on my heart such cruel blows arrive
 That they would seem to threaten me with death:
 Kind ladies, then, wherever ye may see her,
 If you by chance should meet her on your way,
O rest with her awhile for pity's sake,
 And with humility make known to her
 That my life bears for her the weight of death:
And if in mercy she will comfort me,
 And ease the mind deep laden with my griefs,
 O send to me, far distant, the glad news.

All thoughts that meet within my mind expire,
 Fair jewel, when I come to gaze on you;
 And when I am near you, I hear Love exclaim,
 O flee, if thy destruction thou would'st shun!
The countenance the heart's complexion wears,
 Which panting seeks support where'er it can;

And through the intoxication of great fear,
The very stones, methinks, cry out, Die, die!
He sins who can behold me, then, unmoved,
Nor comfort gives to the affrighted soul,
At least in showing that he pities me
For the distress occasioned by your scorn,
Which is apparent in the deadly hue
Of these sad eyes, that fain would close in death.

Many the times that to my memory comes
The cheerless state imposed on me by Love;
And o'er me comes such sadness, then, that oft
I say, Alas, was ever fate like mine!
For Love assaulteth me so suddenly,
That life itself almost abandons me;
One spirit alone escapes alive, and that
Is left, fair lady, for it speaks of you.
At length I make an effort for relief,
And so, all pale and destitute of power,
I come to gaze on you, in hope of cure:
And if I raise the eyes that I may look,
A trembling at my heart begins, so dread,
It makes the soul take flight from every vein.

So noble and so modest doth appear
My lady when she any one salutes,
That every tongue becomes in trembling mute,
And none dare raise the eyes to look on her.
Robed in humility she hears her praise,
And passes on with calm benignity;
Appearing not a thing of earth, but come
From heaven, to show mankind a miracle.
So pleasing is the sight of her, that he
Who gazes feels a sweetness reach the heart
That must be proved or cannot be conceived.
And from her countenance there seems to flow

A spirit full of mildness and of love,
Which says forever to the soul, O sigh.

He the perfection sees of every grace,
Who doth my lady among ladies see.
They who partake her company are bound
To render thanks to heaven for boon so fair.
Her beauty, too, has virtue so benign,
That it excites no envy in another,
But a resolve to walk like her, arrayed
In gentleness, fidelity, and love.
Her look on all things sheds humility,
And makes her not alone delight the eye,
But everything through her receiveth honor.
And she so perfect is in all her acts,
That no one can recall her to the mind
Who doth not sigh amid the sweets of Love.

A lady, piteous, and of tender age,
Richly adorned with human gentleness,
Stood where I oft was calling upon death;
And seeing that my eyes were full of grief,
And listening to the folly of my words,
Was moved by fear to weep with bitterness.
And other ladies, who were kindly drawn
To notice me, through her who wept with me,
Removed her from my side,
And then approached, to rouse me by their voice.
And one said, Sleep no more!
Another said, Why thus discomfort thee?
Then fled the strange distressing fantasy,
As I was calling on my lady's name.
So indistinct and mournful was my voice,
And broken so by anguish and by tears,
That in my heart I only heard the name:
And with a countenance o'erspread with shame,

So strongly it had mounted to my face,
Love made me turn to them distractedly;
And such was my complexion to the sight,
That it led others to discourse of death.
O let us comfort him,
Said each one to the other tenderly.
And oft they said to me,
What hast thou seen that has unmanned thee thus?
And when I had regained some strength, I said,
Ladies, to you I will relate the whole.
Whilst I lay pondering on my ebbing life,
And saw how brief its tenure and how frail,
Love wept within my heart, where he abides;
For my unhappy soul was wandering so,
That sighing heavily, it said, in thought,
My lady too most certainly shall die.
Such consternation then my reason seized,
That my eyes closed through fear, and heaviness;
And scattered far and wide
My spirits fled, and each in error strayed:
Imagination then,
Bereft of understanding and of truth,
Showed me the forms of ladies in distress,
Who said to me, Thou die'st, ay, thou shalt die.
Many the doubtful things which next I saw,
While wandering in imagination's maze;
I seemed to be I know not in what place,
And to see ladies pass with hair all loose,
Some weeping, and some uttering loud laments,
Which darted burning grief into the soul.
And then methought I saw a thickening veil
Obscure the sun, and night's fair star appear,
And sun and star both weep;
Birds flying through the dusky air drop down,
And earth itself to shake;
And then appeared a man, feeble, and pale,
Saying, What dost thou here? Hast thou not heard?
Dead is thy lady, she who was so fair.

I raised mine eyes, oppressed and bathed in tears,
And saw what like a shower of manna seemed,
And angels re-ascending up to heaven;
And spread before them was a little cloud,
Behind which they were chanting loud, Hosanna.
And if they more had added, you should hear.
Then Love thus spoke: Concealment here shall end;
Come now and see our lady on her bier.
Deceitful fancy then
Conducted me to see my lady dead:
And while I gazed, I saw
That ladies with a veil were covering her;
And in her face humility so true
There was, it seemed to say, I am in peace.
So humble in my sorrow I became,
Seeing such humbleness in her expressed,
That I exclaimed, O Death! I hold thee sweet;
Thou must be deemed, henceforth, a gentle thing,
Since thou hast been united to my lady,
And pity thou should'st have, and not disdain:
Behold me so desirous to be one
Of thine, that I resemble thee in faith:
Come, for the heart entreats thee.
Then, all sad rites being o'er, I went my way;
And when I was alone,
I said, with eyes upraised to realms above;
Blesséd is he who sees thee, beauteous soul!
'Twas then you called to me, thanks to your love.

Say, pilgrims, ye who go thus pensively,
Musing, perchance, on things that distant are,
Come ye from land and men so far away,
As by your outward mien ye show to us,
That ye weep not when passing through the midst
Of the dejected city, in her woe,
Seeming as persons who have never heard
Of the calamity oppressing her?

If ye remain and have the will to hear,
This heart of sighs assures me ye will then
Share in our grief, and weep when ye depart.
The desolate city mourns her Beatrice,
And in the tale that may be told of her
Is virtue to force every one to weep.

Remembrance had brought back into my mind
That gentle lady for whom Love doth weep,
At the same instant that his influence
Drew your regard to what engagéd me.
Love, who perceived her presence in the mind,
Had waked from slumber in my wretched heart,
And calling to the sighs, exclaimed, Go forth!
They heard, and each departed mournfully.
Weeping they issued from my breast, with voice
Of grief, which often brings to the sad eyes
The bitter tears of my unhappiness.
But those which issued forth with greater pain
Went saying, Noble intellect, this day
Completes the year since thy ascent to heaven.

Farewell, alas! farewell those tresses bright,
From whence the hills around
Drew and reflected tints of shining gold;
Farewell the beauteous cheer, and glances sweet,
Implanted in my heart
By those fair eyes on that thrice happy day;
Farewell the graceful bloom
Of sparkling countenance;
Farewell the soft sweet smile,
Disclosing pearls of snowy white, between
Roses of vermeil hue, throughout the year;
Why without me, O Death,
These hast thou carried off in beauty's spring?

Farewell the endearing mirth, and wise reserve,
The welcome frank and sweet;
The prudent mind, and well-directed heart;
Farewell the beautiful, meek, proud disdain,
Which strengthened my resolve
All baseness to detest, and greatness love.
Farewell desire, the child
Of beauty so abounding;
Farewell the aspiring hope,
Which every other made me leave behind,
And rendered light to me Love's heaviest load;
These hast thou broken, Death,
As glass and me to living death exposed.

Lady, farewell! Of every virtue queen,
Goddess, for whom, through Love,
I have refused all others to adore;
Farewell! What column, of what precious stone,
On earth were worthy found
To build thy fane, and lift thee high in air?
Farewell! thou vessel filled
With nature's miracles.
By fortune's evil turn
High on the rugged mountains thou wast led,
Where death has closed thee in the cruel tomb;
And of my eyes hath formed
Two fountains wearied with incessant tears.

Farewell! and O unpardonable Death,
Pity these sorrowing eyes, and own at least,
That till thy hand destroy me,
Endless should be my cry, Alas! Farewell!

FRANCESCO PETRARCH.

1304—1374.

LAURA.

As Petrarch was at his devotions in the church of Santa Clara of Avignon, on the morning of the 6th of April, 1327, he saw a lady near him in a green mantle sprinkled with violets. Her youth and beauty impressed him; he forgot the sacredness of the time and place, and, giving himself up to the feelings which she inspired, was soon in love with her. He awoke from his reverie when the service was over, and finding her gone, followed her and learned her name. It was Laura de Sade. She belonged to a noble Provençal family, and was the wife of Hugo de Sade, a rich citizen of Avignon. This last intelligence, which ought to have discouraged Petrarch, does not seem to have affected him much, for he was a priest, and could not have married her, even if she had been free. We are not told what her emotions were when she discovered, as she soon did, that she was loved by another than her husband, but considering the character of that gentleman, who had a habit of scolding her until she wept, it could not have grieved her very deeply. She did not exactly encourage Petrarch, for she was a good wife and mother, with a keen eye to the proprieties of life; but neither did she discourage him. As long as he kept within bounds, she admitted him to her society and friendship, but when he forgot himself, as he sometimes did, and devoured her with passionate looks, her virtue took the alarm, and she withdrew; or, if that were not always practicable, covered her face with a veil. Their meetings were probably few and far between, or we should have heard more of them from Petrarch, who was as communicative in all that related to her as he well could be. It was her absence that made him a lover and a poet; in her presence he was a silent madman. He poured out his soul in song in the solitude of his study, ransacking heaven and earth for metaphors and comparisons. Her eyes were stars, her hair sunbeams. She was the Air; she was the Laurel. Her smile was his life, her frown his death. He ran up and down the gamut of passion as no poet before had ever done, and made himself and Laura famous, wherever the Italian language was spoken or read. Some of his friends doubted the reality of his passion, as they well might after reading some of his glittering conceits; others even questioned the existence of Laura, greatly to Petrarch's surprise. "As to Laura," he wrote to the Bishop of Lombes, who bantered him on the subject, in 1335, "would to Heaven that she were only an imaginary personage, and my passion for her only a pastime! Alas! it is a madness which it would be difficult and painful to feign for any length of time; and what an extravagance it would be to affect such a passion! One may counterfeit illness by action, by voice, and by manner, but no one in health can give himself the true air and complexion of disease. How often have you yourself been witness of my paleness and my sufferings! I know very well that you speak only in irony; it is your favorite figure of speech; but I hope that time will cicatrize the wounds of my spirit, and that Augustine, whom I pretend to love, will furnish me with a defence against a Laura, who does not exist." He tried to divert his mind by travel, and made an extensive tour, but to no purpose; he returned to Avignon as he left it—the lover of Laura. He then took a mistress, as was the fashion of clerical gentlemen of his time, but neither her blandishments, nor the children she bore him, effected his cure. At last he determined to remove from Avignon. He bought a cottage at Vaucluse, a wild and picturesque spot near the windings of the Sorgue. Here he repaired with his books, and devoted himself to study and meditation. He commenced his great Latin epic, "Africa," and planned a history of Rome from Romulus down to Titus Vespasian. He was a happy man as long as he kept at work, but the moment he became idle his thoughts reverted to Laura. He found some consolation in the society of his friends, but unfortunately they seldom came to see him, for travelling even short distances was difficult then. He threw aside his books, and took to rambling about Vaucluse—the very worst thing he could have done, for one day in the course of his rambles he found himself at Avignon. It was accidental, no doubt—a piece of absent-mindedness on his part, but somehow it did not end here, for a few days after he found himself at Avignon again, and this time in the neighborhood of Laura's house! She met him in the street, coquette that she was, and whispered, "Petrarch, you are tired of loving me." Tired of loving her—it was impossible! And to prove it he went home and wrote her a sonnet. About this time he was visited by Simone Martini, of Sienna, a pupil of Giotto, famous for taking spirited likenesses. He sat to Simone for his portrait, and was so much pleased with it when it was finished, that he persuaded him to paint him a miniature of Laura, which miniature he ever after carried about with him.

Twenty years passed, and his passion was unabated. Laura had aged somewhat in that time, having borne her husband ten children; but it made no difference to Petrarch. Her wise chastity towards him had kept her young in his eyes. He had enjoyed no favours, not even a kiss: the most that she had granted him was her hand, which she had once permitted him to hold for a little while!

In 1347, he made up his mind to depart for Italy. "Before he left Avignon, he went to take leave of Laura. He found her at an assembly which she often frequented. 'She was seated,' he says, 'among those ladies who are generally her companions, and appeared like a beautiful rose surrounded with flowers smaller and less blooming.' Her air was more touching than usual. She was dressed perfectly plain, and without pearls or garlands, or any gay colour. Though she was not melancholy, she did not appear to have her wonted cheerfulness, but was serious and thoughtful. She did not sing as usual, nor speak with that voice that used to charm every one. She had the air of a person who fears an evil not yet arrived. 'In taking leave of her,' says Petrarch, 'I sought in her looks for a consolation of my sufferings. Her eyes had an expression which I had never seen in them before. What I saw in her face seemed to predict the sorrows that threatened me.'"

They parted, never to meet again, for in the following spring Laura died of the plague. Her death shocked Petrarch, who made a note of it in his Virgil, which is now in the Ambrosian Library at Milan. "Laura, illustrious for her virtues, and for a long time celebrated in my verses, for the first time appeared to my eyes on the 6th of April, 1327, in the church of St. Clara, at the first hour of the day. I was then in my youth. In the same city, and at the same hour, in the year 1348, this luminary disappeared from our world. I was then at Verona, ignorant of my wretched situation. Her chaste and beautiful body was buried the same day, after vespers, in the church of the Cordeliers. Her soul returned to her native mansion in Heaven. I have written this with a pleasure mixed with bitterness, to retrace the melancholy remembrance of 'MY GREAT LOSS.' This loss convinces me that I have nothing now left worth living for, since the strongest cord of my life is broken. By the grace of God I shall easily renounce a world where my hopes have been vain and perishing. It is time for me to fly from Babylon, when the knot that bound me to it is untied."

There are many portraits of Laura, but none, I fancy, that can be relied upon as being authentic. The one that I have selected comes the nearest to the descriptions of her by Petrarch and his biographers. It is from Tomasini's "PETRARCHA REDIVIVVS"—an old Latin work on the love of Petrarch and Laura, and is probably a copy of the portrait painted by Simone of Sienna. So, at least, I gather from the rather obscure text.

TO LAURA IN LIFE.

HE CONFESSES THE VANITY OF HIS PASSION.

Ye who in rhymes dispersed the echoes hear
Of those sad sighs with which my heart I fed
When early youth my mazy wanderings led,
Fondly diverse from what I now appear,
Fluttering 'twixt frantic hope and frantic fear,
From those by whom my various style is read,
I hope, if e'er their hearts for love have bled,
Not only pardon, but perhaps a tear.
But now I clearly see that of mankind
Long time I was the tale: whence bitter thought

And self-reproach with frequent blushes teem:
While of my frenzy, shame the fruit I find,
And sad repentance, and the proof, dear-bought,
That the world's joy is but a flitting dream.

CHARLEMONT.

HE BLAMES LOVE FOR WOUNDING HIM ON A HOLY DAY.

'Twas on the morn, when heaven its blessèd ray
In pity to its suffering master veiled,
First did I, Lady, to your beauty yield,
Of your victorious eyes th' unguarded prey.
Ah! little recked I that, on such a day,
Needed against Love's arrows any shield;
And trod, securely trod, the fatal field:
Whence, with the world's, began my heart's dismay.
On every side Love found his victim bare,
And through mine eyes transfixed my throbbing heart;
Those eyes which now with constant sorrows flow:
But poor the triumph of his boasted art,
Who thus could pierce a naked youth, nor dare
To you in armour mailed even to display his bow!

WRANGHAM.

ON THE PORTRAIT OF LAURA, PAINTED BY SIMON MEMMI.

Had Policletus seen her, or the rest
Who, in past time, won honour in this art,
A thousand years had but the meaner part
Shown of the beauty which o'ercame my breast.
But Simon sure, in Paradise the blest,
Whence came this noble lady of my heart,
Saw her, and took this wondrous counterpart,
Which should on earth her lovely face attest.
The work, indeed, was one, in heaven alone
To be conceived, not wrought by fellow-men,

Over whose souls the body's veil is thrown:
'Twas done of grace; and failed his pencil when
To earth he turned our cold and heat to bear,
And felt that his own eyes but mortal were.

MACGREGOR.

RECOLLECTIONS OF LOVE.

That window where my sun is often seen
Refulgent, and the world's at morning hours;
And that where Boreas blows, when winter lowers,
And the short days reveal a clouded scene;
That bench of stone, where, with a pensive mien,
My Laura sits, forgetting beauty's powers;
Haunts where her shadow strikes the walls or flowers,
And her feet press the paths or herbage green:
The place where Love assailed me with success;
And spring, the fatal time that, first observed,
Revives the keen remembrance every year;
With looks and words, that o'er me have preserved
A power no length of time can render less,
Call to my eyes the sadly-soothing tear.

PENN.

HE IS BEWILDERED AT THE UNEXPECTED ARRIVAL OF LAURA.

As Love his arts in haunts familiar tried,
Watchful as one expecting war is found,
Who all foresees, and guards the passes round,
I in the armour of old thoughts relied:
Turning, I saw a shadow at my side
Cast by the sun, whose outline on the ground
I knew for hers, who (be my judgment sound)
Deserves in bliss immortal to abide.
I whispered to my heart, Nay, wherefore fear?
But scarcely did the thought arise within,

Than the bright rays in which I burn were here.
As thunders with the lightning-flash begin,
So was I struck at once both blind and mute,
By her dear dazzling eyes and sweet salute.

MACGREGOR.

COULD HE BUT SEE THE HOUSE OF LAURA, HIS SIGHS MIGHT REACH HER MORE QUICKLY.

If, which our valley bars, this wall of stone,
From which its present name we closely trace,
Were by disdainful nature rased, and thrown
Its back to Babel and to Rome its face:
Then had my sighs a better pathway known
To where their hope is yet in life and grace:
They now go singly, yet my voice all own,
And, where I send, not one but finds its place.
There too, as I perceive, such welcome sweet
They ever find, that none returns again,
But still delightedly with her remain.
My grief is from the eyes, each morn to meet—
Not the fair scenes my soul so longed to see—
Toil for my weary limbs and tears for me.

MACGREGOR.

THOUGH HE IS UNHAPPY, HIS LOVE REMAINS EVER UNCHANGED.

My sixteenth year of sighs its course has run,
I stand alone, already on the brow
Where Age descends: and yet it seems as now
My time of trial only were begun.
'Tis sweet to love, and good to be undone;
Though life be hard, more days may Heaven allow
Misfortune to outlive; else Death may bow
The bright head low my loving praise that won.
Here am I now, who fain would be elsewhere;

More would I wish, and yet no more I would;
I could no more, and yet did all I could:
And new tears born of old desires declare
That still I am as I was wont to be,
And that a thousand changes change not me.

MACGREGOR.

TO THE FOUNTAIN OF VAUCLUSE—CONTEMPLATIONS OF DEATH.

Clear, fresh, and dulcet streams,
Which the fair shape, who seems
To me sole woman, haunted at noon-tide;
Fair bough, so gently fit,
(I sigh to think of it,)
Which lent a pillow to her lovely side;
And turf, and flowers bright-eyed,
O'er which her folded gown
Flowed like an angel's down;
And you, O holy air and hushed,
Where first my heart at her sweet glances gushed;
Give ear, give ear, with one consenting,
To my last words, my last and my lamenting.

If 'tis my fate below,
And Heaven will have it so,
That Love must close these dying eyes in tears,
May my poor dust be laid
In middle of your shade,
While my soul, naked, mounts to its own spheres.
The thought would calm my fears,
When taking, out of breath,
The doubtful step of death;
For never could my spirit find
A stiller port after the stormy wind;
Nor in more calm, abstracted bourne,
Slip from my travailed flesh, and from my bones outworn.

Perhaps, some future hour,
To her accustomed bower
Might come the untamed, and yet the gentle she;
And where she saw me first,
Might turn with eyes athirst,
And kinder joy to look again on me;
Then, O the charity!
Seeing amidst the stones
The earth that held my bones,
A sigh for very love at last
Might ask of Heaven to pardon me the past:
And Heaven itself could not say nay,
As with her gentle veil she wiped the tears away.

How well I call to mind,
When from those boughs the wind
Shook down upon her bosom flower on flower;
And there she sat, meek-eyed,
In midst of all that pride,
Sprinkled and blushing through an amorous shower.
Some to her hair paid dower,
And seemed to dress the curls,
Queenlike, with gold and pearls;
Some, snowing, on her drapery stopped,
Some on the earth, some on the water dropped;
While others, fluttering from above,
Seemed wheeling round in pomp, and saying, "Here reigns
Love!"

How often then I said,
Inward, and filled with dread,
"Doubtless this creature came from Paradise!"
For at her look the while,
Her voice, and her sweet smile,
And heavenly air, truth parted from mine eyes;
So that, with long-drawn sighs,

I said, as far from men,
"How came I here, and when?"
I had forgotten; and alas!
Fancied myself in heaven, not where I was;
And from that time till this, I bear
Such love for the green bower, I cannot rest elsewhere.

LEIGH HUNT.

HE ENVIES EVERY SPOT THAT SHE FREQUENTS.

O bright and happy flowers and herbage blessed,
On which my lady treads! O favoured plain,
That hears her accents sweet, and can retain
The traces by her fairy steps impressed!
Pure shrubs, with tender verdure newly dressed,
Pale amorous violets, leafy woods, whose reign
Thy sun's bright rays transpierce, and thus sustain
Your lofty stature, and umbrageous crest;
O thou, fair country, and thou, crystal stream,
Which bathes her countenance and sparkling eyes,
Stealing fresh lustre from their living beam;
How do I envy thee those precious ties!
Thy rocky shores will soon be taught to gleam
With the same flame that burns in all my sighs.

WROTTESLEY.

TO THE SUN, WHOSE SETTING HID LAURA'S DWELLING FROM HIS VIEW.

O blessèd Sun! that sole sweet leaf I love,
First loved by thee, in its fair seat, alone,
Bloometh without a peer, since from above
To Adam first our shining ill was shown.
Pause we to look on her! Although to stay
Thy course I pray thee, yet thy beams retire;
Their shades the mountains fling, and parting day
Parts me from all I most on earth desire.

The shadows from yon gentle heights that fall,
Where sparkles my sweet fire, where brightly grew
That stately laurel from a sucker small,
Increasing, as I speak, hide from my view
The beauteous landscape and the blessèd scene,
Where dwells my true heart with its only queen.

MACGREGOR.

TO LOVE, ON LAURA WALKING ABROAD.

Here stand we, Love, our glory to behold,
How, passing Nature, lovely, high, and rare!
Behold! what showers of sweetness falling there!
What floods of light by heaven to earth unrolled!
How shine her robes, in purple, pearls, and gold,
So richly wrought, with skill beyond compare!
How glance her feet! her beaming eyes how fair
Through the dark cloister which these hills enfold!
The verdant turf, and flowers of thousand hues
Beneath yon oak's old canopy of state,
Spring round her feet to pay their amorous duty.
The heavens, in joyful reverence, cannot choose
But light up all their fires, to celebrate
Her praise, whose presence charms their awful beauty.

MERIVALE.

HE LEAVES VAUCLUSE, BUT HIS SPIRIT REMAINS THERE WITH LAURA.

The loved hills where I left myself behind,
Whence ever 'twas so hard my steps to tear,
Before me rise; at each remove I bear
The dear load to my lot by Love consigned.
Often I wonder inly in my mind,
That still the fair yoke holds me, which despair
Would vainly break, that yet I breathe this air;
Though long the chain, its links but closer bind.

And as a stag, sore struck by hunter's dart,
Whose poisoned iron rankles in his breast,
Flies, and more grieves the more the chase is pressed,
So I, with Love's keen arrow in my heart,
Endure at once my death and my delight,
Racked with long grief, and weary with vain flight.

MACGREGOR.

HEARING NO TIDINGS OF HER, HE BEGINS TO DESPAIR.

Still do I wait to hear, in vain still wait,
Of that sweet enemy I love so well:
What now to think or say I cannot tell,
'Twixt hope and fear my feelings fluctuate.
The beautiful are still the marks of fate;
And sure her worth and beauty most excel:
What if her God have called her hence, to dwell
Where virtue finds a more congenial state?
If so, she will illuminate that sphere
Even as a sun: but I—'tis done with me!
I then am nothing, have no business here!
O cruel absence! why not let me see
The worst? My little tale is told, I fear;
My scene is closed ere it accomplished be.

MOREHEAD.

TO LAURA IN DEATH.

HE DESIRES TO DIE, THAT HIS SOUL MAY BE WITH HER, AS HIS THOUGHTS ALREADY ARE.

E'en in youth's fairest flower, when Love's dear sway
Is wont with strongest power our hearts to bind,
Leaving on earth her fleshly veil behind,
My life, my Laura, passed from me away;
Living, and fair, and free from our vile clay,

From heaven she rules supreme my willing mind:
Alas! why left me in this mortal rind
That first of peace, of sin that latest day?
As my fond thoughts her heavenward path pursue,
So may my soul, glad, light, and ready be
To follow her, and thus from troubles flee.
Whate'er delays me as worst loss I rue:
Time makes me to myself but heavier grow:
Death had been sweet to-day three years ago!

MACGREGOR.

HE PRAYS THAT SHE WILL BE NEAR HIM AT HIS DEATH, WHICH HE FEELS APPROACHING.

Go, plaintive verse, to the cold marble go,
Which hides in earth my treasure from these eyes,
There call on her who answers from yon skies,
Although the mortal part dwells dark and low.
Of life how I am wearied make her know,
Of stemming these dread waves that round me rise:
But, copying all her virtues I so prize,
Her track I follow, yet my steps are slow.
I sing of her, living or dead, alone,
(Dead, did I say? She is immortal made!)
That by the world she should be loved, and known.
O in my passage hence may she be near,
To greet my coming that's not long delayed;
And may I hold in heaven the rank herself holds there!

NOTT.

HE WOULD DIE OF GRIEF, WERE SHE NOT SOMETIMES TO CONSOLE HIM WITH HER PRESENCE.

To that soft look which now adorns the skies,
The graceful bending of the radiant head,
The face, the sweet angelic accents fled,

That soothed me once, but now awake my sighs:
O when to these imagination flies,
I wonder that I am not long since dead!
'Tis she supports me, for her heavenly tread
Is round my couch when morning visions rise!
In every attitude how holy, chaste!
How tenderly she seems to hear the tale
Of my long woes, and their relief to seek!
But when day breaks she then appears in haste
The well-known heavenward path again to scale,
With moistened eye and soft expressive cheek!

MOREHEAD.

SINCE HER DEATH HE HAS CEASED TO LIVE.

Death cannot make that beauteous face less fair,
But that sweet face may lend to death a grace;
My spirit's guide, from her each good I trace;
Who learns to die, may seek his lesson there.
That Holy One, who not his blood would spare,
But did the dark Tartarean bolts unbrace;
He, too, doth from my soul death's terrors chase:
Then welcome, death, thy impress I would wear.
And linger not, 'tis time that I had fled;
Alas! my stay hath little here availed,
Since she, my Laura blest, resigned her breath:
Life's spring in me hath since that hour lain dead,
In I her lived, my life in hers exhaled,
The hour she died I felt within me death!

WOLLASTON.

Leonora.

TORQUATO TASSO.

1544—1595.

LEONORA.

EARLY in the autumn of 1565, Tasso left the University of Bologna, where he had been for three years, studying poetry and philosophy, to enter the service of Cardinal Luigi d'Este, who was at that time in Ferrara. He arrived at Ferrara in October, and found the city alive with preparations for the approaching marriage of Duke Alphonso the Second with the Archduchess Barbara of Austria, daughter of the Emperor Ferdinand the First. The appearance of the bride elect, on the 31st of October, ushered in a series of magnificent entertainments, balls, tournaments, etc., which lasted an entire week. We are not told what part Tasso took in them (it could scarcely have been a prominent one, he was so newly arrived at court), but we know that it appealed strongly to his imagination, ever on the alert for the picturesque and the gorgeous. The death of Pius the Fifth terminated the festivities, and Cardinal Luigi departed for Rome to assist in the election of a new Pope: as the presence of Tasso was not necessary at that ceremony, he remained at Ferrara. Already a favourite with the Duke and his sister, the Princess Lucretia, he was now introduced to the Princess Leonora, who was just recovering from a long illness. She received him graciously, and waiving her rank in his behalf, admitted him to her favour and intimacy. Various reasons have been assigned for this condescension on her part—such as his youth and beauty, the elegance of his mind and manners—but the strongest one was undoubtedly her fondness for an art, in which he had already attained a reputation. The fact of his being a poet, levelled, as it should have done, the barriers of rank and custom, and opened the way to her friendship.

It is not known at what time Tasso began to look upon the Princess Leonora with the eyes of love, for the whole subject is wrapt in profoundest mystery; but circumstances render it probable that it was not long after his introduction to her. There was from the first a marked difference between the poems which he addressed to her, and those which he addressed to her sister; the one being complimentary—the fanciful effusions of a young poet, celebrating a noble lady, because it was expected of him; the others breathing the most ardent attachment—the passionate but guarded confessions of a lover. How the Princess

Leonora received these poetical declarations from Tasso—whether she saw and encouraged his passion from the beginning, or only perceived it when it was too late, can never be known. That she returned it I have no doubt. Not openly, of course, for that would have been fatal to both; but in secret, by something in her voice or look—a tone meant only for his ear, a glance imperceptible to all but him—there were a thousand ways of showing him that he was dear, as every lover divines. It was necessary that they should exercise the greatest caution, and they did so, for their love remained unsuspected for years; indeed, that of Leonora was never suspected, for she died and made no sign. Tasso was equally discreet, for he not only addressed the sonnets which he wrote to her to other ladies, but paid his court to them with a great show of reality. There were two ladies in Ferrara with whom he was supposed to be in love—Laura Peperara, and Lucretia Bendidio. He met the former at Mantua, about a year before he entered the service of Cardinal Luigi; the latter, I believe, was a native of Ferrara, where she was celebrated for her beauty and accomplishments. She had two poets in her train, Pigna, the Duke's secretary, and Guarini, the author of "PASTOR FIDO." Tasso entered the lists (possibly at the suggestion of Leonora), and undertook on her account to support at the Academy, against every disputant, fifty amorous Theses or Conclusions. The trial, which lasted three days, redounded to his credit for ingenuity and learning.

The marriage of the Princess Lucretia to the Duke of Urbino, in the spring of 1570, and her subsequent departure from Ferrara, made a blank in the life of Leonora, into which Tasso insensibly glided. He read his great epic, "JERUSALEM DELIVERED," to her as it was composed, for the benefit of her advice and criticism, and wrote her a great number of sonnets, canzones, and madrigals. He was assiduous in his attentions till autumn, when he was obliged to quit Ferrara, and accompany Cardinal Luigi to France. A difficulty with his Eminence while in that country, led him to return to Ferrara, and enter the service of Duke Alphonso. He was allowed a pension of fifteen crowns of gold a month, and exempted from any particular duty, that he might have leisure to attend to his studies. He set himself diligently to the completion of his epic, polishing what he had already written, and adding many new episodes. Growing at length weary of his application, he resolved to rest his mind on a new theme; and taking advantage of a visit of the Duke to Rome, he composed in two months his celebrated pastoral, "AMINTA." It was represented on the Duke's return, in the spring of 1573, and greeted with unbounded applause. Its reputation reached the ears of the Duchess of Urbino, who invited Tasso to her palace at Pesaro, to read it to her. The intrigues of his enemies during his absence from Ferrara embittered his mind, and laid the foundation of that singular suspicion which ever after marked his character. We are ignorant of the means they employed against him, but they must have been powerful ones, for they seem for a time to have prejudiced the mind of Leonora. They may have discovered, or at least guessed, the secret of his love. That one of the most active and talented of them, Guarini, did so, is evident from the paper war which ensued between him and Tasso. Tasso opened the campaign with an angry madrigal, addressed to Leonora, whose preference for Guarini, who had somehow insinuated himself into her good graces, was extremely distasteful to him. Guarini answered with another, assuming to speak the language of Leonora, and told him that his love and hate were alike indifferent to her. Whether he wrote this by her authority, or volunteered it, because he thought it would please her and annoy Tasso, cannot be ascertained. Indeed, the whole affair is shrouded in obscurity. That it pained Tasso exceedingly, is evident from the following extract from a letter, which he wrote Leonora from Casteldurante, where he spent the summer of 1573, with the Duchess of Urbino: "I have not written to your highness for so many months, rather from want of subject than of will, since now that an occasion, however small, presents itself for paying my respects, it is not neglected. I send your highness, then, a sonnet, which may be allowed to recall me to your memory, inasmuch as it seems to me I promised to send you everything new of mine. It will not be found at all to resemble those beautiful ones your highness is now accustomed oftentimes to hear, but is as poor in wit and art as I am in fortune; nor in my present state can anything better be expected of me. I send it, however, trusting that, whether good or bad, it will have the effect I desire. But, that you may not deem me so vacant of thought as to give love a place in my bosom, know that it was not written for myself (or perhaps it might have been better), but at the request of a poor lover, who, being for a while in anger with his lady, and now unable to hold out longer, is obliged to surrender and beg for mercy." That Tasso himself was the poor lover, and Leonora the lady alluded to, it does not require much penetration to discover.

The next event of consequence in the life of Tasso (I pass over his poetical labors, as not essential to an understanding of his love for Leonora), was the opening of his apartments with false keys, in the autumn of 1576. The person who was guilty of this treachery was named Maddalo, but in what relation he stood to Tasso has never been settled. Some of Tasso's biographers say that he was a servant, others that he was a notary of his acquaintance; but the earliest of them, Manso, declares that he was "a friend with whom he had everything in common, even to his very thoughts, and from whom he had not altogether concealed the secret of his loves." He entered Tasso's apartments during a visit of the latter to Modena, and opened a box, or chest, in which he kept his private papers. Tasso discovered his baseness on his return, and meeting him in the palace court-yard, taxed him with it; but instead of apologizing, or attempting to clear himself of the charge, the villain gave him the lie. Tasso struck him in the face. He did not resent the blow at the time, but slunk away and collected his three brothers, and then waylaid the poet as he was walking alone in the piazza of the palace. They attacked him suddenly from behind, but he wheeled about, and drawing his sword, soon put them to flight.

This circumstance troubled Tasso greatly—why, we can only conjecture. There must have been more in it than meets the eye—more than the mere rummaging of a box of letters from his friends—or it would not have unsettled his mind, as it did. Maddalo must have obtained some secret connected with Leonora, some proof of Tasso's love, and possibly of hers, which, if divulged, would ruin both. Could it have been her letters to him? I suspect so. And what strengthens this suspicion in my mind is, that immediately after the rupture with Maddalo, Tasso visited Leonora at Consaldoli. The ostensible object of this visit was to divert his melancholy, but its real object, I am persuaded, was to concert measures for their safety, in case their love should come to the knowledge of the Duke.

We reach now one of the saddest periods of Tasso's life—a period which perplexes all his biographers, as well, indeed, it may. I mean the beginning of his insanity, for that he was, or feigned to be, insane, shortly after his visit to Leonora, there can be no doubt. He was in a pitiable state of mind, depressed, melancholy, restless. He fancied that he had been denounced to the Inquisition; that he had been accused of treachery to the Duke; that his enemies were seeking to poison him: there was no end to his phantasies. On the evening of the 17th of June, 1577, he drew his dagger on a domestic in the apartments of the Duchess of Urbino. He was arrested and imprisoned, not so much for the offence, which the Duke was willing to overlook, as because he seemed to need restraint. He petitioned to be released, declaring that he was not mad, though he feared he should be, if he were compelled to remain in confinement; above all, he begged to be restored to his apartments. The Duke granted his request, and sent the ablest physicians to attend him. Their prescriptions, or his recovered freedom, appeared to calm him, and he accompanied the Duke to his beautiful villa at Belriguardo, but relapsing in a few days, he was sent back to Ferrara, and confined in the convent of Saint Francis. He contrived to escape on the 20th of July, and, disguised as a shepherd, took his way to the kingdom of Naples. On arriving at Sorrento he sought out the dwelling of his sister Cornelia, and presented himself to her as a messenger from her brother Tasso, whose life, he said, was in danger, and who implored her assistance. He told his story so pathetically that she fainted, whereupon he threw off his disguise, and revealed himself, being fully satisfied of her affection. He remained at Sorrento until his health began to improve, when he was seized with a desire to return to Ferrara. He wrote to the Duke, asking to be restored to his favour, and to the possession of his books and manuscripts, and to the Duchess of Urbino and the Princess Leonora, urging them to second his request with their influence. Leonora alone replied, and in such terms as showed that she could not help him. This, however, did not discourage him, but rather increased his determination to return. He departed from Sorrento in November, in defiance of the advice of his friends, and on arriving at Rome proceeded at once to the house of the Duke's agent. Still harping on his manuscripts and the Duke's favour, he persuaded Cardinal Albano to write to Alphonso on his behalf. Six weeks passed before an answer was received, and then it was anything but satisfactory. Alphonso said nothing about restoring Tasso to his favour, or what little he did say was too vague to mean anything, but he promised to send his manuscripts. Tasso waited a month or two patiently, and the manuscripts being still withheld, made up his mind to return to Ferrara at all hazards. He was influenced in this decision, Manso says, by the letters which he received from Leonora. The Duke consented to his return on certain conditions, viz.: that he would admit that his suspicions of persecution had no other origin than his melancholy whims: that he would promise to be quiet and submissive; and, above all, that he would be doctored for his infirmity. "If he thinks to make disturbance and use such expressions as he has done heretofore, we mean not to call him to account, but if he will not allow himself to be cured, to expel him immediately from our dominions, with orders never to return." Tasso accepted these conditions, and started for Ferrara in March or April, 1578. His reception was courteous but cool. The Duke admitted him to his presence as formerly, but did not restore his manuscripts, and took no interest in his poetry. On the contrary, it seemed to offend him. "It was his wish," Tasso afterwards wrote to the Duke of Urbino, "that I should aspire to no praise of genius or fame in letters, but that amid ease, luxury, and pleasure, I should lead an effeminate, idle, and slothful life." The Duke and his creatures were ashamed to clothe this degrading wish in words, so they communicated it to Tasso by signs, which he feigned not to understand. "These signs," he wrote, "still continuing on their part, though not on mine, I attempted to speak to the Duchess, and Madame Leonora, but found audience always denied me; and many times, without necessity or respect, I was forbidden by the porters to enter their apartments. I sought to talk to the Duke about it, but he abhorred the subject; I spoke to his confessor, but in vain." He fled again from Ferrara, and wandered to Padua, Mantua, and Venice, and finally to Pesaro and Turin. From the latter place he wrote to Cardinal Albano, and entreated him to use his influence with the Duke, "that his highness may be content, not only to restore my books, writings, and other trifles, but to give me also some hundreds of crowns, that I may finish the work begun under his protection." The Cardinal wrote, and "his highness" being in good humor, for he was about to marry Margherita Gonzaga, daughter of Duke William of Mantua, consented that Tasso should come back, provided he would allow himself to be cured. He arrived at Ferrara on the 21st of February, 1579, and sought an audience of the Duke, but he was too busy to receive him, being entirely taken up with the ceremonies of his marriage. He turned his steps to the apartments of the Duchess of Urbino and the Princess Leonora, where a similar disappointment awaited him. The ministers and courtiers treated him with rudeness and inhumanity. No habitation had been assigned him, and he was obliged to seek temporary lodgings, now in one place, and now in another. He bore up under this neglect and indignity till the middle of March, when he was confined in the Hospital of Saint Anne, as a lunatic. The pretended cause of his confinement was abusive and injurious language towards the Duke and the whole house of Este; the probable cause, the discovery of his love for the Princess Leonora. My reasons for this supposition are various. First, the sagacity of the Duke, who must by this time have discovered the true cause of Tasso's persistent returns to Ferrara—an unconquerable desire to be near the person of Leonora; and, second, the length of Tasso's imprisonment—over seven years—a punishment utterly disproportioned to his supposed offence. My third reason is a tradition current in the days of Muratori, who heard it from Francesco Caretta, of Modena, an *élève* of Alessandro Tassoni, one of Tasso's contemporaries. It is to this effect: Tasso was one day at court near Alphonso and his sisters, and having occasion to come closer to the Princess Leonora, for the purpose of replying to some question which she had asked him, was so transported on the sudden by a more than poetical enthusiasm, that he kissed her. Whereupon the Duke, like a wise prince, turned to his courtiers, and said, "See what a heavy misfortune has befallen a great genius, who in a moment has become mad." This, the tradition says, was the cause of Tasso's imprisonment in the Hospital of Saint Anne.

I shall not pursue the subject further, having already made this note much longer than I intended, but refer the reader to Mr. Wilde's interesting work on "The Love, Madness and Imprisonment of Torquato Tasso," where he will find it treated at length.

An extract from the manuscript History of Ferrara, and I have done:

"On the 10th of February, 1581, died Madame Leonora, daughter of Duke Hercules II., who preferred a life of celibacy."

The accompanying portrait of Leonora is based on a medal of the time.

If Love his captive bind with ties so dear,
How sweet to be in amorous tangles caught!
If such the food to snare my freedom brought,
How sweet the baited hook that lured me near!
How tempting sweet the liméd twigs appear!
The chilling ice that warmth like mine has wrought!
Sweet, too, each painful unimparted thought!
The moan how sweet that others loathe to hear!
Nor less delight the wounds that inward smart,
The tears that my sad eyes with moisture stain,
And constant wail of blow that deadly smote.
If this be life—I would expose my heart
To countless wounds, and bliss from each should gain;
If death—to death I would my days devote.

London Magazine.

I see the anchored bark with streamers gay,
The beckoning pilot, and unruffled tide,
The south and stormy north their fury hide,
And only zephyrs on the waters play:
But winds and waves and skies alike betray;
Others who to their flattery dared confide,
And late when stars were bright sailed forth in pride,
Now breathe no more, or wander in dismay.
I see the trophies which the billows heap,
Torn sails, and wreck, and graveless bones that throng
The whitening beach, and spirits hovering round:
Still, if for woman's sake this cruel deep
I must essay, not shoals and rocks among,
But 'mid the Sirens, may my bones be found!

London Magazine.

Thou, in thy unripe years, wast like the rose,
    Which shrinketh from the summer dawn, afraid,
    And with her green veil, like a bashful maid,
Hideth her bosom sweet, and scarcely blows:
Or rather, (for what shape ever arose
    From the dull earth like thee,) thou did'st appear
    Heavenly Aurora, who, when skies are clear,
Her dewy pearls o'er all the country sows.
Time stealeth nought: thy rare and careless grace
    Surpasseth still the youthful bride when neatest,
Her wealth of dress, her budding blooming face;
    So is the full-blown rose for age the sweetest,
So doth the mid-day sun outshine the morn,
With rays more beautiful, and brighter born.

Anon.

Till Laura comes, who now, alas, elsewhere
    Breathes, amid fields and forests hard of heart,
    Bereft of joy I stray from crowds apart,
In this dark vale, 'mid grief and ire's foul air,
Where there is nothing left of bright or fair,
    Since Love has gone a rustic to the plough,
    Or feeds his flocks, or in the summer now
Handles the rake, now plies the scythe with care.
Happy the mead and valley, hill and wood,
    Where man and beast, and almost tree and stone,
Seem by her look with sense and joy endued!
    What is not changed on which her eyes e'er shone?
The country courteous grows, the city rude,
    Even from her presence or her loss alone.

Wilde.

I saw two ladies once, illustrious, rare;
    One a sad sun, her beauties at mid-day
    In clouds concealed; the other, bright and gay,
Gladdened, Aurora-like, earth, sea, and air.

One hid her light, lest men should call her fair,
And of her praises no reflected ray
Suffered to cross her own celestial way;
To charm, and to be charmed, the other's care.
Yet this her loveliness veiled not so well,
But forth it broke; nor could the other show
All hers, which wearied mirrors did not tell.
Nor of this one could I be silent, though
Bidden in ire; nor that one's triumphs swell,
Since my tired verse, o'ertasked, refused to flow.

WILDE.

'Twas night, and underneath her starry vest
The prattling Loves were hidden, and their arts
Practised so cunningly upon our hearts,
That never felt they sweeter scorn and jest:
Thousands of amorous thefts their skill attest,
All kindly hidden by the gloom from day;
A thousand visions in each trembling ray
Flitted around, in bright, false splendour dressed.
The clear, pure moon rolled on her starry way
Without a cloud to dim her silver light;
And high-born beauty made our revels gay,
Reflecting back on heaven beams as bright,
Which even with the dawn fled not away,
When chased the sun such lovely ghosts from night.

WILDE.

Ah me! it is a cruel destiny,
Which, envying, robs the world of thy clear voice,
And hence it is that men no more rejoice,
Impoverished in their greatest blessing—thee!
Its harmony, like some celestial wind,
Its bright and burning thoughts, like vestal fires,
Dispersed the clouds of sense from every mind,
And kindled honour, and divine desires.

It was too much for us to merit long;
    Enough your smile, and your serenest eyes
        That sacred joy inspired, and endless grace;
    For beautiful no more were Paradise,
Could men but hear the angel in your song,
        As they behold the angel in your face.

R. H. S.

One day my lady at a balcony
Alone was standing, when I chanced to stretch
My arm on hers; I straightway begged her pardon,
For I was fearful of offending her.
"Not by the placing of thy arm on mine,
But by withdrawing it, hast thou offended,"
She sweetly answered me. O happy words!
Dear little love-words, short, but sweet and courteous,
Courteous as sweet, affectionate as courteous!
If it were true and certain what I heard,
I shall be always seeking not t' offend thee,
Repeating the great bliss; but, my sweet life,
By all my eagerness therein, remember,
Where no offence is, there must be no vengeance!

Anon.

Three high-born dames it was my lot to see,
    Not all alike in beauty, yet so fair,
    And so akin in act, and look, and air,
That Nature seemed to say, "Sisters are we!"
I praised them all, but one of all the three
    So charmed me, that I loved her, and became
    Her bard, and sung my passion, and her name,
Till to the stars they soared past rivalry.
Her only I adored, and if my gaze
    Was turned elsewhere, it was but to admire
Of her high beauty some far-scattered rays,
    And worship her in idols, fond desire,
False incense hid; yet I repent my praise,
    As rank idolatry 'gainst Love's true fire.

Wilde.

She, who, a maiden, taught me, Love, thy woes,
    To-morrow may become a new-made bride,
Like, if I err not, a fresh-gathered rose,
    Opening her bosom to the sun with pride:
But him, for whom thus flushed with joy it blows,
    Whene'er I see, my blood will scarcely glide;
If jealousy my ice-bound heart should close,
    Will any ray of pity thaw its tide?
Thou only know'st. And now, alas! I haste
    Where I must mark that snowy neck and breast
By envied fingers played with and embraced:
    How shall I live, or where find peace or rest,
If one kind look on me she will not waste,
    To hint not vain my sighs, nor all unblest?

WILDE.

[This is the sonnet which Tasso sent to Leonora, from Casteldurante.]

Anger, a champion bold but warrior weak,
    Led me with feeble armour to the field,
    Against Love's bow and shafts blunt arms to wield,
And Freedom or Revenge in battle seek.
Fool that I was! what human arms avail
    In conflict with that torch of heavenly fire,
    Whose light alone turns anger to desire?
Peace, I implore, and own me rash and frail.
Mercy I beg, and my weak hands extend,
    And kneel, and bow, and bare my humble breast;
If fight I must, pity her aid shall lend,
    And win the palm for me, or death and rest:
If with my blood some tears of hers should blend,
    Defeat is triumph, and I perish blest.

WILDE.

Wandering Ulysses on the storm-vexed shore
    Lay amid wrecks, upon the sand scarce dry,
Naked and sad; hunger and thirst he bore,
    And hopeless gazed upon the sea and sky;

Where there appeared — so willed the Fates on high—
A royal dame to terminate his woe:
"Sweet fruits," she said, "sun-tinged with every dye,
My father's garden boasts; would'st taste them? Go!"
For me, alas! though shivering in the blast
I perish, a more cruel shipwreck mine,
Who from the beach, where famishing I'm cast,
Will point to royal roofs, for which I pine,
If 'tis not thou,—moved by my prayers at last?
What shall I call thee? Goddess! by each sign.

WILDE.

A hell of torment is this life of mine;
My sighs are as the Furies breathing flame;
Desires around my heart like serpents twine,
A bold, fierce throng no skill or art may tame.
As the lost race to whom hope never came,
So am I now, for me all hope is o'er;
My tears are Styx, and my complaint and shame
The fires of Phlegethon but stir the more.
My voice is that of Cerberus, whose bark
Fills the abyss, and echoes frightfully
Over the stream, dull as my mind, and dark:
In this alone less hard my fate may be,
That there poor ghosts are of foul fiends the mark,
While here an earthly goddess tortures me.

WILDE.

SIR THOMAS WYATT.

1503—1542.

IT is a disputed point among the biographers of Wyatt, whether his amatory poems were the result of a real attachment, or merely poetical exercises. Some maintain that they are Petrarchian studies; others consider them life-sketches, drawn from his heart, and coloured by his love for Anne Boleyn. The weight of proof should rest with the latter; but unfortunately there can be no proof in the case: there was none in the time of the parties themselves, and there can be none now. When Anne Boleyn fell into disfavour with her capricious and tyrannical husband, who was casting about for a way to elevate Jane Seymour in her place, she was charged with having been unfaithful to him, and it was whispered that she was guilty of criminal intercourse with Wyatt. So, at least, Hearne says, though no evidence of such a charge exists. It was not made at her trial, for Wyatt's name is said not to have been mentioned in it. Certain it is that Henry never for a moment believed it, for after her death, no man in England stood higher in his good graces than Wyatt. That Wyatt was intimate with Anne Boleyn, does not admit of a doubt. She was the cousin of his friend Surrey, and her brother, Lord Rochfort, and himself, were fast friends. He probably met her for the first time when she was maid of honour to Queen Katharine, and as they were both about the same age, with the same taste for music and poetry, it was natural that he should admire her, and write verses to her. That she admired him and his verses, even in her darkest days, is shown by the fragment of a letter, in the Cotton collection, written by Sir William Kingston, and containing an account of all that she said and did in the Tower. She retained Wyatt's sister about her person, as her favourite and confidential attendant, and shortly before laying her head on the block, gave her, as a memento, a little manuscript prayer-book, set in gold and black enamel. This relic was preserved for a long time in the Wyatt family, as was also the tradition of Wyatt's attachment to Anne Boleyn. They rebutted all aspersions on her character after her death, and one of them, in his younger years, gathered many particulars concerning her, to refute the slanders which were then afloat. All this proves nothing, I am aware; but weighed in connection with Wyatt's poems, by those who can read between the lines, it is pretty strong circumstantial evidence. For my own part, I believe that Wyatt, at one time, loved Anne Boleyn. My friend Boker, I see, is of the same opinion, for in his touching tragedy, "ANNE BOLEYN," he puts the following lines in the mouth of Wyatt:

> "O Anne, Anne,
> The world may banish all regard for thee,
> Mewing thy fame in frigid chronicles,
> But every memory that haunts my mind
> Shall cluster round thee still. I'll hide thy name
> Under the coverture of even lines,
> I'll hint it darkly in familiar songs,
> I'll mix each melancholy thought of thee
> Through all my numbers: so that heedless men
> Shall hold my love for thee within their hearts,
> Not knowing of the treasure."

Wyatt's poems were first published in 1557, fifteen years after his death, in a work called Tottel's Miscellany, the earliest collection of the kind in the language.

THE LOVER PRAYETH HIS OFFERED HEART TO BE RECEIVED.

How oft have I, my dear and cruel foe,
With my great pain to get some peace or truce,
Given you my heart; but you do not use
In so high things, to cast your mind so low.
If any other look for it, as you trow,
Their vain weak hope doth greatly them abuse:
And that I thus disdain, that you refuse;
It was once mine, it can no more be so.
If you it chafe, that it in you can find,
In this exile, no manner of comfort,
Nor live alone, nor where he is called resort;
He may wander from his natural kind.
So shall it be great hurt unto us twain,
And yours the loss, and mine the deadly pain.

THE LOVER FORSAKETH HIS UNKIND LOVE.

My heart I gave thee, not to do it pain,
But to preserve, lo, it to thee was taken.
I served thee, not that I should be forsaken;

But, that I should receive reward again,
I was content thy servant to remain;
And not to be repaid on this fashion.
Now, since in thee there is none other reason,
Displease thee not, if that I do refrain.
Unsatiate of my woe, and thy desire;
Assured by craft for to excuse thy fault:
But, since it pleaseth thee to feign default,
Farewell, I say, departing from the fire.
  For he that doth believe, bearing in hand,
  Plougheth in the water, and soweth in the sand.

THE LOVER, DESPAIRING TO ATTAIN UNTO HIS LADY'S GRACE, RELINQUISHETH THE PURSUIT.

Whoso list to hunt? I know where is an hind!
But as for me, alas! I may no more,
The vain travail hath wearied me so sore;
I am of them that furthest come behind.
Yet may I by no means my wearied mind
Draw from the deer; but as she fleeth afore,
Fainting I follow: I leave off therefore,
Since in a net I seek to hold the wind.
Who list her hunt, I put him out of doubt
As well as I, may spend his time in vain;
And graven with diamonds in letters plain,
There is written her fair neck round about:
  "Noli me tangere; for Cæsar's I am,
  And wild for to hold, though I seem tame."

THE DESERTED LOVER CONSOLETH HIMSELF WITH REMEMBRANCE THAT ALL WOMEN ARE BY NATURE FICKLE.

Divers doth use, as I have heard and know,
When that to change their ladies do begin,
To mourn, and wail, and never for to lynn;

Hoping thereby to 'pease their painful woe.
And some there be that when it chanceth so
That women change, and hate where love hath been,
They call them false, and think with words to win
The hearts of them which otherwhere doth grow.
But as for me, though that by chance indeed
Change hath outworn the favour that I had,
I will not wail, lament, nor yet be sad,
Nor call her false that falsely did me feed;
  But let it pass, and think it is of kind
  That often change doth please a woman's mind.

THE LOVER CURSETH THE TIME WHEN FIRST HE FELL IN LOVE.

When first mine eyes did view and mark
Thy fair beauty to behold,
And when my ears listened to hark
The pleasant words, that thou me told;
  I would as then I had been free
  From ears to hear, and eyes to see.
And when my lips 'gan first to move,
Whereby my heart to thee was known,
And when my tongue did talk of love
To thee, that hast true love down thrown;
  I would my lips and tongue also
  Had then been dumb, no deal to go.
And when my hands have handled aught
That thee hath kept in memory,
And when my feet have gone and sought
To find and get thee company,
  I would each foot a hand had been,
  And I each foot a hand had seen.
And when in mind I did consent,
To follow this my fancy's will,
And when my heart did first relent
To taste such bait, my life to spill,
  I would my heart had been as thine,
  Or else thy heart had been as mine.

AN EARNEST SUIT TO HIS UNKIND MISTRESS NOT TO FORSAKE HIM.

And wilt thou leave me thus?
Say nay! say nay! for shame!
To save thee from the blame
Of all my grief and grame.
And wilt thou leave me thus?
Say nay! say nay!
And wilt thou leave me thus?
That hath loved thee so long,
In wealth and woe among?
And is thy heart so strong
As for to leave me thus?
Say nay! say nay!
And wilt thou leave me thus?
That hath given thee my heart,
Never for to depart;
Neither for pain nor smart:
And wilt thou leave me thus?
Say nay! say nay!
And wilt thou leave me thus!
And have no more pity,
Of him that loveth thee?
Alas, thy cruelty!
And wilt thou leave me thus?
Say nay! say nay!

THE FORSAKEN LOVER CONSOLETH HIMSELF WITH REMEMBRANCE OF PAST HAPPINESS.

Spite hath no power to make me sad,
Nor scornfulness to make me plain.
It doth suffice that once I had,
And so to leave it is no pain.

Let them frown on that least doth gain,
Who did rejoice must needs be glad;
And though with words thou ween'st to reign,
It doth suffice that once I had.

Since that in checks thus overthwart,
And coyly looks thou dost delight;
It doth suffice that mine thou wert,
Though change hath put thy faith to flight.

Alas! it is a peevish spite,
To yield thyself, and then to part;
But since thou force thy faith so light,
It doth suffice that mine thou wert.

And since thy love doth thus decline,
And in thy heart such hate doth grow;
It doth suffice that thou wert mine,
And with good-will I quite it so.

Sometime my friend, farewell my foe,
Since thou change I am not thine;
But for relief of all my woe,
It doth suffice that thou wert mine.

Praying you all that hear this song,
To judge no wight, nor none to blame;
It doth suffice she doth me wrong,
And that herself doth know the same.

And though she change it is no shame,
Their kind it is, and hath been long;
Yet I protest she hath no name;
It doth suffice she doth me wrong.

THE LOVER LAMENTS THE DEATH OF HIS LOVE.

The pillar perished is whereto I leant,
The strongest stay of mine unquiet mind;
The like of it no man again can find,
From east to west still seeking though he went,
To mine unhap. For hap away hath rent

Of all my joy the very bark and rind:
And I, alas, by chance am thus assigned
Daily to mourn, till death do it relent.
But since that thus it is by destiny,
What can I more but have a woeful heart;
My pen in plaint, my voice in care-full cry,
My mind in woe, my body full of smart;
    And I myself, myself always to hate,
    Till dreadful death do ease my doleful state.

Geraldine

HENRY HOWARD,

EARL OF SURREY.

1516—1547.

GERALDINE.

The story of Surrey's love for the fair Geraldine, as related by all his early biographers, is as marvellous in its way, as any of the old knightly romances. According to Anthony à Wood, Surrey made a tour in Italy, where he proclaimed the surpassing beauty of his lady, at her express command, and maintained the same at Florence, in a tournament, after the manner of the knights errant of old, coming off victorious, of course, to his and her great glory. He also visited the palace of her ancestors, the Geraldi, and was admitted into the very chamber in which she was born, where he broke forth into magnificats in her praise! This story, which Anthony relates as a veritable bit of biography, has been traced back to Michael Drayton, from whom he *professed* to derive it, and to Thomas Nash, from whom he really did derive it, though he carefully avoids mentioning Nash's name. The work of Drayton, which he quotes as his authority, was published in 1598, under the name of "England's Heroical Epistles." It consists of a series of rhymed letters, many of them of great beauty, supposed to be written by sundry royal and noble personages, male and female. Among these are two by our hero and heroine. The epistle of Surrey purports to be written from Florence, and in addition to the incidents of the chamber and the tournament, contains an account of a visit which he paid to Rotterdam, where he saw Erasmus and Sir Thomas More, and of a visit to the famous wizard, Cornelius Agrippa, who showed him a wonderful magic mirror, wherein he saw the counterfeit presentment of the fair Geraldine, lying sick in her own chamber in England, and reading one of his poems! All this, and more of the same sort, may be found in the "Athenæ Oxonienses," where it is laid at the door of Drayton, who obtained it from Nash, as nobody knew better than Wood, who, in many parts of his narration, adopts the very language of Nash himself! The work of Nash is in prose. It was published in 1594, four years before the appearance of Drayton's "Heroical Epistles," and was entitled "The Unfortunate Traveller; or, The Life of Jack Wilton." Jack Wilton, the imaginary hero (for the whole thing bears on its face every mark of a romance), is an English Bohemian of the most unmistakable stamp, who, in the course of his rambles on the Continent, pretends to have met Surrey in Germany; to have entered his service; and to have witnessed the adventures above mentioned. That Drayton, being a poet, should have adopted Nash's fiction, is not to be wondered at, considering the poetical requirements of his subject, and the little that was then known of Surrey and his supposed passion; but that the prosaic Anthony should have been deceived by it, if he was deceived, and should have suppressed all mention of Nash, is not at all to his credit. The nonsense of Wood and Nash stood a fair chance of becoming an essential part of all future biographies of Surrey—Winstanley, Cibber, Walpole, Warton, and others repeating it, until Dr. Nott proved its absurdity. In his biography of Surrey, published in 1815, he showed that Erasmus was at Basle, when Nash, *alias* Jack Wilton, pretended that Surrey visited him in Rotterdam; that More was beheaded in England the previous year, and that "The Praise of Folly," and the "Utopia," both of which were said to be then unwritten, were written in 1509, and 1516! Besides this, he showed that it was doubtful whether Surrey was ever in Italy at all! He was betrothed to his cousin, the Lady Frances Vere, in 1532, his sixteenth year, and was married to her in 1535. His eldest son, Thomas, was born on the 10th of March, 1536, the year in which he was said to be wandering over the continent in search of madcap adventures in honor of the fair Geraldine! So much being proved false, the reader may doubt the existence of the lady herself; but he will be mistaken if he does so, for she was a real personage. She was the Lady Elizabeth Gerald, daughter of Gerald Fitz-Gerald, ninth Earl of Kildare. The family is said to have descended from the Geraldi, as Drayton states in his epistles. She was born in Ireland, probably at Maynooth, the seat of the Geralds. Her earliest years were passed in England, principally at Hunsdon, in attendance on the Princess Mary, with whom she seems to have been a favourite, and to whom she was related. She became one of the Ladies of the Chamber in 1542, or thereabouts; was married to Sir Anthony Brown in 1543; and after his death, which took place in 1549, she became the third wife of Henry Clinton, Earl of Lincoln. She died in 1589, and was followed to her grave by sixty-one old women, one, we are told, for each year of her age. If she was sixty-one at her death, as this would seem to indicate, she was born in 1528, and was a mere child when Surrey is said to have fallen in love with her. She was only seven years old at his marriage, and fifteen at her own! Dates are awkward things, but I do not see what we can do in this case, unless we suppose the old Countess to have dropped a few years from her age. (Could she have done so without detection?) We must otherwise suppose Surrey to have been in love with a child. That he met the Lady Elizabeth Gerald, or Garrat, as she was more commonly called, at Hunsdon, and admired her, we have no reason to doubt; but that he had a passion for her, I do not believe. She happened to come in his way when he was fresh from the reading of Petrarch, and, as he wanted some lady to celebrate, she became for the nonce his Laura. Such, at least, is my opinion, after a careful consideration of the whole matter.

Surrey's poems were first published in Tottel's Miscellany.

The only original portrait of Geraldine, is in the gallery of the Duke of Bedford, at Woburn. It was probably painted when she was Countess of Lincoln.

DESCRIPTION AND PRAISE OF HIS LOVE GERALDINE.

From Tuscane came my lady's worthy race;
Fair Florence was sometime their ancient seat.
The western isle, whose pleasant shore doth face
Wild Camber's cliffs, did give her lively heat.
Fostered she was with milk of Irish breast;
Her sire an earl, her dame of prince's blood.
From tender years in Britain doth she rest,
With king's child, where she tasteth costly food.
Hunsdon did first present her to mine eyen:
Bright is her hue, and Geraldine she hight.
Hampton me taught to wish her first for mine;
And Windsor, alas! doth chase me from her sight.
    Her beauty of kind; her virtues from above;
    Happy is he that can obtain her love!

COMPLAINT,

THAT HIS LADY, AFTER SHE KNEW HIS LOVE, KEPT HER FACE ALWAYS HIDDEN FROM HIM.

I never saw my lady lay apart
Her cornet black, in cold, nor yet in heat,
Sith first she knew my grief was grown so great;
Which other fancies driveth from my heart,
That to myself I do the thought reserve,
The which unwares did wound my woeful breast;
But on her face mine eyes might never rest.
Yet since she knew I did her love and serve,
Her golden tresses clad alway with black,
Her smiling looks that hid thus evermore,
And that restrains which I desire so sore.
So doth this cornet govern me, alack!
    In summer, sun, in winter's breath, a frost;
    Whereby the light of her fair looks I lost.

REQUEST TO HIS LOVE TO JOIN BOUNTY WITH BEAUTY.

The golden gift that Nature did thee give,
To fasten friends, and feed them at thy will,
With form and favour, taught me to believe,
How thou art made to show her greatest skill,
Whose hidden virtues are not so unknown,
But lively dooms might gather at the first
Where beauty so her perfect seed hath sown,
Of other graces follow needs there must.
Now certes, Garret, since all this is true,
That from above thy gifts are thus elect,
Do not deface them then with fancies new;
Nor change of minds, let not the mind infect:
  But mercy him thy friend that doth thee serve,
  Who seeks alway thine honour to preserve.

A PRAISE OF HIS LADY.

WHEREIN HE REPROVETH THEM THAT COMPARE THEIR LADIES WITH HIS.

Give place, ye lovers, here before
That spent your boasts and brags in vain;
My lady's beauty passeth more
The best of yours, I dare well sayen,
Than doth the sun the candle light,
Or brightest day the darkest night.

And thereto hath a troth as just
As had Penelope the fair;
For what she saith, ye may it trust,
As it by writing sealéd were:
And virtues hath she many mo'
Than I with pen have skill to show.

I could rehearse, if that I would,
The whole effect of Nature's plaint,
When she had lost the perfect mould,
The like to whom she could not paint:
With wringing hands, how she did cry,
And what she said, I know it, aye.

I know she swore with raging mind,
Her kingdom only set apart,
There was no loss by law of kind,
That could have gone so near her heart;
And this was chiefly all her pain:
"She could not make the like again."

Sith Nature thus gave her the praise,
To be the chiefest work she wrought;
In faith, methink, some better ways
On your behalf might well be sought,
Than to compare, as ye have done,
To match the candle with the sun.

JOHN HARRINGTON.

1534—1582.

ISABELLA MARKHAM.

Of John Harrington and Isabella Markham but little is known, except that the former was the son of Sir James Harrington, who was attainted in the reign of Henry the Seventh, for bearing arms at the battle of Towton, and taking Henry the Sixth prisoner, and that the latter was one of the maids of honor of the Princess Elizabeth. The poems below are copied from the "Nugæ Antiquæ," where they bear the dates of 1549, and 1564, both of which dates I believe to be erroneous; the first, because Harrington was only fifteen years old at the time—if the year of his birth be given correctly—the last, because he was then more than ten years married to the fair Isabella, who was confined with him in the Tower by Queen Mary, in 1554, for carrying a letter to the Princess Elizabeth. I should place the first poem some years later, the last some years earlier.

TO ISABELLA MARKHAM.

QUESTION.

Alas! I love you overwell,
Mine own sweet dear delight;
Yet, for respects, I fear to tell
What moves my troubled sprite:
What works my woe, what breeds my smart,
What wounds mine heart and mind,
Reason restrains me to impart
Such perils as I find.

ANSWER.

If present peril reason find,
    And hope for help do haste;
Unfold the secrets of your mind,
    Whilst hope of help may taste.
And I will ease your pain and smart,
    As if it were mine own;
Respects and peril put apart,
    And let the truth be known.

QUESTION.

The words be sound, the sound is sweet,
    The sweet yields bounty free;
No wight hath worth to yield meed meet
    For grace of such degree:
Now, sith my plaint doth pity move,
    Grant grace that I may taste
Such joys as angels feel above,
    That lovingly may last.

ANSWER.

I yield with heart and willing mind
    To do all you desire;
Doubting no deal such faith to find
    As such truth doth require:
Now you have wealth at your own will,
    And law at your own lust,
To make or mar, to save or spill;
    Then be a conqueror just.

ANSWER.

First shall the sun in darkness dwell,
    The moon and stars lack light,
Before in thought I do rebel
    Against my life's delight:

Tried is my trust, known is my truth,
In time, my sweet, provide,
Whilst beauty flourish in thine youth,
And breath in me abide.

A SONNET.

Made on Isabella Markham, when I first thought her fair, as she stood at the Princess's window in goodly attire, and talked to divers in the court-yard.

Whence comes my love, O heart, disclose!
'Twas from cheeks that shamed the rose;
From lips that spoil the rubies' praise;
From eyes that mock the diamond's blaze.
Whence comes my woe, as freely own:
Ah, me! 'twas from a heart like stone.

The blushing cheek speaks modest mind,
The lips befitting words most kind;
The eye does tempt to love's desire,
And seems to say, 'tis Cupid's fire;
Yet all so fair but speak my moan,
Sith nought doth say the heart of stone.

Why thus, my love, so kind bespeak
Sweet lip, sweet eye, sweet blushing cheek,
Yet not a heart to save my pain?
O Venus, take thy gifts again;
Make not so fair to cause our moan,
Or make a heart that's like our own.

THOMAS WATSON.

1560—1591.

[“*Ekatompathia, or Passionate Centurie of Love.*” 1581.]

SONNET.

When May is in his prime, and youthful Spring
  Doth clothe the tree with leaves, and ground with flowers,
And time of year reviveth everything,
  And lovely Nature smiles, and nothing lowers;
Then Philomela most doth strain her breast
With night complaints, and sits in little rest.

This bird's estate I may compare with mine,
  To whom fond Love doth work such wrongs by day,
That in the night my heart must needs repine,
  And storm with sighs, to ease me as I may,
Whilst others are becalmed, or lie them still,
Or sail secure, with tide and wind at will.

And as all those which hear this bird complain,
  Conceive in all her tunes a sweet delight,
Without remorse, or pitying her pain;
  So she, for whom I wail both day and night,
Doth sport herself in hearing my complaint,
A just reward for serving such a saint!

SONNET.

All ye that grieve to think my death so near,
  Take pity on yourselves, whose thought is blind:
Can there be day unless some light appear?
  Can fire be cold, which yieldeth heat by kind?
If love were passed, my life would soon decay;
Love bids me hope, and hope is all my stay.

And you that see in what estate I stand,
  Now hot, now cold, and yet am living still,
Persuade yourselves Love hath a mighty hand,
  And custom frames what pleaseth best her will:
A lingering use of Love hath taught my breast
To harbour strife, and yet to live in rest.

The man that dwells far north hath seldom harm
  With blast of winter's wind, or nipping frost;
The negro seldom feels himself too warm,
  If he abide within his native coast;
So love in me a second nature is,
And custom makes me think my woes are bliss.

SONNET.

Youth made a fault through lightness of belief,
  Which fond belief Love placéd in my breast;
But now I find that reason gives relief,
  And time shows truth, and wit that's bought is best:
Muse not therefore although I change my vein,
He runs too far which never turns again.

Henceforth my mind shall have a watchful eye,
  I'll scorn fond love, and practice of the same;
The wisdom of my heart shall soon descry
  Each thing that's good from what deserveth blame.

My song shall be, "Fortune hath spit her spite,
And Love can hurt no more with all his might."

Therefore all you, to whom my cause is known,
  Think better comes, and pardon what is past:
I find that all my wildest oats are sown,
  And joy to see what now I see at last;
And since that Love was cause I trod awry,
I here take off his bells, and let him fly.

THOMAS LODGE.

1556—1625.

[*"Rosalynde: Euphues Golden Legacie."* 1581.]

ROSADOR'S SONNETO.

TURN I my looks unto the skies,
Love with his arrows wounds mine eyes;
If so I look upon the ground,
Love then in every flower is found;
Search I the shade to flee my pain,
Love meets me in the shades again;
Want I to walk in secret grove,
E'en there I meet with sacred Love.
If so I bathe me in the spring,
E'en on the brink I hear him sing;
If so I meditate alone,
He will be partner of my moan;
If so I mourn, he weeps with me,
And where I am there will he be;
When as I talk of Rosalind,
The God from coyness waxeth kind,
And seems in self-same frame to fly,
Because he loves as well as I.
Sweet Rosalind, for pity rue,
For why, than Love I am more true:
He, if he speed, will quickly fly,
But in thy love I live and die.

["*The Phœnix Nest.*" 1593.]

THE SHEPHERD'S SORROW FOR HIS PHŒBE'S DISDAIN.

O woods! unto your walks my body hies,
To loose the traitorous bonds of 'ticing Love,
Where trees, where herbs, where flowers,
Their native moisture pours,
From forth their tender stalks, to help mine eyes,
Yet their united tears may nothing move.

When I behold the fair adornéd tree,
Which lightning's force and winter's frost resists,
Then Daphne's ill betide,
And Phœbus' lawless pride
Enforce me say, even such my sorrows be;
For self-disdain in Phœbe's heart consists.

If I behold the flowers by morning tears,
Look lovely sweet, ah! then forlorn I cry:
Sweet showers for Memnon shed,
All flowers by you are fed.
Whereas my piteous plaint, that still appears,
Yields vigour to her scorns, and makes me die.

When I regard the pretty, gleeful bird,
With tearful (yet delightful) notes complain,
I yield a tenor with my tears,
And whilst her music wounds mine ears,
Alas! say I, when will my notes afford
Such like remorse, who still beweep my pain?

When I behold upon the leafless bough
The hapless bird lament her love's depart,
I draw her biding nigh,
And, sitting down, I sigh,
And sighing say, Alas! that birds avow
A settled faith, yet Phœbe scorns my smart.

Thus weary in my walk, and woeful too,
    I spend the day, forespent with daily grief:
        Each object of distress
        My sorrow doth express;
I doat on that which doth my heart undo,
    And honour her that scorns to yield relief.

[“*The Phœnix Nest.*”]

Now I find thy looks were feignéd,
Quickly lost and quickly gainéd;
Soft thy skin, like wool of wethers,
Heart unstable, light as feathers:
Tongue untrusty, subtle-sighted,
Wanton will, with change delighted,
    Siren pleasant, foe to reason,
    Cupid plague thee for this treason!

Of thine eyes I made my mirror;
From thy beauty came mine error:
All thy words I counted witty,
All thy smiles I deeméd pity;
Thy false tears, that me aggrievéd,
First of all my heart deceivéd;
    Siren pleasant, foe to reason,
    Cupid plague thee for this treason!

Feigned acceptance, when I askéd,
Lovely words, with cunning maskéd;
Holy vows, but heart unholy;
Wretched man! my trust was folly!
Lily white, and pretty winking;
Solemn vows, but sorry thinking.
    Siren pleasant, foe to reason,
    Cupid plague thee for this treason!

Now I see (O seemly cruel!)
Others warm them at my fuel:
Wit shall guide me in this durance,
Since in love is no assurance:
Change thy pasture, take thy pleasure;
Beauty is a fading treasure.
    Siren pleasant, foe to reason,
    Cupid plague thee for this treason!

Prime youth lasts not, age will follow,
And make white these tresses yellow:
Wrinkled face, for looks delightful,
Shall acquaint thee, dame despiteful!
And when time shall date thy glory,
Then, too late, thou wilt be sorry.
    Siren pleasant, foe to reason,
    Cupid plague thee for this treason!

JOHN LILY.

1553—1600.

["*A tragical comedie of Alexander and Campaspe.*" 1584.]

Cupid and my Campaspe played
At cards for kisses; Cupid paid.
He stakes his quiver, bow and arrows,
His mother's doves, and team of sparrows;
Loses them too; then down he throws
The coral of his lip, the rose
Growing on 's cheek, but none knows how;
With these, the crystal of his brow,
And then the dimple of his chin;
All these did my Campaspe win.
At last he set her both his eyes;
She won, and Cupid blind did rise.
O Love, has she done this to thee?
What shall, alas, become of me?

["*Gallathea.*" 1592.]

O yes, O yes, if any maid
Whom leering Cupid has betrayed
To powers of spite, to eyes of scorn,
And would in madness now see torn
The boy in pieces, let her come
Hither, and lay on him her doom.

O yes, O yes, has any lost
A heart which many a sigh hath cost?
Is any cozened of a tear,
Which, as a pearl, Disdain does wear?
Here stands the thief; let her but come
Hither, and lay on him her doom.

Is any one undone by fire,
And turned to ashes by desire?
Did ever any lady weep,
Being cheated of her golden sleep
Stolen by sick thoughts? The pirate 's found,
And in her tears he shall be drowned.
Read his indictment, let him hear
What he 's to trust to. Boy, give ear.

SIR PHILIP SYDNEY.

1554—1586.

STELLA.

The Stella of Sydney's sonnets, was the Lady Penelope Devereux, daughter of Walter Devereux, the first Earl of Essex. They were acquainted in their childhood, and in 1575, when Sydney returned from his travels on the Continent, a match was proposed between them; but for some reason or other it was eventually broken off, and she was married to Robert, Lord Rich. Shortly afterwards Sydney married Frances, the daughter of Sir Francis Walsingham. Neither Stella, nor Astrophel (the name by which Sydney designated himself in his sonnets), were happy in their new relation. Lord Rich was a notorious profligate and brute, while Lady Sydney, who is said to have been very handsome, never acquired anything beyond her husband's respect. From the first the course of true love never ran smooth with Sydney; for when he was a youth at the University of Oxford, his uncle, Lord Leicester, planned an alliance between him and Anne Cecil, the daughter of Lord Burleigh; but the wily old Treasurer married her to Edward Vere, Earl of Oxford, to whom we indirectly owe the "Arcadia." The occasion was this: Sir Philip was one day at tennis, when my Lord Oxford abruptly entered the court, and ordered him to depart, calling him at the same time a puppy. Sydney, in the words of his biographer, Fulke Grevile, Lord Brooke, "gave my lord a lie impossible (as he averred) to be retorted; in respect all the world knows puppies are gotten by dogs, and children by men." The next day he challenged his lordship. The Council heard of it, and laboured in vain to reconcile them. At last it came to the ears of the Queen, who undertook to lay before Sydney, "the difference in degree between earls and gentlemen; the respect inferiors owed to their superiors;" etc., etc. He listened to her Majesty's arguments, says Lord Brooke, "with such reverence as became him," and adroitly rebutted them one by one. The upshot of the matter was, that, rather than bate his pride, he retired to Wilton, the abode of his sister, the Countess of Pembroke, where he planned and composed the "Arcadia." Lord Oxford, by the way, was the first to introduce embroidered gloves and perfumes into England from Italy. A ludicrous reason for his Italian journey, may be found in D'Israeli's

"Curiosities of Literature." But there was another reason not so creditable to him. His friend the Duke of Norfolk, being condemned on account of Mary Queen of Scots, my Lord Oxford solicited his father-in-law, Lord Burleigh, to save the Duke's life; but not succeeding, he swore to be revenged on him by ruining his daughter. He forsook her bed, and studied how he might squander his immense estate. This led him to Italy, where he resided for seven years in more than ducal state. So much for Edward Vere, Lord Oxford, the husband of Sydney's first love, Anne Cecil. To return to his second, Stella. She was married in 1583, or thereabouts, and from that time till the death of Sydney in 1586, she was the theme of his sonnets and songs. We have every reason to think that he loved her, but no reason to think that she loved him. She was doubtless flattered by his poetical worship—as what lady would not have been? she coquetted with him, perhaps, giving him an interview now and then, a flower, or ribbon, or some such amorous trifle; but love him she did not. Her heart belonged to Charles Blount, Lord Montjoy, afterwards Duke of Devonshire, to whom she is said to have engaged herself before her unhappy marriage with Lord Rich. A guilty intercourse was kept up between them for several years, and only made public by her flying from the house of her husband to that of her lover, and carrying with her her five children, whom she declared to be the issue of the latter. She was divorced from Lord Rich in 1605, and united to the Duke of Devonshire by his chaplain, Laud, who fell under the censure of the Church for marrying them, and ever after kept a fast on the anniversary of their marriage. The moral sense of the English nation, which has always set itself against divorce of any kind, was shocked, and a great outcry was raised against them, but they were soon beyond its reach. The Duke died in a few months, some said of a burning fever and putrefaction of the lungs, others of the "grief of unsuccessful love." He left Stella fifteen hundred pounds a year, and most of his moveables, and provided for some of her children, giving a daughter six thousand pounds in money, and her eldest son, who afterwards became Lord Warwick, three or four thousand pounds a year. Stella survived him but a little while, living and dying in miserable obscurity. Sydney's widow, by the way, had previously married Stella's brother, Robert Devereux, the famous Earl of Essex, the favourite of Elizabeth, with whose execution all the readers of English history are familiar.

Sydney's sonnets were first published in 1591, five years after his death. In 1593 they were annexed to the "Arcadia," in all the subsequent editions of which they appear.

In truth, O Love, with what a boyish kind
Thou dost proceed, in thy most serious ways,
That when the heaven to thee his best displays,
    Yet of that best, thou leav'st the best behind!
    For, like a child, that some fair book doth find,
With gilded leaves, or coloured vellum plays,
Or, at the most, on some fine picture stays,
    But never heeds the fruit of writer's mind:

So when thou saw'st in Nature's cabinet,
Stella, thou straight looked'st babies in her eyes,
In her cheeks' pit, thou did'st thy pitfold set,
And in her breast, bo-peep, or couching, lies,
Playing, and shining in each outward part:
But, fool! seek'st not to get into her heart.

You that do search for every purling spring,
Which from the ribs of old Parnassus flows,
And every flower, not sweet, perhaps, which grows
Near thereabouts, into your poesy wring;
You that do dictionary's method bring
Into your rhymes, running in rattling rows;
You that poor Petrarch's long-deceaséd woes
With new-born sighs, and denizened wit do sing:
You take wrong ways; those far-fetched helps be such,
As do bewray a want of inward touch.
And sure, at length, stolen goods do come to light;
But if (both for your love and skill) your name
You seek to nurse at fullest breasts of fame,
Stella behold, and then begin t' indite.

Because I oft, in dark abstracted guise,
Seem most alone in greatest company;
With dearth of words, or answers quite awry,
To them that would make speech of speech arise:
They deem, and of their doom the rumour flies,
That poison foul of bubbling pride doth lie
So in my swelling breast, that only I
Fawn on myself, and others do despise:
Yet pride, I think, doth not my soul possess,
Which looks too oft in his unflattering glass:
But one worse fault, ambition, I confess,
That makes me oft my best friends overpass,
Unseen, unheard, while thought to highest place
Bends all his power, even unto Stella's grace.

Come, Sleep, O Sleep! the certain knot of peace,
The baiting place of wit, the balm of woe,
The poor man's wealth, the prisoner's release,
Th' indifferent judge between the high and low;
With shield of proof, shield me from out the prease
Of those fierce darts, Despair at me doth throw:
O make in me those civil wars to cease;
I will good tribute pay, if thou do so.
Take thou of me, smooth pillows, sweetest bed:
A chamber deaf to noise, and blind to light;
A rosy garland, and a weary head:
And if these things, as being thine by right,
Move not thy heavy grace, thou shalt, in me,
Livelier than elsewhere, Stella's image see.

Having this day my horse, my hand, my lance,
Guided so well, that I obtained the prize,
Both by the judgment of the English eyes,
And of some sent from that sweet enemy, France;
Horsemen, my skill in horsemanship advance;
Town-folks my strength; a daintier judge applies
His praise to sleight, which from good use doth rise:
Some lucky wits impute it but to chance:
Others, because of both sides I do take
My blood from them who did excel in this,
Think Nature me a man of arms did make;
How far they shot awry! the true cause is,
Stella looked on, and from her heavenly face
Sent forth the beams which made so fair my race.

In martial sports I had my cunning tried,
And yet to break more staves did me address,
While, with the people's shouts, I must confess,
Youth, luck, and praise e'en filled my veins with pride;
When Cupid, having me, his slave, descried
In Mars' livery, prancing in the press:

What now, Sir Fool? said he, I would no less:
    Look here, I say; I looked, and Stella spied;
Who, hard by, made a window send forth light;
    My heart then quaked, then dazzled were mine eyes,
One hand forgot to rule, th' other to fight;
    Nor trumpet's sound I heard, nor friendly cries:
My foe came on, and beat the air for me,
Till that her blush taught me my shame to see.

    Because I breathe not love to every one,
Nor do not use set colours for to wear;
Nor nourish special locks of vowéd hair;
    Nor give each speech a full point of a groan;
    The courtly nymphs, acquainted with the moan
Of them who, in their lips, Love's standard bear;
What he? say they of me, now dare I swear,
    He cannot love; no, no; let him alone.
And think so still, so Stella know my mind;
    Profess, indeed, I do not, Cupid's art;
But you, fair maids, at length this true shall find,
    That his right badge is worn but in the heart.
Dumb swans, not chattering pies, do lovers prove;
They love indeed who quake to say they love.

    Dear! why make you more of a dog than me?
If he do love, I burn, I burn in love;
If he wait well, I never thence would move:
    If he be fair, yet but a dog can be:
    Little he is, so little worth is he;
He barks, my songs thine own voice oft doth prove;
Bidden, perhaps, he fetcheth thee a glove,
    But I, unbid, fetch even my soul to thee.
Yet, while I languish, him that bosom clips,
    That lap doth lap, nay lets, in spite of spite,
This sour-breathed mate taste of those sugared lips:
    Alas! if you grant only such delight

To witless things, then Love, I hope (since wit
Becomes a clog) will soon ease me of it.

Highway, since you my chief Parnassus be,
And that my Muse, to some ears not unsweet,
Tempers her words to trampling horses' feet,
More oft than to a chamber melody:
Now blessèd you, bear onward blessèd me,
To her, where I my heart, safe left, shall meet;
My Muse and I must you of duty greet
With thanks and wishes, wishing thankfully.
Be you still fair, honoured by public heed;
By no encroachment wronged, nor time forgot:
Nor blamed for blood, nor shamed for sinful deed;
And that you know I envy you no lot
Of highest wish, I wish you so much bliss,
Hundreds of years you Stella's feet may kiss.

Stella! think not that I by verse seek fame,
Who seek, who hope, who love, who live but thee;
Thine eyes my pride, thy lips my history:
If thou praise not, all other praise is shame.
Nor so ambitious am I, as to frame
A nest for my young praise, in laurel tree:
In truth I swear, I wish not there should be
Graved in my epitaph a Poet's name:
Ne, if I would, I could just title make,
That any laud to me thereof should grow,
Without my plumes from others' wings I take;
For nothing from my wit, or will, doth flow:
Since all my words thy beauty doth indite,
And Love doth hold my hand, and makes me write.

O happy Thames! that did'st my Stella bear,
I saw thee with full many a smiling line,

Upon thy cheerful face joy's livery wear;
While those fair planets on thy streams did shine,
The boat for joy could not to dance forbear,
While wanton winds, with beauties so divine
Ravished, stayed not, till in her golden hair
They did themselves (O sweetest prison!) twine.
And fain those Æol's youth there would their stay
Have made, but forced by Nature still to fly,
First did with puffing kiss those locks display:
She, so dishevelled blushed; from window I
With sight thereof cried out, "O fair disgrace!
Let Honour's self to thee grant highest place."

Unhappy sight, and hath she vanished by
So near, in so good time, so free a place?
Dead glass, dost thou thy object so embrace,
As what my heart still sees thou can'st not spy?
I swear by her I love, and lack, that I
Was not in fault, who bent thy dazzling race
Only unto the heaven of Stella's face;
Counting but dust what in the way did lie.
But cease, mine eyes, your tears do witness well,
That you, guiltless thereof, your nectar missed.
Cursed be the page, from whom the bad torch fell;
Cursed be the night which did your will resist:
Cursed be the coachman which did drive so fast,
Which no less curse than absence makes me taste.

ROBERT GREENE.

1560—1592.

["*Menaphon.*" 1587.]

DORON'S DESCRIPTION OF SAMELA.

LIKE to Diana in her summer weed,
Girt with a crimson robe of brightest dye,
Goes fair Samela;
Whiter than be the flocks that straggling feed,
When washed by Arethusa faint they lie,
Is fair Samela.

As fair Aurora in her morning gray,
Decked with the ruddy glister of her love,
Is fair Samela;
Like lovely Thetis on a calméd day,
When as her brightness Neptune's fancy move,
Shines fair Samela;

Her tresses gold, her eyes like glassy streams,
Her teeth are pearl, the breasts are ivory
Of fair Samela;
Her cheeks, like rose and lily yield forth gleams,
Her brows' bright arches framed of ebony;
Thus fair Samela

Passeth fair Venus in her bravest hue,
And Juno in the show of majesty,
For she's Samela,
Pallas in wit; all three, if you well view,
For beauty, wit, and matchless dignity
Yield to Samela.

["*Pandosto. The Triumph of Time.*" 1588.]

THE PRAISE OF FAWNIA.

Ah, were she pitiful as she is fair,
Or but as mild as she is seeming so,
Then were my hopes greater than my despair,
Then all the world were heaven, nothing woe.
Ah! were her heart relenting as her hand,
That seems to melt even with the mildest touch,
Then knew I where to seat me in a land,
Under wide heavens, but yet (I know) not such.
So as she shows, she seems the budding rose,
Yet sweeter far than is an earthly flower,
Sovereign of beauty, like the spray she grows,
Compassed she is with thorns and cankered flower,
Yet were she willing to be plucked and worn,
She would be gathered, though she grew on thorn.

Ah, when she sings, all music else be still,
For none must be comparéd to her note;
Ne'er breathed such glee from Philomela's bill,
Nor from the morning-singer's swelling throat.
Ah, when she riseth from her blissful bed,
She comforts all the world as doth the sun,
And at her sight the nights' foul vapour's fled;
When she is set, the gladsome day is done.
O glorious sun, imagine me the west,
Shine in my arms, and set thou in my breast!

SAMUEL DANIEL.

1562—1619.

DELIA.

THE biographers of Daniel have not been able to ascertain the name of the lady who was his first love, and whom he celebrated under the poetical name of Delia. We learn from the sonnets that she lived on the River Avon,

("But Avon, poor in fame and poor in waters,
Shall have my songs, where Delia hath her seat,")

and that his love was not returned. He married Justina Florio, the sister of John Florio, a noted philologist of the time—the Holofernes of Shakespeare's "LOVE'S LABOUR LOST." Daniel's sonnets were published in 1592.

Unto the boundless ocean of thy beauty,
Runs this poor river, charged with streams of zeal,
Returning thee the tribute of my duty,
Which here my love, my youth, my plaints reveal.
Here I unclasp the book of my charged soul,
Where I have cast th' accounts of all my care:
Here have I summed my sighs; here I enroll
How they were spent for thee; look what they are.
Look on the dear expences of my youth,
And see how just I reckon with thine eyes:
Examine well thy beauty with my truth;
And cross my cares, ere greater sums arise.
Read it, sweet maid, though it be done but slightly;
Who can show all his love, doth love but lightly.

Fair is my love, and cruel as she's fair;
Her brow shades frowns, although her eyes are sunny;
Her smiles are lightning, though her pride despair;
And her disdains are gall, her favours honey.
A modest maid, decked with a blush of honour;
Whose feet do tread green paths of youth and love;
The wonder of all eyes that look upon her;
Sacred on earth; designed a saint above!
Chastity and beauty, which were deadly foes,
Live reconciléd friends within her brow:
And had she pity to conjoin with those,
Then who had heard the plaints I utter now?
For had she not been fair, and thus unkind,
My muse had slept, and none had known my mind.

Restore thy tresses to the golden ore;
Yield Citherea's son those arks of love:
Bequeath the heavens the stars that I adore;
And to th' orient do thy pearls remove.
Yield thy hands' pride unto the ivory white;
T' Arabian odours give thy breathing sweet:
Restore thy blush unto Aurora bright;
To Thetis give the honour of thy feet.
Let Venus have thy graces, hers resigned;
And thy sweet voice give back unto the spheres:
But yet restore thy fierce and cruel mind
To Hyrcan tygers, and to ruthless bears.
Yield to the marble thy hard heart again;
So shalt thou cease to plague, and I to pain.

Look, Delia, how w' esteem the half-blown rose,
The image of thy blush, and summer's honour!
Whilst yet her tender bud doth undisclose
That full of beauty, time bestows upon her.
No sooner spreads her glory in the air,
But straight her wide-blown pomp comes to decline;

She then is scorned that late adorned the fair:
So fade the roses of those cheeks of thine!
No April can revive thy withered flowers,
Whose springing grace adorns thy glory now;
Swift speedy time, feathered with flying hours,
Dissolves the beauty of the fairest brow.
Then do not thou such treasure waste in vain;
But love now, whilst thou may'st be loved again.

But love whilst that thou may'st be loved again,
Now whilst that May hath filled thy lap with flowers;
Now whilst thy beauty bears without a stain;
Now use the summer's smiles, ere winter lowers.
And whilst thou spread'st unto the rising sun,
The fairest flower that ever saw the light,
Now joy the time before thy sweet be done;
And, Delia, think thy morning must have night;
And that thy brightness sets at length to West,
When thou wilt close up that which now thou show'st,
And think the fame becomes thy fading best,
Which then shall most inveil and shadow most.
Men do not weigh the stalk for what it was,
When once they find her flower, her glory pass.

When men shall find thy flower, thy glory pass,
And thou with careful brow sitting alone,
Receivéd hast this message from thy glass,
That tells the truth, and says that all is gone,
Fresh shalt thou see in me the wounds thou mad'st;
Though spent thy flame, in me the heat remaining:
I that have loved thee thus before thou fad'st,
My faith shall wax when thou art in thy waning.
The world shall find this miracle in me,
That fire can burn when all the matter 's spent:
Then what my faith hath been, thyself shall see;
And that thou wast unkind thou may'st repent.

Thou may'st repent that thou hast scorned my tears,
When winter snows upon thy sable hairs.

Read in my face a volume of despairs,
    The wailing Iliads of my tragic woe;
    Drawn with my blood, and painted with my cares,
    Wrought by her hand that I have honoured so.
Who, whilst I burn, she sings at my soul's wrack,
    Looking aloft from turret of her pride;
    There my soul's tyrant joys her, in the sack
    Of her own seat, whereof I made her guide.
There do these smokes that from affliction rise,
    Serve as an incense to a cruel dame;
    A sacrifice thrice grateful to her eyes,
    Because their power serves to exact the same.
Thus ruins she, (to satisfy her will,)
The temple where her name was honoured still.

Beauty, sweet love, is like the morning dew,
    Whose short refresh upon the tender green
    Cheers for a time, but till the sun doth shew;
    And straight 'tis gone, as it had never been.
Soon doth it fade that makes the fairest flourish;
    Short is the glory of the blushing rose:
    The hue which thou so carefully dost nourish,
    Yet which at length thou must be forced to lose.
When thou, surcharged with burden of thy years,
    Shalt bend thy wrinkles homeward to the earth;
    And that in beauty's lease expired, appears
    The date of age, the calends of our death.
But ah, no more, this must not be foretold;
For women grieve to think they must be old.

I must not grieve my love, whose eyes would read
    Lines of delight, whereon her youth might smile;

Flowers have time before they come to seed,
And she is young, and now must sport the while.
And sport, sweet maid, in season of these years,
And learn to gather flowers before they wither;
And where the sweetest blossom first appears,
Let love and youth conduct thy pleasures thither.
Lighten forth smiles to clear the clouded air,
And calm the tempest which my sighs do raise;
Pity and smiles do best become the fair;
Pity and smiles must only yield thee praise.
Make me to say, when all my griefs are gone,
Happy the heart that sighed for such a one!

And whither, poor forsaken, wilt thou go,
To go from sorrow, and thine own distress?
When every place presents like face of woe,
And no remove can make thy sorrows less?
Yet go, forsaken; leave these woods, these plains;
Leave her and all, and all for her, that leaves
Thee and thy love forlorn, and both disdains;
And of both wrongful deems, and ill conceives.
Seek out some place; and see if any place
Can give the least release unto thy grief:
Convey thee from the thoughts of thy disgrace;
Steal from thyself, and be thy cares' own thief.
But yet what comforts shall I hereby gain?
Bearing the wound, I needs must feel the pain.

MICHAEL DRAYTON.

1563—1631.

Nothing is known of the lady who inspired the love-sonnets of Drayton, except that she resided on the banks of the Ankor. As Drayton himself was born near that river (in the village of Harshull, or Hartshill, in the parish of Atherston), it is probable that he met her there in his youth. She was born on the 4th of August, in Coventry, if his "Hymn to his Lady's Birth Place," may be taken as evidence, and resided at one time in Mich-Parke, a noted street of that town. He celebrated her under the singular name of Idea. His sonnets were first published in 1593. The Hymn was written some ten or twelve years later, certainly after the death of Queen Elizabeth, in 1603.

Bright star of beauty, on whose eyelids sit
A thousand nymph-like and enamoured graces,
The goddesses of memory and wit,
Which there in order take their several places;
In whose dear bosom sweet, delicious Love
Lays down his quiver which he once did bear:
Since he that blesséd paradise did prove,
And leaves his mother's lap to sport him there:
Let others strive to entertain with words,
My soul is of a braver metal made,
I hold that vile, which vulgar wit affords;
In me's that faith which time can not invade.
Let what I praise be still made good by you:
Be you most worthy whilst I am most true.

'Mongst all the creatures in this spacious round,
Of the birds' kind, the phenix is alone,

Which best by you, of living things, is known;
None like to that, none like to you is found.
Your beauty is the hot and splendorous Sun,
The precious spices be your chaste desire,
Which being kindled by that heavenly fire,
Your life so like the phenix's begun;
Yourself thus burnéd in that sacred flame,
With so rare sweetness all the heavens perfuming,
Again increasing, as you are consuming,
Only by dying, born the very same;
    And winged by fame, you to the stars ascend,
    So you of time shall live beyond the end.

I hear some say, "This man is not in love:
Who? Can he love? A likely thing," they say;
"Read but his verse, and it will easily prove."
O, judge not rashly (gentle sir) I pray,
Because I loosely trifle in this sort,
As one that fain his sorrows would beguile:
You now suppose me all this time in sport,
And please yourself with this conceit the while.
Ye shallow censors, sometimes see ye not,
In greatest perils some men pleasant be,
Where fame by death is only to be got,
They resolute? So stands the case with me;
    Where other men in depth of passion cry,
    I laugh at fortune, as in jest to die.

Dear, why should you command me to my rest,
When now the night doth summon all to sleep?
Methinks this time becometh lovers best;
Night was ordained together friends to keep:
How happy are all other living things,
Which through the day disjoin by several flight,
The quiet evening yet together brings,
And each returns unto his love at night!

O, thou that art so courteous else to all!
Why should'st thou, Night, abuse me only thus?
That every creature to his kind dost call,
And yet 'tis thou dost only sever us?
    Well could I wish it would be ever day,
    If when night comes, you bid me go away.

Why should your fair eyes with such sovereign grace
Disperse their rays on every vulgar spirit,
Whilst I in darkness, in the self-same place,
Get not one glance to recompence my merit?
So doth the ploughman gaze the wandering star,
And only rest contented with the light,
That never learned what constellations are,
Beyond the bent of his unknowing sight.
O, why should beauty (custom to obey)
To their gross sense apply herself so ill!
Would God I were as ignorant as they,
When I am made unhappy by my skill;
    Only compelled on this poor good to boast,
    Heavens are not kind to them that know them most.

Clear Ankor, on whose silver-sanded shore,
My soul-shrined saint, my fair Idea lies,
O blesséd brook, whose milk-white swans adore
Thy crystal stream refinéd by her eyes,
Where sweet myrrh-breathing Zephyr in the spring
Gently distils his nectar-dropping showers,
Where nightingales in Arden sit and sing,
Amongst the dainty dew-impearléd flowers;
Say thus, fair brook, when thou shalt see thy queen,
Lo, here thy shepherd spent his wandering years,
And in these shades, dear nymph, he oft hath been,
And here to thee he sacrificed his tears:
    Fair Arden, thou my Tempe art alone,
    And thou, sweet Ankor, art my Helicon.

You, best discerned of my mind's inward eyes,
And yet your graces outwardly divine,
Whose dear remembrance in my bosom lies,
Too rich a relic for so poor a shrine:
You, in whom Nature chose herself to view,
When she her own perfection would admire,
Bestowing all her excellence on you,
At whose pure eyes Love lights his hallowed fire.
Even as a man that in some trance had seen
More than his wondering utterance can unfold,
That wrapt in spirit, in better worlds hath been,
So must your praise distractedly be told:
    Most of all short, when I should show you most,
    In your perfections so much am I lost.

Since there's no help, come, let us kiss and part,
Nay, I have done, you get no more of me;
And I am glad, yea, glad with all my heart,
That thus so cleanly I myself can free:
Shake hands forever, cancel all our vows,
And when we meet at any time again,
Be it not seen in either of our brows,
That we one jot of former love retain;
Now at the last gasp of love's latest breath,
When his pulse failing, passion speechless lies,
When faith is kneeling by his bed of death,
And innocence is closing up his eyes,
    Now, if thou would'st, when all have given him over,
    From death to life thou might'st him yet recover.

AN HYMN.

TO HIS LADY'S BIRTH PLACE.

Coventry, that dost adorn
The country wherein I was born,

Yet therein lies not thy praise,
Why I should crown thy towers with bays:
'Tis not thy wall me to thee weds,
Thy ports, nor thy proud pyramids,
Nor thy trophies of the boar,
But that she which I adore,
Which scarce Goodness' self can pair,
First there breathing blessed thy air.
  Idea, in which name I hide
Her, in my heart deified,
For what good man's mind can see,
Only her ideas be;
She, in whom the virtues came
In woman's shape, and took her name,
She, so far past imitation,
As but Nature our creation
Could not alter, she had aimed
More than woman to have framed:
She, whose truly-written story,
To thy poor name shall add more glory,
Than if it should have been thy chance
T' have bred our kings that conquered France.
  Had she been born the former age,
That house had been a pilgrimage,
And reputed more divine,
Than Walsingham or Becket's shrine.
  That princess, to whom thou dost owe
Thy freedom, whose clear blushing snow
The envious Sun saw, when as she
Naked rode to make thee free,
Was but her type, as to foretell
Thou should'st bring forth one, should excell
Her bounty, by whom thou should'st have
More honour, than she freedom gave;
And that great queen, which but of late
Ruled this land in peace and state,
Had not been, but Heaven had sworn
A maid should reign when she was born.

Of thy streets which thou hold'st best,
And most frequent of the rest,
Happy Mich-Parke, of the year,
On the fourth of August there,
Let thy maids from Flora's bowers,
With their choice and daintiest flowers
Deck thee up, and from their store
With brave garlands crown that door.
The old man passing by that way,
To his son in time shall say,
"There was that lady born, which long
To after ages shall be sung;"
Who unawares being passed by,
Back to that house shall cast his eye,
Speaking my verses as he goes,
And with a sigh shut every close.
Dear city, travelling by thee,
When thy rising spires I see,
Destined her place of birth;
Yet methinks the very earth
Hallowed is, so far as I
Can thee possibly descry:
Then thou, dwelling in this place,
Hearing some rude hind disgrace
Thy city with some scurvy thing,
Which some jester forth did bring,
Speak these lines where thou dost come,
And strike the slave forever dumb.

CHRISTOPHER MARLOW.

1563—1593.

[“*England's Helicon.*” 1600.]

THE PASSIONATE SHEPHERD TO HIS LOVE.

Come live with me, and be my love,
And we will all the pleasures prove,
That vallies, groves, hills and fields,
Woods, or steepy mountains yields.

And we will sit upon the rocks,
Seeing the shepherds feed their flocks,
By shallow rivers, to whose falls
Melodious birds sing madrigals.

And I will make thee beds of roses,
And a thousand fragrant posies,
A cap of flowers, and a kirtle
Embroidered all with leaves of myrtle.

A gown made of the finest wool,
Which from our pretty lambs we pull,
Fair linéd slippers for the cold,
With buckles of the purest gold:

A belt of straw, and ivy buds,
With coral clasps and amber studs.

And if these pleasures may thee move,
Come live with me, and be my love.

The shepherd swains shall dance and sing
For thy delights each May morning;
If these delights thy mind may move,
Then live with me, and be my love.

EDWARD VERE,

EARL OF OXFORD.

1534(?)—1604.

[" *The Phœnix Nest.*" 1593.]

HE SHEPHERD'S COMMENDATION OF HIS NYMPH.

WHAT shepherd can express
The favour of her face,
To whom in this distress
I do appeal for grace?
    A thousand Cupids fly
    About her gentle eye:

From which each throws a dart,
That kindleth soft sweet fire
Within my sighing heart,
Possessèd by desire.
    No sweeter life I try,
    Than in her love to die.

The lily in the field,
That glories in his white,
For pureness now must yield,
And render up his right.
    Heaven pictured in her face
    Doth promise joy and grace.

Fair Cynthia's silver light,
That beats on running streams,
Compares not with her white,
Whose hairs are all sunbeams.
So bright my nymph doth shine
As day unto mine eyen.

With this there is a red
Exceeds the damask rose;
Which in her cheeks is spread,
Where every favour grows.
In sky there is no star,
But she surmounts it far.

When Phœbus from the bed
Of Thetis doth arise,
The morning blushing red,
In fair carnation-wise;
He shows in my nymph's face,
As queen of every grace.

This pleasant lily white,
This taint of roseate red,
This Cynthia's silver light,
This sweet fair Dea spread,
These sunbeams in mine eye,
These beauties make me die.

EDMUND SPENSER.

1552–1598.

SPENSER is said to have been in love twice; once in his youth with a hard-hearted damsel, who scorned him, and married a rival, and again in his riper years with a lady whom he married. Nothing is known of either, except that the name of the last was Elizabeth. He is supposed to have met the first, somewhere in the north of England, in 1577 or '78, certainly not later than '79, when he published "THE SHEPHERD'S CALENDAR," in which she figured as Rosalinde. E. K., who wrote a gloss to the poem, tells us that Rosalinde is "a fained name, which being well ordered will bewray the verie name of his love and mistresse, whom by that name he coloureth." Who E. K. was, and how he happened to know Spenser's secret, if he did know it, is a mystery. Some real name was undoubtedly hidden in the fictitious one of Rosalinde, but what name? Of whom was Rosalinde the anagram? The question has never been answered satisfactorily. A writer in "THE ATLANTIC MONTHLY," for November, 1858, conjectures it to have been that of Rose Daniel, a sister of Samuel Daniel, the poet. This theory is ingenious, to say the least, but there are, it seems to me, some chronological objections to it. That Spenser and Daniel were acquainted, and that the latter had a sister named Rose, is true; but that Spenser was acquainted with her, especially when he is said to have been in love with Rosalinde, is mere conjecture. There is no reason to believe that he knew Daniel then: for Daniel was his junior by nine or ten years; was from a different county, (Spenser being born in London, and Daniel near Taunton, in Somersetshire,) and was about entering, if he had not already entered, college. He was admitted a Commoner of Magdalen Hall, Oxford, in 1579, at which time Spenser, who was educated at Pembroke Hall, Cambridge, was in Kent, having left college in 1576, or '77. The chances are rather against this early acquaintance of the two poets. Still, they *may* have known each other, and Rose Daniel *may* have been the Rosalinde of "THE SHEPHERD'S CALENDAR." All that is known of Miss Rose is, that she married Resolute John Florio, and at his death, in 1625, was remembered in his will. Daniel, the reader will remember, married Florio's sister, Justina.

After the publication of "THE SHEPHERD'S CALENDAR," Spenser proceeded to Ireland, where he remained for a number of years. In 1586, he received from Queen Elizabeth, the grant of the manor and castle of Kilcolman, with other lands, amounting in all to

3,028 acres, in the barony of Fermoy, county of Cork. He took possession of his Irish estate, and began, it would seem, to look about for a wife. His courtship commenced in the latter part of 1592, and he was married on St. Barnabas's day, (the 11th of June, O. S.) 1594. How he fared in this interval—what hopes and fears were his—the old yet ever new story of a lover's life—is seen in his sonnets. He sent them to England after his marriage, and they were published in 1595, under the title of "AMORETTI."

The name of Spenser's wife was Elizabeth, as I have already mentioned, but who she was is unknown. She is called a country lass in "THE FAIRY QUEEN," and in "THE EPITHALAMION" is said to live near the sea. The writer of the article in "THE ATLANTIC MONTHLY" has a similar theory in relation to her. He transposes the word "Angel," which occurs quite often in the sonnets—too often, he thinks, for poetical purposes merely—and produces the word "Nagle," which he assumes to have been her name. A family of Nagles lived in the county of Cork in Spenser's day. They were divided into two branches, and distinguished according to the colour of their hair, as the Red Nagles, and the Black Nagles. The lord, or chieftain, of the former resided at Moneanymmy, an ancient preceptory of the Knights of St. John, situated on the banks of the Mulla, at a little distance from Kilcolman. It is not certain that there was an Elizabeth in this family in 1592–94, (the records, unfortunately, preserve only the name of the male heir,) but if there was one, there is no reason why Spenser should not have married her. I have no more objection to this theory than to the former one, so, with the reader's permission, the supposititious Elizabeth Nagle shall be Spenser's wife, and Rose Daniel his first love, Rosalinde.

New Year, forth looking out of Janus' gate,
Doth seem to promise hope of new delight,
And, bidding th' old adieu, his passéd date,
Bids all old thoughts to die in dumpish sprite;
And calling forth out of sad Winter's night
Fresh Love, that long hath slept in cheerless bower,
Wills him awake, and soon about him dight
His wanton wings and darts of deadly power.
For lusty Spring now in his timely hour
Is ready to come forth, him to receive;
And warns the Earth with divers-coloured flower
To deck herself, and her fair mantle weave.
  Then you, fair flower! in whom fresh youth doth reign,
  Prepare yourself new love to entertain.

The merry cuckoo, messenger of Spring,
His trumpet shrill hath thrice already sounded,

That warns all lovers wait upon their king,
Who now is coming forth with garland crownéd.
With noise whereof the quire of birds resounded
Their anthems sweet, deviséd of love's praise,
That all the woods their echoes back rebounded,
As if they knew the meaning of their lays.
But 'mongst them all which did Love's honour raise,
No word was heard of her that most it ought;
But she his precept proudly disobeys,
And doth his idle message set at nought.
    Therefore, O Love, unless she turn to thee
    Ere cuckoo end, let her a rebel be!

This holy season, fit to fast and pray,
Men to devotion ought to be inclined:
Therefore, I, likewise, on so holy day,
For my sweet saint some service fit will find.
Her temple fair is built within my mind,
In which her glorious image placéd is;
On which my thoughts do day and night attend,
Like sacred priests that never think amiss.
There I to her, as th' author of my bliss,
Will build an altar to appease her ire,
And on the same my heart will sacrifice,
Burning in flames of pure and chaste desire:
    The which vouchsafe, O Goddess, to accept,
    Amongst thy dearest relics to be kept.

What guile is this, that those her golden tresses
She doth attire under a net of gold,
And with sly skill so cunningly them dresses,
That which is gold or hair may scarce be told?
Is it that men's frail eyes, which gaze too bold,
She may entangle in that golden snare;
And, being caught, may craftily enfold
Their weaker hearts, which are not well aware?

Take heed therefore, mine eyes, how ye do stare
Henceforth too rashly on that guileful net,
In which if ever ye entrappéd are,
Out of her bands ye by no means shall get.
    Fondness it were for any, being free,
    To covet fetters, though they golden be!

Mark when she smiles with amiable cheer,
And tell me whereto can ye liken it;
When on each eyelid sweetly do appear
An hundred Graces as in shade to sit.
Likest it seemeth, in my simple wit,
Unto the fair sunshine in summer's day,
That, when a dreadful storm away is flit,
Through the broad world doth spread his goodly ray;
At sight whereof, each bird that sits on spray,
And every beast that to his den was fled,
Comes forth afresh out of their late dismay,
And to the light lift up their drooping head.
    So my storm-beaten heart likewise is cheered
    With that sunshine, when cloudy looks are cleared.

When my abode's prefixéd time is spent,
My cruel fair straight bids me wend my way:
But then from heaven most hideous storms are sent,
As willing me against her will to stay.
Whom then shall I—or heaven, or her—obey?
The heavens know best what is the best for me:
But as she will, whose will my life doth sway,
My lower heaven, so it perforce must be.
But ye, high heavens, that all this sorrow see,
Sith all your tempests cannot hold me back,
Assuage your storms, or else both you and she
Will both together me too sorely wrack.
    Enough it is for one man to sustain
    The storms which she alone on me doth rain.

The glorious image of the Maker's beauty,
My sovereign saint, the idol of my thought,
Dare not henceforth, above the bounds of duty,
T' accuse of pride, or rashly blame for aught.
For being, as she is, divinely wrought,
And of the brood of angels heavenly born,
And with the crew of blessed saints up-brought,
Each of which did her with their gifts adorn,
The bud of joy, the blossom of the morn,
The beam of light, whom mortal eyes admire,
What reason is it then but she should scorn
Base things, that to her love too bold aspire!
    Such heavenly forms ought rather worshipped be,
    Than dare be loved by men of mean degree.

Like as an huntsman, after weary chase,
Seeing the game from him escaped away,
Sits down to rest him in some shady place,
With panting hounds, beguiléd of their prey;
So, after long pursuit and vain essay,
When I all-weary had the chase forsook,
The gentle deer returned the self-same way,
Thinking to quench her thirst at the next brook.
There she, beholding me with milder look,
Sought not to fly, but fearless still did 'bide,
Till I in hand her yet half trembling took,
And with her own good will her firmly tied.
    Strange thing, me seemed, to see a beast so wild
    So goodly won, with her own will beguiled.

The famous warriours of the antique world
Used trophies to erect in stately wise,
In which they would the records have enrolled
Of their great deeds and valorous emprize.
What trophy then shall I most fit devise,
In which I may record the memory

Of my love's conquest, peerless beauty's prize,
Adorned with honour, love, and chastity?
Even this verse, vowed to eternity,
Shall be thereof immortal monument,
And tell her praise to all posterity,
That may admire such world's rare wonderment;
    The happy purchase of my glorious spoil,
    Gotten at last with labour, and long toil.

Fresh Spring, the herald of Love's mighty king,
In whose coat-armour richly are displayed
All sorts of flowers the which on earth do spring,
In goodly colours gloriously arrayed,
Go to my love, where she is careless laid,
Yet in her winter's bower not well awake:
Tell her the joyous time will not be stayed,
Unless she do him by the forelock take;
Bid her therefore her self soon ready make,
To wait on Love amongst his lovely crew,
Where every one that misseth then her make
Shall be by him amerced with penance due.
    Make haste therefore, sweet love, while it is prime,
    For none can call again the passéd time.

Being myself captivéd here in care,
My heart (whom none with servile bands can tie,
But the fair tresses of your golden hair),
Breaking his prison, forth to you doth fly.
Like as a bird, that in one's hand doth spy
Desiréd food, to it doth make his flight,
Even so my heart, that wont on your fair eye
To feed his fill, flies back unto your sight.
Do you him take, and in your bosom bright
Gently encage, that he may be your thrall:
Perhaps he there may learn, with rare delight,
To sing your name and praises over all:

That it hereafter may you not repent,
Him lodging in your bosom to have lent.

Since I did leave the presence oi my love,
Many long weary days I have outworn,
And many nights, that slowly seemed to move
Their sad protract, from even until morn.
For, when as day the heaven doth adorn,
I wish that night the noyous day would end:
And when as night hath us of light forlorn,
I wish that day would shortly re-ascend.
Thus I the time with expectation spend,
And feign my grief with changes to beguile,
That further seems his term still to extend,
And maketh every minute seem a mile.
So sorrow still doth seem too long to last;
But joyous hours do fly away too fast.

Like as the culver, on the baréd bough
Sits mourning for the absence of her mate,
And in her songs sends many a wishful vow
For his return, that seems to linger late;
So I alone, now left disconsolate,
Mourn to myself the absence of my love:
And wandering here and there all desolate,
Seek with my plaints to match that mournful dove:
Ne joy of aught that under heaven doth hove,
Can comfort me, but her own joyous sight,
Whose sweet aspect both God and man can move,
In her unspotted pleasaunce to delight.
Dark is my day, whiles her fair light I miss,
And dead my life that wants such lively bliss.

B. GRIFFIN.

[*"Fidessa, more chaste than kind."* 1596.]

Fair is my love that feeds among the lilies,
  The lilies growing in that pleasant garden,
Where Cupid's mount, that well-belovéd hill is,
  And where that little god himself is warden.
See, where my love sits in the beds of spices,
  Beset all round with camphor, myrrh, and roses,
And interlaced with curious devices,
  Which her from all the world apart incloses.
There doth she tune her lute for her delight,
  And with sweet music makes the ground to move,
Whilst I (poor I) do sit in heavy plight
  Wailing alone my unrespected love;
Not daring rush into so rare a place,
That gives to her and she to it a grace.

I have not spent the April of my time,
  The sweet of youth in plotting in the air:
But do at first adventure seek to climb,
  Whilst flowers of blooming years are green and fair.
I am no leaving of all-withering age,
  I have not suffered many winter lowers;
I feel no storm, unless my love do rage,
  And then in grief I spend both days and hours.
This yet doth comfort, that my flower lasted,

Until it did approach my Sun too near;
And then (alas) untimely was it blasted,
So soon as once thy beauty did appear:
But after all my comfort rests in this,
That for thy sake my youth decayéd is.

Sweet stroke, (so might I thrive) as I must praise,
But sweeter hand that gives so sweet a stroke:
The lute itself is sweetest, when she plays;
But what hear I? A string through fear is broke.
The lute doth shake, as if it were afraid,
O sure some goddess holds it in her hand!
A heavenly power that oft hath me dismayed,
Yet such a power as doth in beauty stand.
Cease, lute; my ceaseless suit will ne'er be heard:
(Ah! too hard-hearted she that will not hear it!)
If I but think on joy, my joy is marred,
My grief is great, yet ever must I bear it.
But love 'twixt us will prove a faithful page,
And she will love my sorrows to assuage.

Weep now no more, mine eyes, but be you drowned
In your own tears, so many years distilled:
And let her know that at them long hath frowned,
That you can weep no more, although she willed.
This hap her cruelty hath her allotten,
Who whilom was commandress of each part:
That now her proper griefs must be forgotten,
By those true outward signs of inward smart.
For how can he that hath not one tear left him,
Stream out those floods that's due unto her moaning,
When both of eyes and tears she hath bereft him?
O yet I'll signify my grief with groaning!
True sighs, true groans shall echo in the air,
And say Fidessa (though most cruel) is most fair.

Shakespeare's Love.

WILLIAM SHAKESPEARE.

1564—1616.

THE sonnets of Shakespeare are a puzzle to his commentators, who cannot agree upon the person to whom they were addressed. They—the sonnets, not the commentators—were published for the first time in 1609, and dedicated by the publisher, T. T. (Thomas Thorpe), to Mr. W. H., whom he declared to be their "onlie begetter." Who Mr. W. H. was, has never been settled. Dr. Farmer supposed the initials were those of William Harte, the poet's nephew; but as that young gentleman was only nine years old when the sonnets were published, his suggestion refuted itself. Tyrwhitt pointed out a line in the twentieth sonnet,

"A man in hue, all hues in his controlling,"

and because the word hues was printed *Hews* in the old edition, inferred that they stood for William Hews, or Hughes. Dr. Drake was for reversing them, when they would stand for those of Henry Wriothesley, the patron and friend of Shakespeare, to whom "VENUS AND ADONIS," and "THE RAPE OF LUCRECE" were dedicated. Mr. Boaden, and Keats' friend, Mr. Charles Armitage Brown, were for letting them remain, and interpreting them as the initials of William Herbert, Sydney's nephew, and the son of the Earl of Pembroke. Whether this young nobleman, who, by the by, was Earl of Pembroke himself, when the sonnets were published, his father dying in 1601, could with propriety be styled *Mr.* William Herbert, is still a subject of dispute. Not being a Shakespearean commentator, I shall not favour the reader with any theory of my own, but leaving him to take his choice of the persons suggested, pass on to what more immediately concerns me, which is, whether the enigmatical Mr. W. H. was what Thorpe declared him to be, the "onlie begetter" of the sonnets. To this there can be but one answer: He was not. That the majority of the sonnets were addressed to a man, is certain; but that a considerable number of them, about one third, I should say, were addressed to a woman, is equally certain. The difficulty hitherto has been the way in which they were originally printed. Instead of being divided into poems of a certain length, they were huddled together carelessly, no order being preserved, except in the first twenty or thirty. Whether the blame rests with Thorpe, or the person who furnished him the copy, can not of course be ascertained, but probably with the latter. There is reason to think that Shakespeare did not assist in their publication, but that they were given to the world without his concurrence, as was the case with all his plays printed in his lifetime. Had he published the sonnets himself, he would have printed them, I am convinced, in a different order to that in which they now stand, and not as sonnets proper, but rather as poems in the sonnet stanza, like Spenser's "VISIONS OF PETRARCH," "VISIONS OF BELLAY," etc. He would have classified them, as Mr. Brown and others have since done. Whether his classification would have corresponded with theirs, is another matter. Mr. Brown divides them into six consecutive poems, or parts. With this division I agree in the main, although it seems to me in some respects imperfect. I would shift some of the stanzas into different poems, and would re-arrange the order of the whole. Especially I would add to the last division, which Mr. Brown christens, "*To his mistress, on her infidelity*," because it is the only writing of Shakespeare's extant, which seems to be autobiographical. Whether it is so, or not, we shall probably never know. For my own part I love to think it is. It is a pleasure to me when I read the sonnets, to think that I am obtaining a glimpse of Shakespeare—an insight, however slight, into the emotions of that great Spirit. He permits me to read a page in the volume of his heart—a page of all others the most interesting—the story of his love.

"And who was she the lady of his love?"

Not Mistress Shakespeare, of Stratford, *née* Anne Hathaway, though he doubtless loved her as his wife, and the mother of his children, but some light dame who consoled him for her absence when he was living in London. Of this Siren, who had black eyes and black hair, we know nothing, except that Shakespeare loved her, and that she was false to him. When this happened we can only conjecture: I imagine it to have been between 1593 and 1598; certainly not much later than the last year, when Shakespeare's "sugred Sonnets" were well enough known to be mentioned in print. (MERE'S WIT'S TREASURY.) My reasons for this supposition are various. First, the form of the verse in which Shakespeare celebrated this mysterious episode in his life—the Sonnet. It was not an early form with him, as far as we can ascertain, for his two earliest poems, "VENUS AND ADONIS," published in 1593, and "THE RAPE OF LUCRECE," published in 1594, are in measures the music of which is utterly at variance with that of the Sonnet. If he had tried the Sonnet before the six and seven line stanzas of these poems, it would have been difficult for him to have avoided its cadences while writing them. He was a master of rhythm, it is true; but it is equally true that at certain periods of his poetical life, he wrote in certain styles, and in no other. He began, like all young poets, with some peculiar rhythm or tune in his head; but as his mind enlarged with practice and knowledge, he learned new ones, and shaped his creations according to their laws. My second reason for thinking the sonnets were written after "VENUS AND ADONIS," and "THE RAPE OF LUCRECE," is, that they are in all respects superior to those poems. It might not be safe to apply this test to the works of some of the modern poets, for their latest works are frequently their worst; but it is safe to apply it to Shakespeare, for his great mind never retrograded. Another reason for thinking that his sonnets were written after 1593, is that at that time the Sonnet was just beginning to be popular in England. There were three causes for this popularity, or rather three poets who contributed to it—Sydney, Daniel, and Drayton, whose sonnets, the reader will remember, were published in 1591, '92, and '93. The fashion was set by them, and Shakespeare was not long in adopting it. His model was Daniel, the linked sweetness of whose versification was in harmony with his own taste. He commenced with "THE PASSIONATE PILGRIM"—admitting it to be his work, which many critics doubt—and finding his studies, so to speak, successful, tried his hand at a poetical portrait of the enigmatical Mr. W. H. As his touch became firmer and more assured, he painted himself and his Delilah. Would that we could know who she was, that dallied with the invincible locks of this greater than Samson! But we can not. What song the sirens sang, or what name Achilles assumed when he hid himself among women, though puzzling questions, are not beyond all conjecture; but Shakespeare's mistress is.

> Gone like a wind that blew
> A thousand years ago.

"I fear," says Mr. Brown, at the conclusion of his dissertation on Shakespeare's sonnets, "I fear some readers may be surprised that I have not yet noticed a certain fault in Shakespeare, a glaring one—his having a wife of his own, perhaps, at Stratford. May no persons be inclined, on this account, to condemn him with a bitterness equal to their own virtue! For myself, I confess I have not the heart to blame him at all—purely because he so keenly reproaches himself for his own sin and folly. Fascinated as he was, he did not, like other poets similarly guilty, directly, or by implication, obtrude his own passions on the world as reasonable laws. Had such been the case, he might have merited our censure, possibly our contempt. On the contrary, he condemned and subdued his fault, and may therefore be cited as a good rather than as a bad example. Should it be contended that he seems to have quitted his mistress more on account of her unworthiness than from conscientious feelings, I have nothing to answer beyond this: I will not seek after questionable motives for good actions, well knowing by experience, that when obtruded on me, they have been nothing but a nuisance to my better thoughts."

So is it not with me as with that muse,
Stirred by a painted beauty to his verse;
Who heaven itself for ornament doth use,
And every fair with his fair doth rehearse;
Making a complement of proud compare
With sun and moon, with earth and sea's rich gems,
With April's first-born flowers, and all things rare
That heaven's air in his huge rondure hems.

O let me, true in love, but truly write,
And then believe me, my love is as fair
As any mother's child, though not so bright
As those gold candles fixed in heaven's air:
    Let them say more that like of hear-say well;
    I will not praise, that purpose not to sell.

My glass shall not persuade me I am old,
So long as youth and thou are of one date;
But when in thee Time's furrows I behold,
Then look I death my days should expiate.
For all that beauty that doth cover thee,
Is but the seemly raiment of my heart,
Which in thy breast doth live, as thine in me;
How then can I be elder than thou art?
O therefore, love, be of thyself so wary,
As I not for myself, but for thee will;
Bearing thy heart, which I will keep so chary
As tender nurse her babe from faring ill.
    Presume not on thy heart when mine is slain;
    Thou gav'st me thine, not to give back again.

Weary with toil, I haste me to my bed,
The dear repose for limbs with travel tired;
But then begins a journey in my head,
To work my mind, when body's work 's expired:
For then my thoughts (from far where I abide)
Intend a zealous pilgrimage to thee,
And keep my drooping eyelids open wide,
Looking on darkness which the blind do see;
Save that my soul's imaginary sight
Presents thy shadow to my sightless view,
Which, like a jewel hung in ghastly night,
Makes black night beauteous, and her old face new.
    Lo! thus by day my limbs, by night my mind,
    For thee, and for myself, no quiet find.

How careful was I when I took my way,
Each trifle under truest bars to thrust,
That, to my use, it might unuséd stay
From hands of falsehood, in sure wards of trust!
But thou, to whom my jewels trifles are,
Most worthy comfort, now my greatest grief,
Thou, best of dearest, and mine only care,
Art left the prey of every vulgar thief.
Thee have I not locked up in any chest,
Save where thou art not, though I feel thou art,
Within the gentle closure of my breast,
From whence at pleasure thou may'st come and part;
    And even thence thou wilt be stolen I fear,
    For truth proves thievish for a prize so dear.

That time of year thou may'st in me behold,
When yellow leaves, or none, or few, do hang
Upon those boughs which shake against the cold,
Bare ruined choirs, where late the sweet birds sang.
In me thou seest the twilight of such day,
As after sunset fadeth in the west,
Which by and by black night doth take away,
Death's second self, that seals up all in rest.
In me thou seest the glowing of such fire,
That on the ashes of his youth doth lie,
As the death-bed whereon it must expire,
Consumed with that which it was nourished by.
    This thou perceiv'st, which makes thy love more strong,
    To love that well which thou must leave ere long.

How like a winter hath my absence been
From thee, the pleasure of the fleeting year!
What freezings have I felt, what dark days seen!
What old December's bareness everywhere!
And yet this time removed was summer's time!
The teeming autumn, big with rich increase,

Bearing the wanton burthen of the prime,
Like widowed wombs after their lords' decease:
Yet this abundant issue seemed to me
But hope of orphans, and unfathered fruit;
For summer and his pleasures wait on thee,
And thou away, the very birds are mute;
Or, if they sing, 'tis with so dull a cheer,
That leaves look pale, dreading the winter's near.

From you have I been absent in the spring,
When proud-pied April, dressed in all his trim,
Hath put a spirit of youth in everything,
That heavy Saturn laughed and leaped with him.
Yet nor the lays of birds, nor the sweet smell
Of different flowers in odour and in hue,
Could make me any summer's story tell,
Or from their proud lap pluck them where they grew:
Nor did I wonder at the lily's white,
Nor praise the deep vermilion in the rose:
They were but sweet, but figures of delight,
Drawn after you, you pattern of all those.
Yet, seemed it winter still, and, you away,
As with your shadow I with these did play.

The forward violet thus did I chide:
Sweet thief, whence didst thou steal thy sweet that smells,
If not from my love's breath? The purple pride
Which on thy soft cheek for complexion dwells,
In my love's veins thou hast too grossly dyed.
The lily I condemnéd for thy hand,
And buds of marjoram had stolen thy hair:
The roses fearfully on thorns did stand,
One blushing shame, another white despair;
A third, nor red nor white, had stolen of both,
And to his robbery had annexed thy breath;
But for his theft, in pride of all his growth,
A vengeful canker eat him up to death.

More flowers I noted, yet I none could see,
But sweet or colour it had stolen from thee.

My mistress' eyes are nothing like the sun;
Coral is far more red than her lips' red:
If snow be white, why then her breasts are dun;
If hairs be wires, black wires grow on her head.
I have seen roses damasked, red and white,
But no such roses see I on her cheeks;
And in some perfumes there is more delight
Than in the breath that from my mistress reeks.
I love to hear her speak, yet well I know
That music hath a far more pleasing sound;
I grant I never saw a goddess go,
My mistress, when she walks, treads on the ground;
And yet, by heaven, I think my love as rare
As any she belied with false compare.

How oft, when thou, my music, music play'st,
Upon that blessèd wood whose motion sounds
With thy sweet fingers, when thou gently sway'st
The wiry concord that mine ear confounds,
Do I envy those jacks, that nimble leap
To kiss the tender inward of thy hand,
Whilst my poor lips, which should that harvest reap,
At the wood's boldness by thee blushing stand!
To be so tickled, they would change their state
And situation with those dancing chips
O'er whom thy fingers walk with gentle gait,
Making dead wood more blest than living lips.
Since saucy jacks so happy are in this,
Give them thy fingers, me thy lips to kiss.

Thine eyes I love, and they, as pitying me,
Knowing thy heart, torment me with disdain;

Have put on black, and loving mourners be,
Looking with pretty ruth upon my pain.
And truly not the morning sun of heaven
Better becomes the grey cheeks of the east,
Nor that full star that ushers in the even,
Doth half that glory to the sober west,
As those two mourning eyes become thy face;
O let it then as well beseem thy heart
To mourn for me, since mourning doth thee grace,
And suit thy pity like in every part.
    Then will I swear beauty herself is black,
    And all they foul that thy complexion lack.

When my love swears that she is made of truth,
I do believe her, though I know she lies;
That she might think me some untutored youth,
Unlearnéd in the world's false subtilties.
Thus vainly thinking that she thinks me young,
Although she knows my days are past the best,
Simply I credit her false-speaking tongue,
On both sides thus is simple truth suppressed.
But wherefore says she not, she is unjust?
And wherefore say not I, that I am old?
O love's best habit is in seeming trust,
And age in love loves not to have years told:
    Therefore I lie with her, and she with me,
    And in our faults by lies we flattered be.

O call me not to justify the wrong,
That thy unkindness lays upon my heart;
Wound me not with thine eye, but with thy tongue;
Use power with power, and slay me not by art.
Tell me thou lov'st elsewhere; but in my sight,
Dear heart, forbear to glance thine eye aside.
What need'st thou wound with cunning, when thy might
Is more than my o'erpressed defence can 'bide?

Let me excuse thee: ah! my love well knows
Her pretty looks have been mine enemies;
And therefore from my face she turns my foes,
That they elsewhere might dart their injuries:
Yet do not so; but since I am near slain,
Kill me outright with looks, and rid my pain.

O me! what eyes hath love put in my head,
Which have no correspondence with true sight?
Or, if they have, where is my judgment fled,
That censures falsely what they see aright?
If that be fair whereon my false eyes doat,
What means the world to say it is not so?
If it be not, then love doth well denote
Love's eye is not so true as all men's: no,
How can it? O how can Love's eye be true,
That is so vexed with watching and with tears?
No marvel then though I mistake my view;
The sun itself sees not till heaven clears.
O cunning Love! with tears thou keep'st me blind,
Lest eyes well-seeing thy foul faults should find.

Canst thou, O cruel! say I love thee not,
When I, against myself, with thee partake?
Do I not think on thee, when I, forgot
Am of myself, all tyrant, for thy sake?
Who hateth thee that I do call my friend?
On whom frown'st thou that I do fawn upon?
Nay, if thou lower'st on me, do I not spend
Revenge upon myself with present moan?
What merit do I in myself respect,
That is so proud thy service to despise,
When all my best doth worship thy defect,
Commanded by the motion of thine eyes?
But, love, hate on, for now I know thy mind;
Those that can see thou lov'st, and I am blind.

SIR WALTER RALEIGH.

1552—1618.

THE SILENT LOVER.

Passions are likened best to floods and streams,
    The shallow murmur, but the deep are dumb.
So, when affections yield discourse, it seems
    The bottom is but shallow whence they come:
They that are rich in words must needs discover,
They are but poor in that which makes a lover.

Wrong not, sweet mistress of my heart,
    The merit of true passion,
With thinking that he feels no smart,
    Who sues for no compassion!

Since, if my plaints were not t' approve
    The conquest of thy beauty,
It comes not from defect of love,
    But fear t' exceed my duty.

For, knowing that I sue to serve
    A saint of such perfection,
As all desire, but none deserve,
    A place in her affection,

I rather choose to want relief,
    Than venture the revealing:

Where glory recommends the grief,
    Despair disdains the healing!

Thus those desires that boil so high
    In any mortal lover,
When Reason cannot make them die,
    Discretion them must cover.

Yet when Discretion doth bereave
    The plaints that I should utter,
Then your Discretion may perceive
    That Silence is a suitor.

Silence in love bewrays more woe
    Than words, though ne'er so witty;
The beggar that is dumb, you know,
    May challenge double pity!

Then wrong not, dearest to my heart!
    My love for secret passion;
He smarteth most that hides his smart,
    And sues for no compassion!

HIS LOVE ADMITS NO RIVAL.

Shall I, like a hermit, dwell
On a rock, or in a cell,
Calling home the smallest part
That is missing of my heart,
To bestow it, where I may
Meet a rival every day?
    If she undervalue me,
    What care I how fair she be?

Were her tresses angel-gold,
If a stranger may be bold,
Unrebuked, unafraid,
To convert them to a braid;

And with little more ado
Work them into bracelets, too!
    If the mine be grown so free,
    What care I how rich it be?

Were her hands as rich a prize
As her hair, or precious eyes:
If she lay them out to take
Kisses, for good manner's sake;
And let every lover skip
From her hand unto her lip;
    If she seem not chaste to me,
    What care I how chaste she be?

No; she must be perfect snow,
In effect as well as show,
Warming but as snow-balls do,
Not like fire, by burning too;
But when she by change hath got
To her heart a second lot,
    Then, if others share with me,
    Farewell her, whate'er she be!

SIR EDWARD DYER.

1540—161-.

["*England's Helicon.*" 1600.]

TO PHILLIS, THE FAIR SHEPHERDESS.

My Phillis hath the morning sun,
At first to look upon her;
My Phillis hath morn-waking birds,
Her risings still to honour.
My Phillis hath prime-feathered flowers,
That smile when she treads on them;
And Phillis hath a gallant flock,
That leaps since she doth own them.
But Phillis hath too hard a heart,
Alas, that she should have it!
It yields no mercy to desert,
Nor grace to those that crave it:
Sweet sun, when thou look'st on,
Pray her regard my moan;
Sweet birds, when you sing to her.
To yield some pity, woo her;
Sweet flowers, that she treads on,
Tell her her beauty deads one.
And if in life her love she will agree me,
Pray her before I die she will come see me.

NICHOLAS BRETON.

1555—1624.

[“*England's Helicon.*”]

A PASTORAL OF PHILLIS AND CORIDON.

On a hill there grows a flower,
    Fair befall the dainty sweet:
For that flower there is a bower,
    Where the heavenly Muses meet.

In that bower there is a chair,
    Fringéd all about with gold,
Where doth sit the fairest fair,
    That ever eye did yet behold.

It is Phillis, fair and bright,
    She that is the shepherd's joy:
She that Venus did despite,
    And did blind her little boy.

This is she, the wise, the rich,
    That the world desires to see:
This is *ipse quæ*, the which
    There is none but only she.

Who would not this face admire?
    Who would not this saint adore?

Who would not this sight desire,
    Though he thought to see no more?

O fair eyes, yet let me see
    One good look, and I am gone;
Look on me, for I am he,
    Thy poor silly Coridon.

Thou that art the shepherd's queen,
    Look upon thy silly swain:
By thy comfort have been seen
    Dead men brought to life again.

CORIDON'S SUPPLICATION TO PHILLIS.

Sweet Phillis, if a silly swain
    May sue to thee for grace,
See not thy loving shepherd slain,
    For looking on thy face.
But think what power thou hast got,
    Upon my flock and me;
Thou see'st they now regard me not,
    But all do follow thee.
And if I have so far presumed,
    With prying in thine eyes;
Yet let not comfort be consumed,
    That in thy pity lies:
But as thou art that Phillis fair,
    That Fortune favour gives,
So let not Love die in despair,
    That in thy favour lives.
The deer do browse upon the brier,
    The birds do pick the cherries:
And will not beauty grant desire
    A handful of her berries?
If it be so that thou hast sworn,
    That none shall look on thee;

Yet let me know thou dost not scorn
 To cast a look on me.
But if thy beauty make thee proud,
 Think then what is ordained:
The heavens have never yet allowed
 That Love should be disdained.
Then lest the fates that favour Love
 Should curse thee for unkind,
Let me report for thy behoove,
 The honour of thy mind;
Let Coridon with full consent
 Set down what he hath seen:
That Phillida, with Love's content,
 Is sworn the Shepherd's Queen.

FULKE GREVILE,

LORD BROOKE.

1554—1628.

"FULKE GREVILE, servant to Queen Elizabeth, Counsellor to King James, and friend to Sir Philip Sydney."—LORD BROOKE'S EPITAPH.

["*England's Helicon.*"]

OF HIS CYNTHIA.

Away with these self-loving lads,
Whom Cupid's arrow never glads;
Away, poor souls that sigh, and weep,
In love of them that lie and sleep.
    For Cupid is a merry god,
    And forceth none to kiss the rod.

God Cupid's shafts, like destiny,
Doth either good or ill decree:
Desert is borne out of his bow,
Reward upon his feet doth go.
    What fools are they that have not known
    That Love likes no laws but his own.

My songs, they be of Cynthia's praise,
I wear her rings on holidays;
On every tree I write her name,
And every day I read the same.

Where Honour, Cupid's rival is,
There miracles are seen of his.

If Cynthia crave her ring of me,
I blot her name out of the tree.
If doubt do darken things held dear,
Then well-fare nothing once a year.
For many run, but one must win;
Fools only hedge the cuckoo in.

The worth that worthiness should move,
Is love, which is the due of love;
And love as well the shepherd can,
As can the mighty nobleman.
Sweet nymph, 'tis true, you worthy be,
Yet without love, nought worth to me.

MYRA'S INCONSTANCY.

I, with whose colours Myra dressed her head,
I, that wore posies of her own hand-making,
I, that mine own name in the chimneys read,
By Myra finely wrought ere I was waking:
Must I look on, in hope time coming may
With change bring back again my turn to play?

I, that on Sunday at the church-stile found
A garland sweet, with true-love knots in flowers,
Which I to wear about mine arm was bound,
That each of us might know that all was ours;
Must I now lead an idle life in wishes,
And follow Cupid for his loaves and fishes?

I, that did wear the ring her mother left,
I, for whose love she gloried to be blamed,
I, with whose eyes her eyes committed theft,
I, who did make her blush when I was named;

Must I lose ring, flowers, blush, theft, and go naked,
Watching with sighs till dead Love be awakéd?

I, that when drowsy Argus fell asleep,
Like Jealousy o'erwatched with Desire,
Was ever warnéd modesty to keep,
While her breath speaking kindled Nature's fire,
Must I look on a-cold while others warm them?
Do Vulcan's brothers in such fine nets arm them?

Was it for this that I might Myra see,
Washing the water with her beauties, white?
Yet would she never write her love to me;
Thinks wit of change, while thoughts are in delight?
Mad girls may safely love, as they may leave:
No man can print a kiss: Lines may deceive.

FRANCIS DAVISON.

1575—161-.

["*A Poetical Rhapsodie.*" 1602.]

OF HIS LADY'S WEEPING.

WHAT need I say how it doth wound my breast,
By fate to be thus ravished from thine eyes,
Since your own tears with me do sympathise,
Pleading with slow departure there to rest?
For when with floods of tears they were oppressed,
Over those ivory banks they did not rise,
Till others, envying their felicities,
Did press them forth, that they might there be blest.
Some of which tears, pressed forth by violence,
Your lips with greedy kissing straight did drink:
And other some, unwilling to part thence,
Enamoured on your cheeks in them did sink;
And some which from your face were forced away,
In sign of love, did on your garments stay.

HIS SIGHS AND TEARS ARE BOOTLESS.

I have entreated, and I have complained;
I have dispraised, and praise I likewise gave;
All means to win her grace I triéd have;
And still I love, and still I am disdained.

So long I have my tongue and pen constrained,
To praise, dispraise, complain, and pity crave,
That now nor tongue, nor pen, to me, her slave,
Remains, whereby her grace may be obtained.
Yet you, my sighs, may purchase me relief;
And ye, my tears, her rocky heart may move:
Therefore, my sighs, sigh in her ear my grief;
And in her heart, my tears, imprint my love.
But cease, vain sighs; cease, cease, ye fruitless tears;
Tears cannot pierce her heart, nor sighs her ears.

HIS FAREWELL,

TO HIS UNKIND AND INCONSTANT MISTRESS.

Sweet, if you like and love me still,
And yield me love for my good will,
And do not from your promise start,
When your fair hand gave me your heart;
If dear to you I be,
As you are dear to me;
Then yours I am and will be ever,
Nor time nor place my love shall sever;
But faithful still I will persever,
Like constant marble stone,
Loving but you alone.

But if you favour more than me,
Who love thee, dear, and none but thee,
If others do the harvest gain,
That's due to me for all my pain;
If you delight to range,
And oft to chop and change;
Then get you some new-fangled mate;
My doating love shall turn to hate,
Esteeming you, though too, too late,
Not worth a pebble stone,
Loving not me alone.

BEN JONSON.

1573—1637.

[“*The Poetaster.*” 1601.]

SONG.

If I freely may discover
What would please me in my lover,
I would have her fair and witty,
Savouring more of court than city;
A little proud, but full of pity;
Light and humorous in her toying;
Oft building hopes, and soon destroying;
Long, but sweet in the enjoying;
Neither too easy, nor too hard,
All extremes I would have barred.

She should be allowed her passions,
So they were but used as fashions;
Sometimes froward, and then frowning,
Sometimes sickish, and then swooning,
Every fit with change still crowning.
Purely jealous I would have her,
Then only constant when I crave her;
'Tis a virtue should not save her.
Thus, nor her delicates would cloy me,
Nor her peevishness annoy me.

[“*Epicœne; or, The Silent Woman.*” 1609.]

SONG.

Still to be neat, still to be dressed,
As you were going to a feast;
Still to be powdered, still perfumed:
Lady, it is to be presumed,
Though art's hid causes are not found,
All is not sweet, all is not sound.

Give me a look, give me a face,
That makes simplicity a grace;
Robes loosely flowing, hair as free:
Such sweet neglect more taketh me,
Than all the adulteries of art;
They strike mine eyes, but not my heart.

[“*The Forest.*” 1616.]

TO CELIA.

Come, my Celia, let us prove,
While we may, the sports of love;
Time will not be ours forever:
He, at length, our good will sever.
Spend not then his gifts in vain:
Suns that set, may rise again;
But if once we lose this light,
'Tis with us perpetual night.
Why should we defer our joys?
Fame and rumour are but toys.
Can not we delude the eyes
Of a few poor household spies?
Or his easier ears beguile,
So removéd by our wile?

'Tis no sin love's fruit to steal,
But the sweet theft to reveal:
To be taken, to be seen,
These have crimes accounted been.

TO THE SAME.

Kiss me, sweet: the wary lover
Can your favours keep, and cover,
When the common courting jay
All your bounties will betray.
Kiss again! no creature comes;
Kiss, and score up wealthy sums
On my lips, thus hardly sundered,
While you breathe. First give a hundred,
Then a thousand, then another
Hundred, then unto the other
Add a thousand, and so more;
Till you equal with the store,
All the grass that Rumney yields,
Or the sands in Chelsea fields,
Or the drops in silver Thames,
Or the stars that gild his streams,
In the silent summers-nights,
When youths ply their stolen delights;
That the curious may not know
How to tell 'em as they flow,
And the envious, when they find
What their number is, be pined.

TO CELIA.

Drink to me only with thine eyes,
    And I will pledge with mine;
Or leave a kiss but in the cup,
    And I'll not look for wine.

The thirst that from the soul doth rise,
    Doth ask a drink divine:
But might I of Jove's nectar sup,
    I would not change for thine.

I sent thee late a rosy wreath,
    Not so much honouring thee,
As giving it a hope that there
    It could not withered be.
But thou thereon did'st only breathe,
    And sent'st it back to me;
Since when it grows, and smells, I swear,
    Not of itself, but thee.

["*Underwoods.*" 1640.]

A CELEBRATION OF CHARIS.

HIS EXCUSE FOR LOVING.

Let it not your wonder move,
Less your laughter, that I love.
Though I now write fifty years,
I have had, and have my peers;
Poets, though divine, are men:
Some have loved as old again.
And it is not always face,
Clothes, or fortune gives the grace;
Or the feature, or the youth;
But the language, and the truth,
With the ardour, and the passion,
Gives the lover weight and fashion.
If you then will read the story,
First, prepare you to be sorry,
That you never knew till now,
Either whom to love, or how:

But be glad, as soon with me,
When you know that this is she,
Of whose beauty it was sung,
She shall make the old man young.
Keep the middle age at stay,
And let nothing high decay,
Till she be the reason, why,
All the world for love may die.

HIS DISCOURSE WITH CUPID.

Noblest Charis, you that are
Both my fortune and my star!
And do govern more my blood,
Than the various moon the flood!
Hear, what late discourse of you,
Love and I have had; and true.
'Mongst my muses finding me,
Where he chanced your name to see
Set, and to this softer strain:
"Sure," said he, "if I have brain,
This, here sung, can be no other
By description, but my mother!
So hath Homer praised her hair;
So Anacreon drawn the air
Of her face, and made to rise,
Just about her sparkling eyes,
Both her brows, bent like my bow;
By her looks I do her know,
Which you call my shafts. And see!
Such my mother's blushes be,
As the bath your verse discloses
In her cheeks, of milk and roses;
Such as oft I wanton in:
And, above her even chin,
Have you placed the bank of kisses,
Where, you say, men gather blisses,

Ripened with a breath more sweet
Than when flowers and west-winds meet.
Nay, her white and polished neck,
With the lace that doth it deck,
Is my mother's! Hearts of slain
Lovers made into a chain!
And between each rising breast,
Lies the valley, called my nest,
Where I sit and proyne my wings
After flight; and put new stings
To my shafts! Her very name,
With my mother's is the same."
I confess all, I replied,
And the glass hangs by her side,
And the girdle 'bout her waist,
All is Venus, save unchaste.
But, alas, thou see'st the least
Of her good, who is the best
Of her sex; but could'st thou, Love,
Call to mind the forms that strove
For the apple, and those three
Make in one, the same were she.
For this beauty yet doth hide
Something more than thou hast spied.
Outward grace weak Love beguiles:
She is Venus when she smiles,
But she 's Juno when she walks,
And Minerva when she talks.

CLAIMING A SECOND KISS BY DESERT.

Charis, guess, and do not miss,
Since I drew a morning kiss
From your lips, and sucked an air
Thence, as sweet as you are fair,
What my muse and I have done:
Whether we have lost or won,

If by us the odds were laid,
That the bride, allowed a maid,
Looked not half so fresh and fair,
With th' advantage of her hair,
And her jewels, to the view
Of th' assembly, as did you.
  Or, that you did sit, or walk,
You were more the eye and talk
Of the court, to-day, than all
Else that glistened in Whitehall;
So, as those that had your sight,
Wished the bride were changed to night,
And did think such rites were due,
To no other grace but you!
  Or, if you did move to-night
In the dances, with what spite
Of your peers you were beheld,
That at every motion swelled
So to see a lady tread,
As might all the graces lead,
And was worthy, being so seen,
To be envied of the queen.
  Or, if you would yet have stayed,
Whether any would upbraid
To himself his loss of time;
Or have charged his sight of crime,
To have left all sight for you:
Guess of these which is the true;
And if such a verse as this,
May not claim another kiss.

WILLIAM ALEXANDER,

EARL OF STIRLING.

1580—1640.

AURORA.

The Aurora of the Earl of Stirling was a reality and not a myth, his biographers tell us, though they have not succeeded in discovering her name. He is said to have fallen in love with her in his fifteenth year, and to have kept her image fresh in his heart during a long tour on the Continent with the Earl of Argyle, whom he accompanied as tutor, or companion. On his return to Scotland he devoted himself to solitude and sonnets. "He now pressed his suit"—(I quote from his biography in the "Lives of Scottish Poets")—"with all the ardour of manhood, and enthusiasm of poetry; but though he actually penned upwards of a hundred songs and sonnets in her praise, the fair enslaver was not to be moved. The object of Alexander's passion," the biographer continues, after quoting one of his songs, "at last gave her hand to another; and as the poet himself poetically tells us, 'the lady, so unrelenting to him, matched her morning to one in the evening of his age.' Alexander sustained his disappointment with great philosophy; he neither drowned himself, nor burnt his sonnets; but, reserving the latter for future use, became again a wooer. In his next attachment he was more fortunate, and after a brief courtship, obtained in marriage the hand of Janet, the daughter and heiress of Sir William Erskine."

Stirling's sonnets were first published in 1604.

I swear, Aurora, by thy starry eyes,
And by those golden locks whose lock none slips,
And by the coral of thy rosy lips,
And by the naked snows which beauty dyes;
I swear by all the jewels of thy mind,
Whose like yet never worldly treasure bought,

Thy solid judgment and thy generous thought,
Which in this darkened age have clearly shined:
I swear by those, and by my spotless love,
And by my secret, yet most fervent fires,
That I have never nursed but chaste desires,
And such as modesty might well approve.
Then since I love those virtuous parts in thee,
Should'st thou not love this virtuous mind in me?

If that so many brave men leaving Greece,
Durst erst adventure through the raging deep,
And all to get the spoils of one poor sheep,
That had been famous for his golden fleece;
O then for that pure gold what should be sought,
Of which each hair is worth a thousand such!
No doubt for it one cannot do too much;
Why should not precious things be dearly bought?
And so they are, for in the Colchic guise,
This treasure many a danger doth defend:
Of which, when I have brought some one to end,
Straight out of that a number doth arise:
Even as the dragon's teeth bred men at arms,
Which, ah, t' o'erthrow I want Medea's charms.

Now when the Siren sings, as one dismayed,
I straight with wax begin to stop mine ears;
And when the crocodile doth shed forth tears,
I fly away, for fear to be betrayed.
I know when as thou seem'st to wail my state,
Thy face is no true table of thy mind;
And thou would'st never show thyself so kind,
Wer't not thy thoughts are hatching some deceit:
Whilst with vain hopes thou go'st about to fill me,
I wot whereto those drams of favour tend;
Lest by my death thy cruelties should end,
Thou think'st by giving life again to kill me:

No, no, thou shalt not thus thy greatness raise,
I'll break the trumpet that proclaimed thy praise.

I dreamed, the nymph that o'er my fancy reigns,
Came to a part whereas I paused alone,
Then said, "What needs you in such sort to moan?
Have I not power to recompense your pains?
Lo! I conjure you by that loyal love
Which you profess, to cast those griefs apart;
It's long, dear love, since that you had my heart,
Yet I was coy your constancy to prove,
But having had a proof, I'll now be free:
I am the echo that your sighs resounds,
Your woes are mine, I suffer in your wounds,
Your passions all they sympathise in me:"
Thus whilst for kindness both began to weep,
My happiness evanished with the sleep.

Ah, thou (my love) wilt lose thyself at last,
Who can to match thyself with none agree:
Thou ow'st thy father nephews, and to me
A recompense for all my passions past.
Ah, why should'st thou thy beauty's treasure waste,
Which will begin for to decay I see?
Erst Daphne did become a barren tree,
Because she was not half so wise as chaste:
And all the fairest things do soonest fade,
Which O, I fear, thou'lt with repentance try:
The roses blasted are, the lilies die,
And all do languish in the summer's shade:
Yet will I grieve to see those flowers fall down,
Which for my temples should have framed a crown.

SIR ROBERT AYTON.

1570—1638.

ON LOVE.

THERE is no worldly pleasure here below,
    Which by experience doth not folly prove;
But amongst all the follies that I know,
    The sweetest folly in the world is love:
But not that passion which, with fools' consent,
    Above the reason bears imperious sway,
Making their life-time a perpetual Lent,
    As if a man were born to fast and pray.
No, that is not the humour I approve,
    As either yielding pleasure, or promotion;
I like a mild and lukewarm zeal in love,
    Although I do not like it in devotion:
For it has no coherence with my creed,
    To think that lovers die, as they pretend:
If all that say they die, had died indeed,
    Sure long ere now the world had had an end.
Besides, we need not love but if we please,
    No destiny can force men's disposition;
And how can any die of that disease,
    Whereof himself may be his own physician?
But some seem so distracted of their wit,
    That I would think it but a venial sin
To take some of those innocents that sit
    In Bedlam out, and put some lovers in.

Yet some men, rather than incur the slander
    Of true apostates, will false martyrs prove:
But I am neither Iphis, nor Leander,
    I'll neither drown, nor hang myself for love.
Methinks a wise man's actions should be such
    As always yields to reason's best advice;
Now for to love too little, or too much,
    Are both extremes, and all extremes are vice.
Yet have I been a lover by report,
    Yea, I have died for love, as others do;
But, praised be God, it was in such a sort,
    That I revived within an hour or two.
Thus have I lived, thus have I loved, till now,
    And find no reason to repent me yet;
And whosoever otherways will do,
    His courage is as little as his wit.

ON A WOMAN'S INCONSTANCY.

I loved thee once, I'll love no more,
    Thine be the grief, as is the blame;
Thou art not what thou wast before,
    What reason I should be the same?
        He that can love, unloved again,
        Hath better store of love than brain.
            God send me love my debts to pay,
            While unthrifts fool their love away.

Nothing could have my love o'erthrown,
    If thou had still continued mine;
Yea, if thou had remained thy own,
    I might perchance have yet been thine.
        But thou thy freedom did recal,
        That if thou might elsewhere enthral;
            And then how could I but disdain
            A captive's captive to remain?

When new desires had conquered thee,
And changed the object of thy will,
It had been lethargy in me,
No constancy to love thee still:
Yea, it had been a sin to go
And prostitute affection so;
Since we are taught no prayers to say
To such as must to others pray.

Yet do thou glory in thy choice,
Thy choice of his good fortune boast;
I'll neither grieve, nor yet rejoice,
To see him gain what I have lost:
The height of my disdain shall be
To laugh at him, to blush for thee;
To love thee still, but go no more
A-begging at a beggar's door.

SONG.

I do confess thou'rt smooth and fair,
And I might have gone near to love thee;
Had I not found the slightest prayer
That lips could speak had power to move thee:
But I can let thee now alone,
As worthy to be loved by none.

I do confess thou'rt sweet, yet find
Thee such an unthrift of thy sweets,
Thy favours are but like the wind,
That kisses everything it meets.
And since thou can with more than one,
Thou'rt worthy to be kissed by none.

The morning rose, that untouched stands,
Armed with her briers, how sweetly smells!

But plucked and strained through ruder hands,
    Her sweets no longer with her dwells;
But scent and beauty both are gone,
And leaves fall from her, one by one.

Such fate, ere long, will thee betide,
    When thou hast handled been awhile,
Like sere flowers to be thrown aside;
    And I will sigh, while some will smile,
To see thy love for more than one,
Hath brought thee to be loved by none.

SONG.

What means this strangeness now of late,
    Since time must truth approve?
This distance may consist with state,
    It cannot stand with love.

'T is either cunning or distrust,
    That may such ways allow:
The first is base, the last unjust,
    Let neither blemish you.

For if you mean to draw me on,
    There needs not half this art:
And if you mean to have me gone,
    You over-act your part.

If kindness cross your wished content,
    Dismiss me with a frown;
I'll give you all the love that's spent,
    The rest shall be my own.

THOMAS HEYWOOD.

15—-16—.

["*Pleasant D alogues and Dramas.*" 1607.]

SONG.

Pack clouds away, and welcome day,
With night we banish sorrow:
Sweet air blow soft, mount lark aloft,
To give my love good morrow!
Wings from the wind to please her mind,
Notes from the lark I'll borrow:
Bird, prune thy wing, nightingale, sing,
To give my love good morrow.
To give my love good morrow,
Notes from them both I'll borrow.

Wake from thy nest, Robin red-breast,
Sing, birds, in every furrow;
And from each bill let music shrill
Give my fair love good morrow.
Blackbird, and thrush, in every bush,
Stare, linnet, and cock-sparrow,
You pretty elves, amongst yourselves,
Sing my fair love good morrow.
To give my love good morrow,
Sing, birds, in every furrow·

["*The Fair Maid of the Exchange.*" 1637.]

Ye little birds that sit and sing
    Amidst the shady valleys,
And see how Phillis sweetly walks
    Within her garden-alleys;
Go, pretty birds, about her bower;
Sing, pretty birds, she may not lower;
Ah, me! methinks I see her frown!
    Ye pretty wantons, warble.

Go, tell her, through your chirping bills,
    As you by me are bidden,
To her is only known my love,
    Which from the world is hidden.
Go, pretty birds, and tell her so;
See that your notes strain not too low,
For still, methinks, I see her frown,
    Ye pretty wantons, warble.

Go, tune your voices' harmony,
    And sing, I am her lover;
Strain loud and sweet, that every note
    With sweet content may move her.
And she that hath the sweetest voice,
Tell her I will not change my choice;
Yet still, methinks, I see her frown,
    Ye pretty wantons, warble.

O fly! make haste! see, see, she falls
    Into a pretty slumber;
Sing round about her rosy bed,
    That waking, she may wonder.
Say to her, 'tis her lover true
That sendeth love to you, to you!
And when you hear her kind reply,
    Return with pleasant warblings.

WILLIAM BROWNE.

1590—1645.

[" *Britannia's Pastorals.*" 1616.]

SHALL I tell you whom I love?
    Hearken then awhile to me;
And if such a woman move,
    As I now shall versify,
Be assured 'tis she, or none
That I love, and love alone.

Nature did her so much right,
    As she scorns the help of art:
In as many virtues dight
    As e'er yet embraced a heart.
So much good so truly tried,
Some for less were deified.

Wit she hath without desire
    To make known how much she hath;
And her anger flames no higher
    Than may fitly sweeten wrath.
Full of pity as may be,
Though, perhaps, not so to me.

Reason masters every sense,
    And her virtues grace her birth;
Lovely as all excellence,
    Modest in her most of mirth:

Likelihood enough to prove
Only worth could kindle love.

Such she is: and if you know
    Such a one as I have sung;
Be she brown, or fair, or so,
    That she be but somewhile young:
Be assured 'tis she, or none,
That I love, and love alone.

WELCOME, WELCOME DO I SING.

[From a manuscript copy of his poems in the Lansdowne collection.]

Welcome, welcome, do I sing,
Far more welcome than the Spring;
He that parteth from you never,
Shall enjoy a spring forever.

Love, that to the voice is near,
    Breaking from your ivory pale,
Need not walk abroad to hear
    The delightful nightingale.
        Welcome, welcome, then I sing, etc.

Love, that looks still on your eyes,
    Though the winter have begun
To benumb our arteries,
    Shall not want the summer's sun.
        Welcome, welcome, then I sing, etc.

Love, that still may see your cheeks,
    Where all rareness still reposes,
'Tis a fool, if e'er he seeks
    Other lilies, other roses.
        Welcome, welcome, then I sing, etc.

Love, to whom your soft lip yields,
    And perceives your breath in kissing,
All the odours of the fields,
    Never, never, shall be missing.
        Welcome, welcome, then I sing, etc.

Love, that question would anew
    What fair Eden was of old,
Let him rightly study you,
    And a brief of that behold.
        Welcome, welcome, then I sing,
        Far more welcome than the Spring,
        He that parteth from you never,
        Shall enjoy a spring forever.

WILLIAM DRUMMOND.

1585—1649.

The fame of Drummond of Hawthornden rests on his sonnets, many of which were inspired by love, and are among the best of the kind in the language. The name of the lady whose name they embalm was Mary Cunningham, a daughter of the Laird of Barns. Drummond fell in love with her, while cultivating his poetical talents at Hawthornden, after the death of his father, in 1610. She returned his passion, and the marriage-day was fixed; but before it arrived she was carried off by a fever. Drummond returned to his poetical studies, and in 1616 published a volume entitled, "Poems: Amorous, Funerall, Pastorall, in Sonnets, Songs, Sextains, Madrigals," from which the following extracts are taken. He travelled several years on the Continent, and made the acquaintance of many of the most learned men in France, Italy, and Germany; and returning to Scotland in 1631 or '32, he accidentally met a lady who bore a striking resemblance to his lost mistress, and married her. Her name was Elizabeth Logan, and she is said to have been a daughter of Sir Robert Logan, of Restelrig. Her pedigree has been disputed on the other side of the water, where they care for such trifles—one account making her "the daughter of a minister, by one whose sire was a shepherd;" but to us, at this late day, it is of no great consequence who she was.

In my first years, and prime yet not at height,
When sweet conceits my wits did entertain,
Ere beauty's force I knew, or false delight,
Or to what oar she did her captives chain,
Led by a sacred troop of Phœbus' train,
I first began to read, then loved to write,
And so to praise a perfect red and white,
But, God wot, wist not what was in my brain:
Love smiled to see in what an awful guise
I turned those antiques of the age of gold,
And, that I might more mysteries behold,
He set so fair a volume to mine eyes,

That I (quires closed which dead, dead sighs but breathe)
Joy on this living book to read my death.

O sacred blush, impurpling cheeks' pure skies
With crimson wings which spread thee like the morn;
O bashful look, sent from those shining eyes,
Which, though cast down on earth, couldst heaven adorn;
O tongue, in which most luscious nectar lies,
That can at once both bless and make forlorn;
Dear coral lip, which beauty beautifies,
That trembling stood ere that her words were born:
And you, her words, words, no, but golden chains,
Which did captive mine ears, ensnare my soul,
Wise image of her mind; mind that contains
A power, all power of senses to control;
Ye all from love dissuade so sweetly me,
That I love more, if more my love could be.

Trust not, sweet soul, those curléd waves of gold,
With gentle tides which on your temples flow,
Nor temples spread with flakes of virgin snow,
Nor snow of cheeks with Tyrian grain enrolled;
Trust not those shining lights which wrought my woe,
When first I did their burning rays behold,
Nor voice whose sounds more strange effects do show
Than of the Thracian harper have been told.
Look to this dying lily, fading rose,
Dark hyacinth, of late whose blushing beams
Made all the neighbouring herbs and grass rejoice,
And think how little is 'twixt life's extremes:
The cruel tyrant that did kill those flowers,
Shall once, ay me! not spare that spring of yours.

Slide soft, fair Forth, and make a crystal plain,
Cut your white locks, and on your foamy face

Let not a wrinkle be, when you embrace
The boat that earth's perfections doth contain.
Winds, wonder, and though wondering hold your peace;
Or if that ye your hearts can not restrain
From sending sighs, moved by a lover's case,
Sigh, and in her fair hair yourselves enchain;
Or take these sighs which absence makes arise
From mine oppresséd breast, and wave the sails,
Or some sweet breath now brought from Paradise:
Floods seem to smile, love o'er the wind prevails,
    And yet huge waves arise; the cause is this,
    The Ocean strives with Forth the boat to kiss.

She whose fair flowers no autumn makes decay,
Whose hue celestial, earthly hues doth stain,
Into a pleasant odoriferous plain
Did walk alone, to brave the pride of May;
And whilst through checkered lists she made her way,
Which smiled about her sight to entertain,
Lo, unawares, where Love did hid remain,
She spied, and sought to make of him her prey;
For which, of golden locks a fairest hair,
To bind the boy, she took; but he, afraid
At her approach, sprang swiftly in the air,
And mounting far from reach, looked back and said,
    Why should'st thou, sweet, me seek in chains to bind,
    Sith in thine eyes I daily am confined?

Are these the flowery banks, is this the mead,
Where she was wont to pass the pleasant hours?
Did here her eyes exhale mine eyes' salt showers,
When on her lap I laid my weary head?
Is this the goodly elm did us o'erspread,
Whose tender rind, cut out in curious flowers
By that white hand, contains those flames of ours?
Is this the rustling spring us music made?

Deflourished mead, where is your heavenly hue?
Bank, where that arras did you late adorn?
How look ye, elm, all withered and forlorn?
Only, sweet spring, nought altered seems in you;
    But while here changed each other thing appears,
    To sour your streams take of mine eyes these tears.

Alexis, here she stayed; among these pines,
Sweet hermitress, she did alone repair;
Here did she spread the treasure of her hair,
More rich than that brought from the Colchian mines.
She sate her by these muskéd eglantines,
The happy place the print seems yet to bear;
Her voice did sweeten here thy sugared lines,
To which winds, trees, beasts, birds, did lend their ear.
Me here she first perceived, and here a morn
Of bright carnations did o'erspread her face;
Here did she sigh, here first my hopes were born,
And I first got a pledge of promised grace:
    But ah! what served it to be happy so,
    Sith passéd pleasures double but new woe?

How many times night's silent queen her face
Hath hid, how oft with stars in silver mask
In Heaven's great hall she hath begun her task,
And cheered the waking eye in lower place!
How oft the sun hath made by Heaven's swift race
The happy lover to forsake the breast
Of his dear lady, wishing in the west
His golden coach to run had larger space!
I ever count, and number since, alas!
I bade farewell to my heart's dearest guest;
The miles I compass, and in mind I chase
The floods and mountains hold me from my rest:
    But, woe is me! long count and count may I,
    Ere I see her whose absence makes me die.

Sweet soul, which in the April of thy years,
So to enrich the heaven mad'st poor this round,
And now with golden rays of glory crowned
Most blest abid'st above the sphere of spheres;
If heavenly laws, alas! have not thee bound
From looking to this globe that all upbears,
If ruth and pity there above be found,
O deign to lend a look unto those tears.
Do not disdain, dear ghost, this sacrifice,
And though I raise not pillars to thy praise,
Mine offerings take; let this for me suffice,
My heart a living pyramid I raise;
    And whilst kings' tombs with laurels flourish green,
    Thine shall with myrtles and these flowers be seen.

Sweet spring, thou turn'st with all thy goodly train,
Thy head with flames, thy mantle bright with flowers;
The zephyrs curl the green locks of the plain,
The clouds for joy in pearls weep down their showers.
Thou turn'st, sweet youth, but ah! my pleasant hours
And happy days with thee come not again;
The sad memorials only of my pain
Do with thee turn, which turn my sweets in sours.
Thou art the same which still thou wast before,
Delicious, wanton, amiable, fair;
But she, whose breath embalmed thy wholesome air,
Is gone; nor gold, nor gems can her restore.
    Neglected virtue, seasons go and come,
    While thine forgot lie closéd in a tomb.

JOHN DONNE.

1573—1631.

In 1597, or thereabouts—the date is rather indefinite—Donne entered the service of Lord Ellesmere, Keeper of the Great Seal, and Lord Chancellor of England. He was his lordship's secretary for five years, during which time, says his biographer Walton, whose account I follow, mostly in his own words, he (I dare not say unhappily) fell into such a liking, as, with her approbation, increased into a love with a young gentlewoman that lived in that family, who was niece to the Lady Ellesmere, and daughter to Sir George More, then Chancellor of the Garter, and Lieutenant of the Tower. Sir George had some intimation of it, and removed her with much haste to his own house at Lothesley, in Surrey, but too late, by reason of some faithful promises, which were so interchangeably passed as never to be violated by either party. Their friends used much diligence, and many arguments, to kill or cool their affections to each other, but in vain. And such an industry did, notwithstanding much watchfulness against it, bring them secretly together, and at last to a marriage without the allowance of their friends. The marriage was broken to Sir George, by his friend and neighbour, the Earl of Northumberland, but it was so immeasurably unwelcome to him, that he engaged his sister, the Lady Ellesmere, to procure her lord to discharge Donne of the place he held under his lordship. Their suit was at last granted, and Donne was discharged by Lord Ellesmere, who said "he parted with a friend, and such a secretary as was fitter to serve a king than a subject." Immediately after his dismission, Donne sent a sad letter to his wife, to acquaint her with it, and after the subscription of his name, wrote,

"John Donne, Anne Donne, un-done:"

And God knows it proved too true; for Sir George was not satisfied till Donne, and his sometime compupil in Cambridge, that married him, namely Samuel Brooke, and his brother, Mr. Christopher Brooke, his chamber-fellow in Lincoln's Inn, who gave him his wife, and witnessed the marriage, were all committed to three several prisons. Donne, who was first enlarged, gave neither rest to his body or brain, nor to any friend in whom he might hope to have an interest, until he had procured their release. He obtained possession of his wife after a tedious and expensive lawsuit, but it was a long time before his father-in-law consented to forgive him. At last, however, his winning behaviour (which, when it would entice, had a strange kind of elegant irresistible art) melted Sir George, and he laboured for his son's restoration to his place; using to that end both his own and his sister's power over her lord, but without success, Lord Ellesmere considering it "inconsistent with his place and credit to discharge and re-admit servants at the request of passionate petitioners." Sir George refusing to contribute to the maintenance of his daughter, Donne was surrounded with many sad thoughts. But his sorrows were lessened, and his wants prevented, by the seasonable courtesy of their noble kinsman, Sir Francis Wolly, of Pirford, in Surrey, who entreated them to a cohabitation with him; where they remained with much freedom to themselves, and equal content to him for some years; and as their charge increased (she had yearly a child) so did his love and bounty. They continued with Sir Francis until his death, when Donne removed to a house in Mitcham. Sir George had previously agreed to pay him eight hundred pounds, as his wife's portion, or, failing in that, to allow him twenty pounds quarterly, as interest upon it, until it should be paid. He seems not to have done either, however, for about this time we find Donne in sad straits. Witness this extract from his letters:

"There is not one person, but myself, well of my family: I have already lost half a child, and with that mischance of hers, my wife has fallen into such a discomposure, as would afflict her too extremely, but that the sickness of all her other children stupefies her: of one of which, in good faith, I have not much hope: and these meet with a fortune so ill provided with physic, and such relief, that if God should ease us with burials, I know not how to perform even that: but I flatter myself with this hope, that I am dying too; for I cannot waste faster than by such griefs.

"From my hospital at Mitcham.

"JOHN DONNE."

They remained at Mitcham about two years, and then removed to London, where one of Donne's friends, Sir Robert Drury, a gentleman of a very noble estate, and a more liberal mind, assigned him and his wife apartments in his own house in Drury Lane. While they were residing with Sir Robert, the latter joined Lord Hay in an embassy to Paris, and pressed Donne to accompany him. Mrs. Donne objected to her husband's leaving her, for she was with child, and "her divining soul boded her some ill in his absence;" but Sir Robert insisting, she gave a faint consent, and the party started for Paris. Two days after their arrival there, Donne was left alone in the room in which Sir Robert, and he, and some other friends had dined together. To this place Sir Robert returned within half an hour; and as he left, so he found, Donne alone; but in such an ecstasy, and so altered as to his looks, as amazed Sir Robert to behold him; insomuch that he earnestly desired Donne to declare what had befallen him in the short time of his absence. To which Donne was not able to make a present answer, but after a long and perplexed pause, did at last say, "I have seen a dreadful vision since I saw you: I have seen my dear wife pass twice by me through this room, with her hair hanging about her shoulders, and a dead child in her arms: this I have seen since I saw you." To which Sir Robert replied, "Sure, sir, you have slept since I saw you, and this is the result of some melancholy dream, which I desire you to forget, for you are now awake." To which Donne's reply was, "I cannot be surer that I now live, than that I have not slept since I saw you; and I am sure, that at her second appearing she stopped, and looked me in the face, and vanished." Rest and sleep had not altered his opinion the next day, for then he affirmed this vision with a more deliberate, and so confirmed a confidence, that he inclined Sir Robert to a faint belief that the vision was true. He immediately sent a servant to Drury-house, with a charge to hasten back, and bring him word, whether Mrs. Donne were alive; and if alive, in what condition she was as to her health. The twelfth day the messenger returned with this account: That he found and left Mrs. Donne very sad and sick in her bed; and that after a very long and dangerous labour, she had been delivered of a dead child: and upon examination the abortion proved to be the same day, and about the very hour, that Donne affirmed he saw her pass by him in his chamber.

The year in which this strange occurrence took place, is not given by Walton, but it was probably in 1608 or '9, certainly before 1610, when Donne published his "PSEUDO-MARTYR." This work, which was written at the command of King James, was the turning point of the poet's fortunes, for it was in consequence of reading it, that his majesty pressed him to enter into the ministry. He hesitated for a long time, thinking it, in his mistaken modesty, to be too weighty for his abilities; but the wishes of the king, joined to the solicitations of his friends, at last decided him, and after several years' incessant study of divinity, he was ordained deacon and priest, by his friend Dr. King, Bishop of London, and shortly after made chaplain in ordinary to the king. This was in the summer of 1617, as far as I can gather from Donne's biographers, all of whom seem to have a great horror of dates. The month that he was ordained and made chaplain, Donne accompanied his majesty to the university of Cambridge, where he was chosen Doctor in Divinity. Immediately after his return from Cambridge, his wife died, leaving him a man of a narrow, unsettled estate, and, having buried five, the careful father of seven children then living: to whom he gave a voluntary assurance, never to bring them under the subjection of a stepmother: which promise he kept most faithfully, burying, with his tears, all his earthly joys in his most dear and deserving wife's grave, and betook himself to a most retired and solitary life. His first motion from his house was to preach where his beloved wife lay buried, (in St. Clement's Church, near Temple-bar, London,) and his text was a part of the prophet Jeremy's lamentation: "*Lo, I am the man that have seen affliction.*"

Donne's poems were first published in 1633, two years after his death. The majority of them—probably all the love-poems—were written between 1597 and 1617.

SONG.

Sweetest Love, I do not go,
For weariness of thee,
Nor in hope the world can show
A fitter love for me;

But since that I
At the last must part, 'tis best
Thus to use myself in jest
By feignèd deaths to die.

Yesternight the sun went hence,
And yet is here to day,
He hath no desire nor sense,
Nor half so short a way:
Then fear not me,
But believe that I shall make
Speedier journeys, since I take
More wings and spurs than he.

O how feeble is man's power,
That, if good fortune fall,
Cannot add another hour,
Nor a lost hour recal!
But come bad chance,
And we join to it our strength,
And we teach it art and length,
Itself o'er us to advance.

When thou sigh'st thou sigh'st no wind,
But sigh'st my soul away;
When thou weep'st, unkindly kind,
My life's blood doth decay.
It cannot be
That thou lov'st me, as thou say'st,
If in thine my life thou waste,
That art the life of me.

Let not thy divining heart
Forethink me any ill,
Destiny may take thy part,
And may thy fears fulfil;
But think that we
Are but turned aside to sleep:

They, who one another keep
Alive, ne'er parted be.

THE SUN-RISING.

Busy old fool, unruly sun,
Why dost thou thus,
Through windows and through curtains call on us?
Must to thy motions lovers' seasons run?
Saucy pedantic wretch, go chide
Late school-boys, and sour 'prentices,
Go tell court-huntsmen, that the King will ride,
Call country ants to harvest offices;
Love, all alike, no season knows nor clime,
Nor hours, days, months, which are the rags of time.

Thy beams so reverend and strong,
Dost thou not think
I could eclipse and cloud them with a wink,
But that I would not lose her sight so long?
If her eyes have not blinded thine,
Look, and to-morrow late tell me
Whether both the Indias of spice and mine
Be where thou left them, or lie here with me:
Ask for those kings, whom thou saw'st yesterday;
And thou shalt hear all here in one bed lay.

She 's all states, and all princes I,
Nothing else is.
Princes do but play us; compared to this,
All honour 's mimic, all wealth alchemy;
Thou sun art half as happy as we,
In that the world 's contracted thus;
Thine age asks ease, and since thy duties be
To warm the world, that 's done in warming us.
Shine here to us, and thou art everywhere;
This bed thy centre is, these walls thy sphere.

THE RELIC.

When my grave is broke up again,
Some second guest to entertain,
(For graves have learned that woman-head,
To be to more than one a bed,)
And he that digs it spies
A bracelet of bright hair about the bone,
Will he not let us alone,
And think that there a loving couple lies,
Who thought that this device might be some way
To make their souls, at the last busy day,
Meet at this grave, and make a little stay?

If this fall in a time, or land,
Where mis-devotion doth command,
Then he, that digs us up, will bring
Us to the Bishop or the King,
To make us relics; then
Thou shalt be a Mary Magdalen, and I
A something else thereby;
All women shall adore us, and some men;
And since at such times miracles are sought,
I would have that age by this paper taught
What miracles we harmless lovers wrought.

First we loved well and faithfully,
Yet knew not what we loved, nor why;
Difference of sex we never knew,
No more than guardian angels do;
Coming and going we
Perchance might kiss, but yet between those meals
Our hands ne'er touched the seals,
Which Nature, injured by late law, set free:
These miracles we did; but now, alas!
All measure and all language I should pass,
Should I tell what a miracle she was.

THE ANNIVERSARY.

All kings, and all their favourites,
All glory of honours, beauties, wits,
The sun itself (which makes times, as these pass)
Is elder by a year now, than it was,
When thou and I first one another saw:
All other things to their destruction draw;
Only our love hath no decay:
This no to-morrow hath, nor yesterday;
Running, it never runs from us away,
But truly keeps his first-last-everlasting day.

Two graves must hide thine and my corse;
If one might, death were no divorce;
Alas! as well as other princes, we,
(Who prince enough in one another be,)
Must leave at last in death these eyes, and ears,
Oft fed with true oaths, and with sweet salt tears.
But souls where nothing dwells but love,
(All other thoughts being inmates) then shall prove
This, or a love increaséd, there above,
When bodies to their graves, souls from their graves remove.

And then we shall be thoroughly blest:
But now no more than all the rest.
Here upon earth we are kings, and none but we
Can be such kings, nor of such subjects be;
Who is so safe as we, where none can do
Treason to us, except one of us two?
True and false fears let us refrain;
Let us love nobly, and live, and add again
Years and years unto years, till we attain
To write three score: this is the second of our reign.

FRANCIS BEAUMONT.

1586—1616.

["*Poems.*" 1640.]

THE INDIFFERENT.

NEVER more will I protest
To love a woman but in jest:
For as they can not be true,
So to give each man his due,
    When the wooing fit is past,
    Their affection cannot last.

Therefore if I chance to meet
With a mistress, fair and sweet,
She my service shall obtain,
Loving her for love again:
    Thus much liberty I crave,
    Not to be a constant slave.

But when we have tried each other,
If she better like another,
Let her quickly change for me,
Then to change am I as free.
    He or she that loves too long.
    Sell their freedom for a song.

SECRECY PROTESTED.

Fear not (dear love) that I'll reveal
Those hours of pleasure we two steal:
No eye shall see, nor yet the sun
Descry, what thou and I have done;
No ear shall hear our love, but we
Silent as the night will be;
The god of love himself (whose dart
Did first wound mine, and then thy heart,)
Shall never know that we can tell
What sweets in stolen embraces dwell.
This only means may find it out,
If when I die physicians doubt
What caused my death, and there to view
Of all their judgments which was true,
Rip up my heart, O then I fear
The world will see thy picture there.

JOHN FLETCHER.

1576—1625.

["*The Mad Lover.*" 1618.]

Go, happy heart! for thou shalt lie
Entombed in her for whom I die,
Example of her cruelty.

Tell her, if she chance to hide
Me for slowness, in her pride,
That it was for her I died.

If a tear escape her eye,
'T is not for my memory,
But thy rites of obsequy.

The altar was my loving breast,
My heart the sacrificéd beast,
And I was myself the priest.

Your body was the sacred shrine,
Your cruel mind the power divine,
Pleased with hearts of men, not kine.

["*The Tragedy of Valentinian.*" About 1618.]

SONG.

Hear, ye ladies that despise
  What the mighty Love has done;
Fear examples, and be wise:
  Fair Calisto was a nun:
Leda, sailing on the stream,
  To deceive the hopes of man,
Love accounting but a dream,
  Doated on a silver swan;
    Danaë, in a brazen tower,
    Where no love was, loved a shower.

Hear, ye ladies that are coy,
  What the mighty Love can do;
Fear the fierceness of the boy:
  The chaste moon he makes to woo;
Vesta, kindling holy fires,
  Circled round about with spies,
Never dreaming loose desires,
  Doting at the altar dies.
    Ilion, in a short hour, higher
    He can build, and once more fire.

["*A Wife for a Month.*" 1624.]

TO THE BLEST EVANTHE.

Let those complain that feel Love's cruelty,
  And in sad legends write their woes;
With roses gently h' has corrected me,
  My war is without rage or blows:
    My mistress' eyes shine fair on my desires,
    And hope springs up inflamed with her new fires.

No more an exile will I dwell,
    With folded arms, and sighs all day,
Reckoning the torments of my hell,
    And flinging my sweet joys away:
        I am called home again to quiet peace,
        My mistress smiles, and all my sorrows cease.

Yet, what is living in her eye,
    Or being blessed with her sweet tongue,
If these no other joys imply?
    A golden gyve, a pleasing wrong:
        To be your own but one poor month, I'd give
        My youth, my fortune, and then leave to live.

["*The Elder Brother.*" About 1624.]

ODE.

Beauty clear and fair,
        Where the air
Rather like a perfume dwells;
    Where the violet and the rose,
    Their blue veins in blush disclose,
And come to honour nothing else.

Where to live near,
        And planted there,
Is to live, and still live new;
    Where to gain a favour is
    More than light, perpetual bliss;
Make me live by serving you.

Dear, again back recall
        To this light,
A stranger to himself and all;
    Both the wonder and the story
    Shall be yours, and eke the glory:
I am your servant, and your thrall.

GEORGE WITHER.

1588—1667.

["*A Description of Love.*" 1620.]

A LOVE SONG.

I LOVED a lass, a fair one,
As fair as e'er was seen;
She was, indeed, a rare one,
Another Sheba queen;
But, fool, as then I was,
I thought she loved me too;
But now, alas! sh' as left me,
Falero, lero, loo.

Her hair like gold did glister,
Her eye was like a star;
She did surpass her sister,
Which passed all others far:
She would me honey call,
She'd, O, she'd kiss me too!
But now, alas! sh' as left me,
Falero, lero, loo.

In summer time, to Medley,
My love and I would go,

The boat-men there stood ready,
    My love and I to row;
For cream there would we call,
    For cakes, and for prunes too;
But now, alas! sh' as left me,
        Falero, lero, loo.

Many a merry meeting
    My love and I have had;
She was my only sweeting,
    She made my heart full glad:
The tears stood in her eyes,
    Like to the morning dew;
But now, alas! sh' as left me,
        Falero, lero, loo.

And, as abroad we walkéd,
    As lovers' fashion is,
Oft, as we sweetly talkéd,
    The sun would steal a kiss;
The wind upon her lips
    Likewise most sweetly blew;
But now, alas! sh' as left me,
        Falero, lero, loo.

Her cheeks were like the cherry,
    Her skin as white as snow;
When she was blythe and merry,
    She angel-like did show:
Her waist exceeding small;
    The fives did fit her shoe:
But now, alas! sh' as left me,
        Falero, lero, loo.

In summer-time, or winter,
    She had her heart's desire;
I still did scorn to stint her
    From sugar, sack, or fire:

The world went round about,
 No cares we ever knew:
But now, alas! sh' as left me,
 Falero, lero, loo.

As we walked home together,
 At midnight, through the town,
To keep away the weather,
 O'er her I'd cast my gown;
No cold my love should feel,
 Whate'er the heavens could do;
But now, alas! sh' as left me,
 Falero, lero, loo.

Like doves we would be billing,
 And clip and kiss so fast,
Yet she would be unwilling
 That I should kiss the last;
They 're Judas kisses now,
 Since that they proved untrue;
For, now, alas! sh' as left me,
 Falero, lero, loo.

To maidens' vows and swearing
 Henceforth no credit give,
You may give them the hearing,
 But never them believe:
They are as false as fair,
 Unconstant, frail, untrue
For mine, alas! hath left me,
 Falero, lero, loo.

'Twas I that paid for all things,
 'Twas others drank the wine;
I cannot now recall things,
 Live but a fool to pine:
'Twas I that beat the bush,
 The bird to others flew;

For she, alas! hath left me,
Falero, lero, loo.

If ever that dame Nature,
For this false lover's sake,
Another pleasing creature,
Like unto her would make,
Let her remember this,
To make the other true;
For this, alas! hath left me,
Falero, lero, loo.

No riches, now, can raise me,
No want make me despair;
No misery amaze me,
Nor yet for want I care:
I have lost a world itself,
My earthly heaven, adieu!
Since she, alas! hath left me,
Falero, lero, loo.

["*Fair Virtue, the mistress of Phil'arete.*" 1622.]

Shall I, wasting in despair,
Die, because a woman's fair?
Or make pale my cheeks with care,
'Cause another's rosy are?
Be she fairer than the day,
Or the flowery meads in May;
If she be not so to me,
What care I how fair she be?

Should my heart be grieved, or pined,
'Cause I see a woman kind?
Or a well disposéd nature
Joinéd with a lovely feature?

Be she meeker, kinder, than
Turtle-dove, or pelican:
    If she be not so to me,
    What care I how kind she be?

Shall a woman's virtues move
Me to perish for her love?
Or, her well-deserving known,
Make me quite forget mine own?
Be she with that goodness blest,
Which may gain her name of Best;
    If she be not such to me,
    What care I how good she be?

'Cause her fortune seems too high,
Shall I play the fool and die?
Those that bear a noble mind,
Where they want of riches find,
Think what with them they would do,
That without them dare to woo.
    And unless that mind I see,
    What care I though great she be?

Great, or good, or kind, or fair,
I will ne'er the more despair;
If she love me, this believe,
I will die ere she shall grieve.
If she slight me when I woo,
I can scorn, and let her go.
    For, if she be not for me,
    What care I for whom she be?

SIR HENRY WOTTON.

1568—1639.

THE QUEEN OF BOHEMIA.

Elizabeth, Queen of Bohemia, the heroine of Wotton's beautiful poem, was the daughter of James the First. She was born in Scotland, on the 19th of August, 1596, and on the 14th of February, 1613, was married to Frederic the Fifth, the Elector Palatine, in the great banqueting-house at Whitehall. The happy pair remained in England until the 10th of April, when they proceeded in great pomp to Heidelburgh, the capital of the Palatinate, where they reigned for some years in peace and prosperity. In 1619, the crown of Bohemia was offered to the Elector. King James endeavoured to persuade him to refuse it, forewarning him that he was to expect no assistance from England, in case his claims should be disputed; but the entreaties of his wife prevailed, and he accepted it, and was crowned at Prague on the 4th of November. The Emperor of Austria declared him a traitor, and a rebel against the Empire; deprived him of his Electoral dignity, and prepared to invade Bohemia and the Palatinate. A year later a decisive battle was fought under the walls of Prague, and the new-made monarch was discomfited, and obliged to fly by night with his Queen, who was great with child. Their first resting-place was Breslau, one hundred and twenty miles from the field of battle. Driven from Breslau, they wandered awhile in Silesia and Brandenburgh, and at length settled in Holland, where they were supported by the House of Nassau, and by occasional contributions from persons of rank in England. King James refused to help them, but consented to negotiate in their behalf, and did so on various occasions, but without success. Of Sir Henry Wotton, who was his ambassador on one of these fruitless missions, in 1621, the following anedote is related by his biographer, Walton. "There were at that time," says honest Izaak, "two opposite armies in the field; and as they were treating, there was a battle fought, in the managery whereof there was so many miserable errors on the one side, (so Sir Henry Wotton expresses it in a dispatch to the King,) and so advantageous events to the Emperor, as put an end to all present hopes of a successful treaty; so that Sir Henry, seeing the face of peace altered by that victory, prepared for a removal from that court; and at his departure from the Emperor, was so bold as to remember him, 'That the events of every battle move on the unseen wheels of fortune, which are this moment up, and down the next; and therefore humbly advised him to use his victory so soberly, as still to put on thoughts of peace.' Which advice, though it seemed to be spoken with some passion, (his dear mistress, the Queen of Bohemia, being concerned in it,) was yet taken in good part by the Emperor, who replied, 'That he would consider his advice. And though he looked on the King, his master, as an abettor of his enemy, the paulsgrave; yet for Sir Henry himself, his behaviour had been such during the manage of the treaty, that he took him to be a person of much honour and merit; and did therefore desire him to accept of that jewel, as a testimony of his good opinion of him;' which was a jewel of diamonds of more value than a thousand pounds.

"This jewel was received with all outward circumstances and terms of honour by Sir Henry Wotton. But the next morning, at his departing from Vienna, he at his taking leave of the Countess of Sabrina, (an Italian lady, in whose house the Emperor had appointed him to be lodged and honourably entertained,) 'acknowledged her merits, and besought her to accept of that jewel, as a testimony of his gratitude for her civilities;' presenting her with the same that was given him by the Emperor: which being suddenly discovered, and told to the Emperor, was by him taken for a high affront, and Sir Henry Wotton told so by a messenger. To which he replied, 'That though he received with thankfulness, yet he found in himself an indisposition to be the better for any gift that came from an enemy to his royal mistress, the Queen of Bohemia;' for so she was pleased he should always call her." It was manly in Wotton to uphold the cause of his fallen mistress, but others were not so loyal. She was an object of ridicule with many, and figured in the caricatures of the time, "as a poor Irish mantler, with her hair hanging about her ears, and her child at her back, and the King, her father, carrying the cradle after her."

Charles the First, on his accession to the throne, declared to his Parliament that the recovery of the Palatinate should be a primary object of his political consideration, but little was done till 1632, when Gustavus of Sweden proffered his aid to that end. His conditions, however, were so unsatisfactory to Charles, with whom he was then at war, that the latter broke up the treaty which had been proposed, and withdrew his ambassador from Stockholm. The Elector then negotiated with Gustavus on his own account, but the death of the Swedish king, who was killed at the battle of Lutzen, on the 6th of November, 1632, frustrated his hopes, and perhaps hastened his death, which took place at Mentz on the 29th of the same month. Elizabeth remained at the Hague, and lived for many years in the utmost privacy, passing her time in educating her children, and in writing letters to eminent men. Her affairs were managed by Lord Craven, who had entered the military service of Holland, in order to be near her, and to whom she is supposed to have been secretly married. The Lower Palatinate was restored to her son, Charles Lewis, in 1648, but she profited but little by it. She lingered in want and exile until the Restoration of Charles the Second, when she was invited to England. She arrived in London on the 17th of May, 1661, and died on the 13th of February of the following year.

The date of Wotton's poem has never been settled, but it must have been written between the 7th of November, 1619, the day of her coronation as Queen of Bohemia, and some time in 1624, when it was printed in "THE SIXT SET OF BOOKES," a musical publication by Michaell Est. I place it in 1620, before the fatal battle of Prague.

ON HIS MISTRESS, THE QUEEN OF BOHEMIA.

You meaner beauties of the night,
    That poorly satisfy our eyes,
More by your number than your light,
    You common-people of the skies,
    What are you when the sun shall rise?

You curious chanters of the wood,
    That warble forth dame Nature's lays,
Thinking your passions understood
    By your weak accents, what 's your praise
    When Philomel her voice shall raise?

You violets that first appear,
    By your pure purple mantles known,
Like the proud virgins of the year,
    As if the spring were all your own,
    What are you when the rose is blown?

So when my mistress shall be seen,
    In form, and beauty of her mind,
By virtue first, then choice, a queen,
    Tell me, if she were not designed
    Th' eclipse and glory of her kind?

THOMAS RANDOLPH.

1605—1634.

["*Poems, with the Muses' Looking Glass.*" 1638.]

TO ONE ADMIRING HERSELF IN A LOOKING GLASS.

Fair lady, when you see the grace
Of beauty in your looking-glass;
A stately forehead, smooth and high,
And full of princely majesty;
A sparkling eye, no gem so fair,
Whose lustre dims the Cyprian star;
A glorious cheek, divinely sweet,
Wherein both roses kindly meet;
A cherry lip that would entice
Even gods to kiss at any price;
You think no beauty is so rare
That with your shadow might compare;
That your reflection is alone
The thing that men most doat upon.
Madam, alas, your glass doth lie,
And you are much deceived; for I
A beauty know of richer grace,
(Sweet, be not angry,) 'tis your face.
Hence then, O learn more mild to be,
And leave to lay your blame on me,
If me your real substance move,
When you so much your shadow love.

Wise Nature would not let your eye
Look on her own bright majesty,
Which had you once but looked upon,
You could, except yourself, love none:
What then you can not love, let me,
That face I can, you can not see.
  Now you have what to love, you'll say,
What is there left for me, I pray?
My face, sweet heart, if it please thee;
That which you can, I can not see:
So either love shall gain his due,
Yours sweet in me, and mine in you.

WILLIAM HABINGTON.

1605—1654.

CASTARA.

The Castara of Habington's poetry was Lucia Herbert, the daughter of William Herbert, the first Lord Powis. By her mother's side she was related to the Percys of Northumberland, who traced their descent back to Charlemagne. Habington's family, though a good one, was not equal to hers, which may have been the reason why her father objected to him as a lover. For my Lord Powis did object, we learn, though Lady Eleanor, his wife, sympathized with the poet from the first. In a poetical epistle which he addressed to her ladyship, he compliments her on the clearness of her judgment of him, and proclaims the unselfishness of his love for her daughter:

> "Would Castara were
> The daughter of some mountaine cottager,
> Who, with his toile worne out, could dying leave
> Her no more dowre, than what she did receive
> From bounteous nature. Her would I then lead
> To th' temple, rich in her own wealth; her head
> Crown'd with her haire's faire treasure; diamonds in
> Her brighter eyes; soft ermines in her skin;
> Each Indie in her cheeke. Then all who vaunt
> That Fortune, them t' enrich, made others want,
> Should set themselves out glorious in her stealth,
> And trie if that could parallel this wealth."

He also addressed an epistle to Lord Powis, but it was after his marriage with Castara. "The holy lights," he says,

> "Smil'd with a cheerful lustre on our rites,
> And every thing presag'd full happinesse
> To mutual love, if you'le the omen blesse.
> * * * * * *
> Nor think in her I courted wealth or blood,
> Or more uncertain hopes: for had I stood
> On th' highest ground of Fortune, the world knowne
> No greatnesse but what waited on my throne;
> And had she onely had that face and mind,
> I, with my selfe, had th' Earth to her resign'd."

The date of Habington's marriage is not mentioned, but from a note to one of his poems in the second part of "CASTARA," which part, by the way, is christened *The Wife*, I should say it took place in or before 1630, his twenty-fifth year. Of his married life, indeed of his life generally, nothing is known, except that it was passed in retirement at the family manor in Hendlip. Devoted to his wife and his books, the contentions of the time swept by, and left him unharmed. In the words of Langbaine, "he was a gentleman who lived in the civil wars, and, slighting Bellona, gave himself entirely to the Muses." His poems were published in 1634.

TO CASTARA.

A SACRIFICE.

Let the chaste Phœnix, from the flowery East,
Bring the sweet treasure of her perfumed nest,
As incense to this altar, where the name
Of my Castara 's graved by th' hand of Fame:
Let purer virgins, to redeem the air
From loose infection, bring their zealous prayer,
T' assist at this great feast, where they shall see,
What rites Love offers up to Chastity.
Let all the amorous youth, whose fair desire
Felt never warmth but from a noble fire,
Bring hither their bright flames, which here shall shine
As tapers fixed about Castara's shrine.
While I, the priest, my untamed heart surprise,
And in this temple make 't her sacrifice.

TO CASTARA.

INTENDING A JOURNEY INTO THE COUNTRY.

Why haste you hence, Castara? Can the Earth,
A glorious mother, in her flowery birth,
Show lilies like thy brow? Can she disclose
In emulation of thy cheeks, a rose,
Sweet as thy blush? Upon thyself then set
Just value, and scorn it thy counterfeit.

The Spring 's still with thee; but perhaps the field,
Not warmed with thy approach, wants force to yield
Her tribute to the plough. O rather let
Th' ungrateful Earth forever be in debt
To th' hope of sweating Industry, than we
Should starve with cold, who have no heat but thee.
  Nor fear the public good; thy eyes can give
  A life to all, who can deserve to live.

TO THE SPRING.

ON THE UNCERTAINTY OF CASTARA'S ABODE.

Fair mistress of the Earth, with garlands crowned,
Rise, by a lover's charm, from the parched ground,
And show thy flowery wealth, that she, where'er
Her stars shall guide her, meet thy beauties there.
Should she to the cold northern climates go,
Force thy affrighted lilies there to grow,
The roses in those gelid fields t' appear;
She absent, I have all their winter here.
Or if to th' torrid zone her way she bend,
Her the cool breathing of Favonius lend.
Thither command the birds to bring their choirs;
That zone is temperate, I have all his fires.
  Attend her, courteous Spring, though we should here
  Lose by it all the treasures of the year.

TO CASTARA.

UPON THE DISGUISING HIS AFFECTION.

Pronounce me guilty of a blacker crime,
Than e'er, in the large volume writ by Time,
The sad historian reads, if not my art
Dissembles love, to veil an amorous heart.

For when the zealous anger of my friend
Checks my unusual sadness, I pretend
To study virtue, which indeed I do;
He must court virtue, who aspires to you.
Or that some friend is dead, and then a tear,
A sigh, or groan steals from me; for I fear
Lest death with love hath struck my heart, and all
These sorrows usher but its funeral:
 Which should revive, should there you a mourner be,
 And force a nuptial in an obsequy.

TO SEYMORS.

THE HOUSE IN WHICH CASTARA LIVED.

Blest temple, hail! where the chaste altar stands,
Which Nature built, but the exacter hands
Of Virtue polished. Though sad fate deny
My profane feet access, my vows shall fly.
May those musicians, which divide the air
With their harmonious breath, their flight prepare
For this glad place, and all their accents frame,
To teach the echoes my Castara's name.
The beauteous troops of Graces, led by Love
In chaste attempts, possess the neighboring grove,
Where may the Spring dwell still. May every tree
Turn to a laurel, and prophetic be,
 Which shall in its first oracle divine
 That courteous Fate decrees Castara mine.

TO CASTARA.

DEPARTING UPON THE APPROACH OF NIGHT.

What should we fear, Castara? The cool air,
That's fallen in love, and wantons in thy hair,
Will not betray our whispers. Should I steal

A nectared kiss, the wind dares not reveal
The pleasure I possess. The wind conspires
To our blest interview, and in our fires
Bathes like a salamander, and doth sip,
Like Bacchus from the grape, life from thy lip.
Nor think of night's approach. The world's great eye,
Though breaking Nature's law, will us supply
With his still-flaming lamp, and to obey
Our chaste desires, fix here perpetual day.
    But should he set, what rebel night dares rise,
    To be subdued i' th' victory of the eyes?

TO CASTARA.

UPON THOUGHT OF AGE AND DEATH.

The breath of Time shall blast the flowery spring,
Which so perfumes thy cheek, and with it bring
So dark a mist, as shall eclipse the light
Of thy fair eyes in an eternal night.
Some melancholy chamber of the earth,
(For that like Time devours whom it gave birth,)
Thy beauties shall entomb, while all whoe'er
Loved nobly, offer up their sorrows there.
But I, whose grief no formal limits bound,
Beholding the dark cavern of that ground,
Will there immure myself. And thus I shall
Thy mourner be, and my own funeral.
    Else by the weeping magic of my verse,
    Thou had'st revived to triumph o'er thy hearse.

LOVE'S ANNIVERSARY.

TO THE SUN.

Thou art returned (great light) to that blest hour
In which I first by marriage, sacred power,

Joined with Castara hearts; and as the same
Thy lustre is, as then, so is our flame;
Which had increased, but that by Love's decree,
'Twas such at first, it ne'er could greater be.
But tell me, (glorious lamp) in thy survey
Of things below thee, what did not decay
By age to weakness? I since that have seen
The rose bud forth and fade, the tree grow green
And wither, and the beauty of the field
With winter wrinkled. Even thyself dost yield
    Something to time, and to thy grave fall nigher;
    But virtuous love is one sweet endless fire.

TO CASTARA.

Why should we fear to melt away in death?
May we but die together! When beneath
In a cool vault we sleep, the world will prove
Religious, and call it the shrine of love.
There, when o' th' wedding eve some beauteous maid,
Suspicious of the faith of man, hath paid
The tribute of her vows, o' th' sudden she
Two violets sprouting from the tomb will see,
And cry out: "Ye sweet emblems of their zeal
Who live below, sprang ye up to reveal
The story of our future joys, how we
The faithful patterns of their love shall be?
    If not, hang down your heads, oppressed with dew,
    And I will weep, and wither hence with you."

TO ROSES,

IN THE BOSOM OF CASTARA.

Ye, blushing virgins, happy are
In the chaste nunnery of her breasts,
For he'd profane so chaste a fair,
Whoe'er should call them Cupid's nests.

Transplanted thus how bright ye grow,
How rich a perfume do ye yield!
In some close garden, cowslips so
Are sweeter than i' th' open field.

In those white cloisters live secure
From the rude blasts of wanton breath;
Each hour more innocent and pure,
Till you shall wither into death.

Then that which living gave you room,
Your glorious sepulchre shall be:
There wants no marble for a tomb,
Whose breast hath marble been to me.

UPON CASTARA'S DEPARTURE.

Vows are vain. No suppliant breath
Stays the speed of swift-heeled Death.
Life with her is gone, and I
Learn but a new way to die.
See the flowers condole, and all
Wither in my funeral.
The bright lily, as if day
Parted with her, fades away.
Violets hang their heads, and lose
All their beauty. That the rose
A sad part in sorrow bears,
Witness all those dewy tears
Which as pearl, or diamond like,
Swell upon her blushing cheek.
All things mourn; but O, behold
How the withered marigold
Closeth up, now she is gone,
Judging her the setting sun.

SIR WILLIAM DAVENANT.

1605—1668.

[“*Madagascar, with other Poems.*” 1635.]

SONG.

THE SOLDIER GOING TO THE FIELD.

PRESERVE thy sighs, unthrifty girl!
    To purify the air;
Thy tears to thread instead of pearl,
    On bracelets of thy hair.

The trumpet makes the echo hoarse,
    And wakes the louder drum;
Expense of grief gains no remorse,
    When sorrow should be dumb.

For I must go where lazy Peace
    Will hide her drowsy head;
And, for the sport of kings, increase
    The number of the dead.

But first I'll chide thy cruel theft:
    Can I in war delight,
Who being of my heart bereft,
    Can have no heart to fight?

Thou know'st the sacred laws of old,
Ordained a thief should pay,
To quit him of his theft, seven-fold
What he had stolen away.

Thy payment shall but double be;
O then with speed resign
My own seducéd heart to me,
Accompanied with thine.

SONG.

The lark now leaves his watery nest,
And climbing, shakes his dewy wings;
He takes this window for the east,
And to implore your light, he sings:
Awake, awake! the morn will never rise,
Till she can dress her beauty at your eyes.

The merchant bows unto the seaman's star,
The ploughman from the sun his season takes;
But still the lover wonders what they are,
Who look for day before his mistress wakes.
Awake, awake! break through your veils of lawn!
Then draw your curtains and begin the dawn.

JOHN MILTON.

1608—1674.

The history of Milton's wives, and his checkered experience of married life, is well known; but the story of his early loves, if he had any, is irrevocably lost. Everybody has read the romantic anecdote of the young Italian lady of rank, who, travelling in England when he was a student at Cambridge, found him one day asleep under a tree, and, alighting from her carriage, was so much struck by his beauty that she wrote in pencil a madrigal of Guarini, "*Occhi stelle mortali*," which she slipped into his hand, and then pursued her journey. When he awoke he read the lines with amazement, and learning the way in which he came by them, conceived such a passion for the fair unknown, that he afterwards journeyed to Italy in search of her. A similar story is told of him in Rome, the scene being shifted to the suburbs of that city, and the date changed to correspond with the period of his visit thither, but it is as mythical as the former one. There is not a word of truth in either. That Milton did travel in Italy, where he met one or two ladies who interested him, is certain; but study, and not love, was the cause of his journey. The first of his Italian heroines, if I may call them such, was the celebrated singer, Leonora Baroni, whom he met at Rome, in the palace of Cardinal Barberini, where he had frequent opportunities of hearing her sing. He celebrated her musical talents in three Latin epigrams, which contain nothing that can be twisted into a declaration of love. Of the second lady, to whom he wrote four Italian sonnets, nothing is known. He is supposed by his latest biographer, Mr. Masson, to have met her in, or near, Bologna, in the spring of 1639. She was for a long time thought to have been a German lady, the word *Rheno* in the second line of one of the sonnets being interpreted to mean the German *Rhine;* but Mr. Masson shows that such an interpretation is unnecessary, there being a river Rheno near Bologna, in which city she probably resided. The "deceased wife" of the last sonnet was Milton's second wife, Catharine Woodcock. She married the poet in 1656, the fourth year of his blindness, and died in childbed within a year after her marriage. His touching tribute to her memory was written shortly after her death.

I have used Cowper's version of the Italian sonnets. It is an elegant one, and, bating the mistake of the Rheno for the Rhine, sufficiently faithful for poetical purposes.

Fair Lady! whose harmonious name the Rhine,
Through all his grassy vales, delights to hear,
Base were indeed the wretch who could forbear
To love a spirit elegant as thine,
That manifests a sweetness all divine,
Nor knows a thousand winning acts to spare,
And graces, which Love's bow and arrows are,
Tempering thy virtues in a softer shine.
When gracefully thou speak'st, or singest gay,
Such strains as might the senseless forest move,
Ah then—turn each his eyes and ears away,
Who feels himself unworthy of thy love!
Grace can alone preserve him ere the dart
Of fond desire yet reach his inmost heart.

As on a hill-top rude, when closing day
Embrowns the scene, some pastoral maiden fair
Waters a lovely foreign plant with care,
Borne from its native genial airs away,
That scarcely can its tender bud display;
So, on my tongue these accents, new and rare,
Are flowers exotic, which Love waters there.
While thus, O sweetly scornful! I essay
Thy praise in verse to British ears unknown,
And Thames exchange for Arno's fair domain;
So Love has willed, and ofttimes Love has shown
That what he wills, he never wills in vain.
O that this hard and sterile breast might be
To Him, who plants from Heaven, a soil as free!

TO CHARLES DEODATI.

Charles, and I say it wondering, thou must know
That I, who once assumed a scornful air,
And scoffed at Love, am fallen in his snare,
(Full many an upright man has fallen so):

Yet think me not thus dazzled by the flow
    Of golden locks, or damask cheeks; more rare
    The heartfelt beauties of my foreign fair;
A mien majestic, with dark brows that show
The tranquil lustre of a lofty mind;
    Words exquisite, of idioms more than one,
And song, whose fascinating power might bind,
    And from her sphere draw down the labouring moon;
With such fire-darting eyes that, should I fill
My ears with wax, she would enchant me still.

Lady! It cannot be but that thine eyes
    Must be my sun, such radiance they display,
    And strike me e'en as Phœbus him whose way
Through horrid Libya's sandy desert lies.
Meantime, on that side steamy vapours rise
    Where most I suffer. Of what kind are they,
    New as to me they are, I can not say,
But deem them, in the lover's language—sighs.
Some, though with pain, my bosom close conceals,
    Which, if in part escaping thence, they tend
To soften thine, thy coldness soon congeals.
    While others to my tearful eyes ascend,
Whence my sad nights in showers are ever drowned,
Till my Aurora comes, her brow with roses bound.

Enamoured, artless, young, on foreign ground,
    Uncertain whither from myself to fly;
    To thee, dear Lady, with an humble sigh
Let me devote my heart, which I have found
By certain proofs, not few, intrepid, sound,
    Good, and addicted to conceptions high:
    When tempests shake the world, and fire the sky,
It rests in adamant self-wrapt around,
As safe from envy, and from outrage rude,
    From hopes and fears that vulgar minds abuse,

As fond of genius, and fixed fortitude,
Of the resounding lyre, and every Muse.
Weak you will find it in one only part,
Now pierced by Love's immedicable dart.

ON HIS DECEASED WIFE.

Methought I saw my late espouséd saint
Brought to me, like Alcestis, from the grave,
Whom Jove's great son to her glad husband gave,
Rescued from death by force, though pale and faint
Mine, as whom, washed from spot of child-bed taint,
Purification in the old Law did save,
And such, as yet once more I trust to have
Full sight of her in Heaven without restraint,
Came vested all in white, pure as her mind:
Her face was veiled, yet, to my fancied sight,
Love, sweetness, goodness, in her person shined
So clear, as in no face with more delight.
But O, as to embrace me she inclined,
I waked, she fled, and day brought back my night.

THOMAS CAREW.

1589—1639

CELIA.

Celia was a real person, but her name is unknown. Carew is said to have fallen in love with her in his youth, and his love not being returned, to have gone to France after leaving the university, to shake off his melancholy. We learn from one of his poems that she demanded her letters back, and from another that she married. Her husband probably died before Carew, for one of the poet's companions bantered him for having a widow for his mistress. Carew stood high in the good graces of his contemporaries. Davenant complimented him and his poetry by telling him there would be more triumphs in King's street, when he died, than in days of Parliament.

"Thy wit's chief virtue is become its vice;
For every beauty thou hast raised so high,
That now coarse faces carry such a price,
As must undo a lover that should buy."

"He was a person of a pleasant and facetious wit," says my Lord Clarendon, "and made many poems (especially in the amorous way), which for the sharpness of the fancy, and the elegance of the language in which that fancy was spread, were at least equal if not superior, to any of that time." "Carew's sonnets," says Oldys, "were more in request than any poet's of his time; that is between 1630 and 1640. They were many of them set to music by the two famous composers, Henry and William Lawes, and other eminent masters, and sung at court in their masques." They were first published in 1640.

SONG.

TO ONE THAT DESIRED TO KNOW MY MISTRESS.

Seek not to know my love, for she
Hath vowed her constant faith to me;

Her mild aspects are mine, and thou
Shalt only find a stormy brow;
For if her beauty stir desire
In me, her kisses quench the fire;
Or, I can to Love's fountain go,
Or dwell upon her hills of snow.
But when thou burn'st, she shall not spare
One gentle breath to cool the air;
Thou shalt not climb those Alps, nor spy
Where the sweet springs of Venus lie;
Search hidden nature and there find
A treasure to enrich thy mind;
Discover arts not yet revealed,
But let my Mistress live concealed;
Though men by knowledge wiser grow,
Yet here 't is wisdom not to know.

SONG.

CELIA SINGING.

You that think love can convey
        No other way,
But through the eyes, into the heart,
        His fatal dart;
Close up those casements, and but hear
        This siren sing;
        And on the wing
Of her sweet voice, it shall appear
That love can enter at the ear:
Then unveil your eyes, behold
        The curious mould
Where that voice dwells; and as we know
        When the cocks crow,
        We freely may
        Gaze on the day:
So may you, when the music 's done,
Awake and see the rising sun.

TO HIS JEALOUS MISTRESS.

Admit, thou darling of mine eyes,
    I have some idol lately framed,
That under such a false disguise,
    Our true loves might the less be famed:
Canst thou that knowest my heart, suppose
I'll fall from thee and worship those?

Remember, dear, how loath and slow
    I was to cast a look or smile,
Or one love-line to misbestow,
    Till thou hadst changed both face and style;
And art thou grown afraid to see
That mask put on thou mad'st for me?

I dare not call those childish fears,
    Coming from love, much less from thee,
But wash away, with frequent tears,
    This counterfeit idolatry,
And henceforth kneel at ne'er a shrine,
To blind the world, but only thine.

UNGRATEFUL BEAUTY THREATENED.

Know, Celia, since thou art so proud,
    'T was I that gave thee thy renown.
Thou hadst, in the forgotten crowd
    Of common beauties, lived unknown,
Had not my verse exhaled thy name,
And with it impt the wings of fame.

That killing power is none of thine,
    I give it to thy voice and eyes;
Thy sweets, thy graces, all are mine,
    Thou art my star, shin'st in my skies;

Then dart not from thy borrowed sphere
Lightning on him that fixed thee there.

Tempt me with such affrights no more,
    Lest what I made I uncreate;
Let fools thy mystic forms adore,
    I'll know thee in thy mortal state:
Wise poets that wrapped truth in tales,
Know her themselves through all her veils.

PARTING, CELIA WEEPS.

Weep not, my dear, for I shall go
Laden enough with my own woe;
Add not thy heaviness to mine;
Since fate our pleasures must disjoin,
Why should our sorrows meet? If I
Must go, and lose thy company,
I wish not theirs; it shall relieve
My grief, to think thou dost not grieve.
Yet grieve, and weep, that I may bear
Every sigh, and every tear
Away with me, so shall thy breast,
And eyes discharged, enjoy their rest:
And it will glad my heart to see
Thou wert thus loath to part with me.

A PRAYER TO THE WIND.

Go, thou gentle whispering wind,
Bear this sigh; and if thou find
Where my cruel fair doth rest,
Cast it in her snowy breast,
So, inflamed by my desire,
It may set her heart a-fire.
Those sweet kisses thou shalt gain,

Will reward thee for thy pain;
Boldly light upon her lip,
There suck odours, and thence skip
To her bosom; lastly fall
Down, and wander over all;
Range about those ivory hills,
From whose every part distils
Amber dew; there spices grow,
There pure streams of nectar flow;
There perfume thyself, and bring
All those sweets upon thy wing:
As thou return'st, change by thy power
Every weed into a flower;
Turn each thistle to a vine,
Make the bramble eglantine:
For so rich a booty made,
Do but this, and I am paid.
Thou can'st, with thy powerful blast,
Heat apace, and cool as fast;
Thou canst kindle hidden flame,
And again destroy the same;
Then for pity, either stir
Up the fire of love in her,
That alike both flames may shine,
Or else quite extinguish mine.

SONG.

Ask me no more where Jove bestows,
When June is past, the fading rose;
For in your beauty's orient deep,
These flowers, as in their causes, sleep.

Ask me no more whither doth stray
The golden atoms of the day:
For, in pure love, heaven did prepare
Those powders to enrich your hair.

Ask me no more whither doth haste
The nightingale when May is past;
For in your sweet dividing throat
She winters, and keeps warm her note.

Ask me no more where those stars light,
That downwards fall in dead of night;
For in your eyes they sit, and there
Fixéd become as in their sphere.

Ask me no more if east or west
The Phœnix builds her spicy nest;
For unto you at last she flies,
And in your fragrant bosom dies.

JAMES GRAHAME,

MARQUIS OF MONTROSE.

1612—1650.

MY DEAR AND ONLY LOVE, I PRAY.

PART FIRST.

My dear and only love I pray
    This noble world of thee,
Be governed by no other sway
    But purest monarchy.
For if confusion have a part,
    Which virtuous souls abhor,
And hold a synod in thy heart,
    I'll never love thee more.

Like Alexander I will reign,
    And I will reign alone;
My thoughts shall evermore disdain
    A rival on my throne.
He either fears his fate too much,
    Or his deserts are small,
That puts it not unto the touch,
    To win or lose it all.

But I must rule and govern still,
    And always give the law,
And have each subject at my will,
    And all to stand in awe.

But 'gainst my battery if I find
    Thou shun'st the prize so sore,
As that thou set'st me up a blind,
    I'll never love thee more.

Or in the empire of thy heart,
    Where I should solely be,
Another do pretend a part,
    And dares to vie with me;
Or if committees thou erect,
    And goes on such a score,
I'll sing and laugh at thy neglect,
    And never love thee more.

But if thou wilt be constant then,
    And faithful of thy word,
I'll make thee glorious by my pen,
    And famous by my sword.
I'll serve thee in such noble ways
    Was never heard before;
I'll crown and deck thee all with bays,
    And love thee evermore.

PART SECOND.

[The authenticity of the second part of this beautiful poem has been doubted. I have omitted one stanza, the text of which seems to me hopelessly corrupt.]

My dear and only love take heed,
    Lest thou thyself expose,
And let all longing lovers feed
    Upon such looks as those.
A marble wall then build about,
    Beset without a door;
But if thou let thy heart fly out,
    I'll never love thee more.

Let not their oaths, like vollies shot,
    Make any breach at all;
Nor smoothness of their language plot
    Which way to scale the wall;
Nor balls of wild-fire love consume
    The shrine which I adore;
For if such smoke about thee fume,
    I'll never love thee more.

I think thy virtues be too strong
    To suffer by surprise;
Which victualled by my love so long,
    The siege at length must rise,
And leave thee rulèd in that health
    And state thou wast before;
But if thou turn a common-wealth
    I'll never love thee more.

For if by fraud, or by consent,
    Thy heart to ruin come,
I'll sound no trumpet as I wont,
    Nor march by tuck of drum;
But hold my arms, like ensigns, up,
    Thy falsehood to deplore,
And bitterly will sigh and weep,
    And never love thee more.

I'll do with thee as Nero did,
    When Rome was set on fire,
Not only all relief forbid,
    But to a hill retire,
And scorn to shed a tear to see
    Thy spirit grown so poor;
But smiling, sing until I die,
    I'll never love thee more.

Yet for the love I bare thee once,
    Lest that thy name should die,

A monument of marble-stone
The truth shall testify;
That every pilgrim passing by,
May pity and deplore
My case, and read the reason why
I can love thee no more.

The golden laws of love shall be
Upon this pillar hung;
A simple heart, a single eye,
A true and constant tongue.
Let no man for more love pretend
Than he has hearts in store;
True love begun shall never end,
Love one and love no more.

Then shall thy heart be set by mine,
But in far different case;
But mine was true, so was not thine,
But looked like Janus' face.
For as the waves with every wind,
So sails thou every shore,
And leaves my constant heart behind.
How can I love thee more?

My heart shall with the sun be fixed,
For constancy most strange,
And thine shall with the moon be mixed,
Delighting aye in change.
Thy beauty shined at first most bright,
And woe is me therefore,
That ever I found thy love so light,
I could love thee no more.

As doth the turtle chaste and true,
Her fellow's death regret,
And daily mourns for his adieu,
And ne'er renews her mate;

So though thy faith was never fast,
Which grieves me wondrous sore,
Yet I shall live in love so chaste,
That I shall love no more.

And when all gallants ride about
These monuments to view,
Whereon is written in and out,
Thou traitorous and untrue;
Then in a passion they shall pause,
And thus say, sighing sore,
Alas! he had too just a cause
Never to love thee more.

And when that tracing goddess Fame
From east to west shall flee,
She shall record it to thy shame,
How thou hast lovéd me;
And how in odds our love was such
As few has been before;
Thou loved too many, and I too much,
That I can love no more.

EDMUND WALLER.

1605—1687.

SACCHARISSA.

WALLER's Saccharissa was the Lady Dorothea Sydney, eldest daughter of Robert Sydney, second Earl of Leicester, and Dorothea Percy, daughter of Henry Percy, ninth Earl of Northumberland. She was born in 1620, and her early years were passed at Penshurst, the famous seat of the Sydneys. As she was reputed beautiful, and her family was rich and distinguished, she was soon beset by admirers. She was much wooed by the young sprigs of nobility, and in her fifteenth year was said to be engaged to Lord Russell, the heir of the great house of Bedford. The gossips were out in their calculations, however, for my Lord Russell was followed by the Earl of Devonshire, who was followed in turn by Lord Lovelace, and others. At what period Waller made his appearance at Penshurst in the character of a lover, we are not told. There is a hiatus of four or five years in his life, which his biographers do not account for. This period embraces his courtship and first marriage. He was married in 1626, or thereabouts, when he was one or two and twenty, or according to another account, which is probably the true one, in 1631. His wife was a Miss Banks, the daughter and heiress of a rich London merchant of that name. Her fortune was large, and she had many suitors, one of whom, Mr. Crofts, afterwards Baron Crofts, was backed by the influence of the court, but Waller succeeded in distancing them all, and won her hand and fortune. At the end of three or four years she died, and left him a wealthy widower, with two children. He mourned her loss a sufficient time, and then cast about for a successor to install in her place. As he was rich enough not to need to marry again for money, he looked for beauty and rank—two charming but expensive qualities, which he however could afford. This drew him to Penshurst, and the Lady Dorothea. The date of his wooing is not given, as I have already mentioned, but circumstances fix it in 1638. He probably followed Lord Lovelace, who seems to have been dismissed the previous year. Waller's suit did not thrive. The Lady Dorothea was doubtless flattered by his attentions, as what young lady would not have been? He was a man of breeding and wit, and, as the saying was then, an ingenious and elegant poet. He wrote beautiful verses about her,

and she admired them, and him too, perhaps, but not as a lover. As a poet he was welcome to praise her; to call her nymph, goddess, and the like; to languish and die for her, He chose: but when it came to making love to her in his own person, it was another matter. And to expect her to return his love, was worst of all. She rejected him with disdain and scorn. Whether she considered herself his superior in rank, or thought him a little too old (there was a difference of fifteen years in their ages), or, what is more likely, loved somebody else better, we are left to conjecture. The Earl, her father, being abroad at the time, Waller wrote to him, and pressed him to come home, and decide the matter.

"That beam of beauty, which begun
To warm us so when thou wert here,
Now scorches like the raging sun,
When Sirius does first appear.
O fix this flame! and let despair
Redeem the rest from endless care."

But he might as well have saved his verses, for the Lady Dorothea fixed the flame herself, by bestowing her heart on Henry, Lord Spencer, afterwards Earl of Sunderland. They were married at Penshurst on the 11th of July, 1639. Waller bore his disappointment like a man of the world, and wrote Lady Lucy Sydney, a younger sister of the bride, a witty letter on the occasion. It may be found in Fenton's edition of Waller's works, and in Mrs. Jameson's "LOVES OF THE POETS." Of the subsequent history of Lady Spencer, or as she is more generally called, Lady Sunderland, little remains to be told. She led a happy life with her lord till the breaking out of the civil war, when he left her to follow the fortunes of the king. His career in the field was a short one, for he was slain by a cannon-ball at the battle of Newbury, on the 20th of September, 1643. She retired to his estate in Northamptonshire with her children, and lived in seclusion, till 1652, when she married Mr. Robert Smythe, a Kentish gentleman of good family. Waller and she met one day at Lady Wharton's, years afterwards, when they were both old people. "Mr. Waller," she asked him, "when will you write such fine verses on me again?" "O madam," the old wit replied, "when your ladyship is as young again." She died on the 25th of February, 1683–4, and was buried at Brinton, in Northamptonshire, in the same vault with her first husband. Waller married a second time, shortly after Saccharissa's marriage with Lord Spencer, but nothing is known of his second wife, save that her name was Bresse, or Breaux, and that she bore him a large family of children.

It is not known with certainty when the love poems of Waller were written, but as they were printed six years after the Lady Dorothea's first marriage, they probably extended over the space of seven years, or from 1638 to 1645. The majority of them were written, I imagine, in 1638–9, and revised at various times until they reached their present state of perfection. Waller was a slow and laborious writer, and was never tired of polishing his trifles. It took him the greater part of a summer on one occasion to write ten lines in a copy of Tasso! There are some twelve or fourteen poems in his works in praise of Saccharissa. She figures in the earlier ones as the Lady Dorothea, or Dorothy; but as Waller's passion (?) increased, she became Saccharissa;

"a name," says his editor, Fenton, "which recalls to mind what is related of the *Turks*, who in their gallantries think *Sucar Birpara*, i. e. bit of sugar, to be the most polite and endearing compliment they can use to the ladies." Besides these poems he wrote others of the same sort, addressed to Amoret, Chloris, Phyllis, Sylvia, Zelinda, etc., all real persons, his biographers assure us, with whom he was in love at various times. The first of these poetical dames shared his heart and song with the cruel Saccharissa. She was the Lady Sophia Murray; Chloris is supposed to have been Mrs. Wharton. The rest are shadows now, whatever they were once.

AT PENSHURST.

Had Dorothea lived when mortals made
Choice of their deities, this sacred shade
Had held an altar to her power, that gave
The peace and glory which these alleys have;
Embroidered so with flowers where she stood,
That it became a garden of a wood.
Her presence has such more than human grace,
That it can civilize the rudest place;
And beauty too, and order, can impart,
Where Nature ne'er intended it, nor art.
The plants acknowledge this, and her admire,
Not less than those of old did Orpheus' lyre.
If she sit down, with tops all towards her bowed,
They round about her into arbours crowd;
Or if she walk, in even ranks they stand,
Like some well-marshalled and obsequious band.
Amphion so made stones and timber leap
Into fair figures from a confused heap;
And in the symmetry of her parts is found
A power like that of harmony in sound.
Ye lofty beeches, tell this matchless dame,
That if together ye fed all one flame,
It could not equalize the hundredth part
Of what her eyes have kindled in my heart!
Go, boy, and carve this passion on the bark
Of yonder tree, which stands the sacred mark
Of noble Sidney's birth; when such benign,
Such more than mortal-making stars did shine,

That there they can not but forever prove
The monument and pledge of humble love;
His humble love whose hope shall ne'er rise higher,
Than for a pardon that he dares admire.

SONG.

Say, lovely dream! where couldst thou find
Shades to counterfeit that face?
Colours of this glorious kind
Come not from any mortal place.

In heaven itself thou sure wert dressed
With that angel-like disguise:
Thus deluded am I blessed,
And see my joy with closéd eyes.

But ah! this image is too kind
To be other than a dream;
Cruel Saccharissa's mind
Never put on that sweet extreme!

Fair dream! if thou intend'st me grace,
Change that heavenly face of thine;
Paint despised love in thy face,
And make it to appear like mine.

Pale, wan, and meagre let it look,
With a pity-moving shape,
Such as wander by the brook
Of Lethe, or from graves escape.

Then to that matchless nymph appear,
In whose shape thou shinest so;
Softly in her sleeping ear,
With humble words, express my woe.

Perhaps from greatness, state, and pride,
Thus surprisèd she may fall;
Sleep does disproportion hide,
And, death resembling, equals all.

TO AMORET.

Fair! that you may truly know
What you unto Thyrsis owe,
I will tell you how I do
Saccharissa love and you.
  Joy salutes me when I set
My blessed eyes on Amoret;
But with wonder I am strook,
When I on the other look.
  If sweet Amoret complains,
I have sense of all her pains;
But for Saccharissa I
Do not only grieve, but die.
  All that of myself is mine,
Lovely Amoret! is thine;
Saccharissa's captive fain
Would untie his iron chain,
And, those scorching beams to shun,
To thy gentle shadow run.
  If the soul had free election
To dispose of her affection,
I would not thus long have borne
Haughty Saccharissa's scorn;
But 't is sure some power above,
Which controls our wills in love!
  If not love, a strong desire
To create and spread that fire
In my heart, solicits me,
Beauteous Amoret! for thee.
  'T is amazement more than love
Which her radiant eyes do move;

If less splendour wait on thine,
Yet they so benignly shine,
I would turn my dazzled sight
To behold their milder light;
But as hard 't is to destroy
That high flame, as to enjoy;
Which how easily I may do,
Heaven (as easily scaled) does know!
  Amoret! as sweet and good
As the most delicious food,
Which, but tasted, does impart
Life and gladness to the heart.
  Saccharissa's beauty 's wine,
Which to madness doth incline;
Such a liquor as no brain
That is mortal can sustain.
  Scarce can I to heaven excuse
The devotion which I use
Unto that adoréd dame;
For 't is not unlike the same
Which I thither ought to send;
So that if it could take end,
'T would to heaven itself be due
To succeed her, and not you,
Who already have of me
All that 's not idolatry;
Which, though not so fierce a flame,
Is longer like to be the same.
  Then smile on me, and I will prove
Wonder is shorter-lived than love.

SIR JOHN SUCKLING.

1609—1641.

SUCKLING was a gay, careless, dissipated fellow, but high-bred and noble withal—a compound of the gentleman and the Bohemian. Addicted to gaming in his younger years, he became the best card-player and bowler in all England, winning and losing large sums of money, occasionally cheating, it is whispered, when the run of luck happened to be against him. His sisters are said to have come one day to the Piccadilly Bowling Green, "crying for the feare he should lose all their portions." "When at his lowest ebb," says his friend Davenant, "he would make himself glorious in apparel, and said that it exalted his spirits; and that then he had the best luck, when he was most gallant, and his spirits high." He was very fond of the ladies, and made them splendid presents. Aubrey mentions a countess "whom he had highly courted, and had spent on her, in treating her, some thousands of pounds." He used to give magnificent assemblies in London, to which all the court dames, who were beautiful, were invited, and at a banquet on one of these occasions he served up to them for the last course, silk stockings, garters, and gloves! The lady of his love, if he had one, is not known. Pope hints a little scandal about Lady Dorset—"old Lady Dorset," he profanely calls her. "That lady took a very odd pride in boasting of her familiarities with Sir John Suckling. She is the Mistress and Goddess in his poems; and several of these pieces were given by herself to the printer. This the Duke of Buckingham used to give as one instance of the fondness she had to let the world know how well they were acquainted."

Suckling's poems were published in 1646, five years after his death. They were popular in his life-time, many of them being set to music by Mr. Henry Lawes, a gentleman of the King's chapel. Milton's nephew, Edward Phillips, who in his criticisms is supposed to reflect the opinions of his illustrious uncle, says they "have a pretty touch of a gentile Spirit, and seem to savour more of the Grape than Lamp."

'Tis now, since I set down before
    That foolish fort, a heart,
(Time strangely spent!) a year, or more,
    And still I did my part;

Made my approaches, from her hand
 Unto her lip did rise;
And did already understand
 The language of her eyes;

Proceeded on with no less art,
 My tongue was engineer;
I thought to undermine the heart,
 By whispering in the ear.

When this did nothing, I brought down
 Great cannon oaths, and shot
A thousand thousand to the town,
 And still it yielded not.

I then resolved to starve the place,
 By cutting off all kisses,
Praising and gazing on her face,
 And all such little blisses.

To draw her out, and from her strength,
 I drew all batteries in,
And brought myself to lie, at length,
 As if no siege had been.

When I had done what man could do,
 And thought the place mine own,
The enemy lay quiet too,
 And smiled at all was done.

I sent to know, from whence, and where,
 These hopes, and this relief?
A spy informed, Honour was there,
 And did command in chief.

March, march (quoth I), the word straight give,
 Let 's lose no time, but leave her;
That giant upon air will live,
 And hold it out forever.

To such a place our camp remove,
As will no siege abide;
I hate a fool that starves her love,
Only to feed her pride.

SONG.

Out upon it! I have loved
Three whole days together,
And am like to love three more,
If it prove fair weather.

Time shalt moult away his wings,
Ere he shall discover
In the whole wide world again,
Such a constant lover.

But the spite on't is, no praise
Is due at all to me;
Love with me had made no stays,
Had it any been but she.

Had it any been but she,
And that very face,
There had been at least ere this
A dozen in her place.

SONNET I.

Do'st see how unregarded now
That piece of beauty passes?
There was a time when I did vow
To that alone;
But mark the fate of faces;
The red and white works now no more on me,
Than if it could not charm, or I not see.

And yet the face continues good,
    And I have still desires;
And still the self-same flesh and blood,
        As apt to melt,
    And suffer from those fires;
O some kind power unriddle where it lies,
Whether my heart be faulty, or her eyes.

She every day her man does kill,
    And I as often die;
Neither her power then, nor my will,
        Can questioned be;
    What is the mystery?
Sure beauty's empires, like to greater states,
Have certain periods set, and hidden fates.

SONNET II.

Of thee (kind boy) I ask no red and white,
        To make up my delight;
        No odd, becoming graces,
Black eyes, or little know-not-whats, in faces:
Make me but mad enough, give me good store
Of love for her I court,
        I ask no more;
'Tis love in love that makes the sport.

There 's no such thing as that we beauty call,
        It is mere cozenage all;
        For though some long ago
Liked certain colours, mingled so, and so,
That doth not tie me now from choosing new;
If I a fancy take
        To black and blue,
That fancy doth it beauty make.

'Tis not the meat, but 'tis the appetite
        Makes eating a delight;

And if I like one dish
More than another, that a pheasant is.
What in our watches, that in us is found;
So to the height and nick
We up be wound,
No matter by what hand, or trick.

SONG.

I prithee send me back my heart,
Since I can not have thine;
For if from your's you will not part,
Why then should'st thou have mine?

Yet now I think on 't, let it lie,
To find it were in vain:
For thou 'st a thief in either eye
Would steal it back again.

Why should two hearts in one breast lie,
And yet not lodge together?
O Love, where is thy sympathy,
If thus our breasts thou sever?

But love is such a mystery,
I cannot find it out;
For when I think I'm best resolved,
I then am in most doubt.

Then farewell care, and farewell woe,
I will no longer pine;
For I'll believe I have her heart,
As much as she has mine.

SIR FRANCIS KINASTON.

1585—1644.

["*Leoline and Sydanis.*" 1642.]

TO CYNTHIA, ON HER CHANGING.

Dear Cynthia, though thou bear'st the name
 Of the pale Queen of night,
Who changing yet is still the same,
 Renewing still her light;
Who monthly doth herself conceal,
 And her bright face doth hide,
That she may to Endymion steal,
 And kiss him unespied;

Do not thou so, not being sure
 When this thy beauty's gone,
That thou another canst procure,
 And wear it as thy own;
For the by-sliding silent hours,
 Conspirators with grief,
May crop thy beauty's lovely flowers,
 Time being a sly thief,

Which with his wings will fly away,
 And will return no more;
As, having got so rich a prey,
 Nature can not restore.

Reserve thou, then, and do not waste
    That beauty which is thine;
Cherish those glories that thou hast,
    Let not grief make thee pine.

Think that the lily, we behold,
    Or July flower may
Flourish, although the mother mould
    That bred them be away;
There is no cause, nor yet no sense,
    That dainty fruits should rot,
Though the tree die and wither, whence
    The apricots were got.

SYDNEY GODOLPHIN.

1610—1643.

SONG.

Or love me less, or love me more;
    And play not with my liberty:
Either take all, or all restore;
    Bind me at least, or set me free!
Let me some nobler torture find
Than of a doubtful wavering mind:
Take all my peace! but you betray
Mine honour too, this cruel way.

'Tis true that I have nursed before
    That hope, of which I now complain;
And, having little, sought no more,
    Fearing to meet with your disdain.
The sparks of favour you did give,
I gently blew, to make them live;
And yet have gained, by all this care,
No rest in hope, nor in despair.

I see you wear that pitying smile
    Which you have still vouchsafed my smart,
Content thus cheaply to beguile
    And entertain an harmless heart:
But I no longer can give way
To hope which doth so little pay;

And yet I dare no freedom owe,
Whilst you are kind, though but in show.

Then give me more, or give me less:
    Do not disdain a mutual sense;
Or your unpitying beauties dress
    In their own free indifference!
But show not a severer eye,
Sooner to give me liberty;
For I shall love the very scorn
Which, for my sake, you do put on.

WILLIAM CARTRIGHT.

1611—1643.

[" *Comedies, Tragi-comedies, with other Poems.*" 1651.]

A SIGH SENT TO HIS ABSENT LOVE.

I sent a sigh unto my blest one's ear,
Which lost its way, and never did come there;
I hastened after, lest some other fair
Should mildly entertain this travelling air;
Each flowery garden I did search, for fear
It might mistake a lily for her ear;
And having there took lodging, might still dwell
Housed in the concave of a crystal bell.
At last, one frosty morning I did spy
This subtle wanderer journeying in the sky;
At sight of me it trembled, then drew near,
Then grieving fell, and dropped into a tear:
I bore it to my saint, and prayed her take
This new-born offspring for the master's sake:
She took it, and preferred it to her ear,
And now it hears each thing that 's whispered there.
O how I envy grief, when that I see
My sorrow makes a gem more blest than me!
Yet, little pendant, porter to the ear,
Let not my rival have admittance there;
Or if by chance a mild access he gain,
Upon her lip inflict a gentle pain

Only for admonition: so when she
Gives ear to him, at least she'll think of me.

TO CHLOE.

WHO WISHED HERSELF YOUNG ENOUGH FOR ME.

Chloe, why wish you that your years
    Would backwards run, till they meet mine?
That perfect likeness, which endears
    Things unto things, might us combine?
Our ages so in date agree,
That twins do differ more than we.

There are two births, the one when light
    First strikes the new-awakened sense;
The other when two souls unite;
    And we must count our life from thence:
When you loved me, and I loved you,
Then both of us were born anew.

Love then to us did new souls give,
    And in those souls did plant new powers;
Since when another life we live,
    The breath we breathe is his, not ours:
Love makes those young, whom age doth chill,
And whom he finds young, keeps young still.

Love, like that angel that shall call
    Our bodies from the silent grave,
Unto one age doth raise us all,
    None too much, none too little have;
Nay, that the difference may be none,
He makes two not alike, but one.

And now since you and I are such,
    Tell me what 's yours, and what is mine?

Our eyes, our ears, our taste, smell, touch,
    Do (like our souls) in one combine:
So by this, I as well may be
Too old for you, as you for me.

A VALEDICTION.

Bid me not go where neither suns nor showers
        Do make or cherish flowers;
Where discontented things in sadness lie,
        And Nature grieves as I;
    When I am parted from those eyes,
    From which my better day doth rise,
        Though some propitious power
        Should plant me in a bower,
Where amongst happy lovers I might see
        How showers and sunbeams bring
        One everlasting spring,
Nor would those fall, nor these shine forth to me:
    Nature herself to him is lost,
    Who loseth her he honours most.
Then fairest to my parting view display
    Your graces all in one full day;
Whose blessèd shapes I'll snatch and keep, till when
    I do return and view agen:
So by this art fancy shall fortune cross,
And lovers live by thinking on their loss.

JAMES SHIRLEY.

1594—1666.

["*Poems.*" 1646.]

TO ODELIA.

HEALTH to my fair Odelia! Some that know
How many months are past
Since I beheld thy lovely brow,
Would count an age at least;
But unto me,
Whose thoughts are still on thee,
I vow
By thy black eyes, 'tis but an hour ago.

That mistress I pronounce but poor in bliss,
That, when her servant parts,
Gives not as much with her last kiss,
As will maintain two hearts
Till both do meet
To taste what else is sweet.
Is 't fit
Time measure love, or our affection it?

Cherish that heart, Odelia, that is mine,
And if the north thou fear,
Dispatch but from thy southern clime
A sigh, to warm thine here;

But be so kind
To send by the next wind;
'Tis far,
And many accidents do wait on war.

TAKING LEAVE WHEN HIS MISTRESS WAS TO RIDE.

How is it my ungentle fate,
When love commanded me to wait
Upon my saint, by break of day,
I brought a heart, but carried none away?

When we joined ceremonious breath,
And lips, that took a leave like death,
With a sad parting thought oppressed,
Did it leave mine, to glide into her breast?

Or was it, when like Pallas she
Was mounted, and I gazed to see,
My heart then looking through mine eye,
Did after her out of that window fly?

'T was so, and 'cause I did not ride,
My heart would lackey by her side,
Or some more careful angel be,
To see my mistress safe conveyed for me.

Nay, then, attend thy charge, nor fear
Storms in the way, and if a tear
By chance, at looking back on thee
Bedew her eye, drink that a health to me.

But smile at night, and be her guest,
At once her music and her feast,
And if at any mention made
Of me, she sigh, say all thy travail's paid.

But when she's gently laid to rest,
O listen softly to her breast,
And thou shalt hear her soul, but see
Thou wake her not, for she may dream of me.

But what's all this, when I am here,
If fancy bid thee welcome there?
Heart! this last duty I implore,
Or bring her back, or see thy cell no more.

THE KISS.

I could endure your eye, although it shot
Lightning at first into me:
Your voice, although it charmed mine ear, had not
The power to undo me:
But, while I on your lip would dwell,
My ravished heart leaped from his cell,
For, looking back into my breast
I found that room without a guest.

Return the heart you stole thus with a kiss,
When last our lips did join;
Or I'll forgive the theft, to change a bliss,
And have your heart for mine.
I ne'er till now believed it truth;
That lovers' hearts were at their mouth;
Now by experience I may say,
That men may kiss their hearts away.

RICHARD CRASHAW.

1615(?)—1650.

["*Steps to the Temple,*" *etc.* 1646.]

OUT OF THE ITALIAN.

A SONG.

To thy lover,
Dear, discover
That sweet blush of thine that shameth
(When those roses
It discloses)
All the flowers that Nature nameth.

In free air
Flow thy hair;
That no more Summer's best dresses
Be beholden
For their golden
Locks to Phœbus' flaming tresses.

O deliver
Love his quiver,
From thy eyes he shoots his arrows,
Where Apollo
Cannot follow,
Feathered with his mother's sparrows.

O envy not
(That we die not)
Those dear lips whose door encloses
All the Graces
In their places,
Brother pearls, and sister roses.

From these treasures
Of ripe pleasures
One bright smile to clear the weather.
Earth and heaven
Thus made even,
Both will be good friends together.

The air does woo thee,
Winds cling to thee;
Might a word once fly from out thee,
Storm and thunder
Would sit under,
And keep silence round about thee.

But if Nature's
Common creatures
So dear glories dare not borrow:
Yet thy beauty
Owes a duty
To my loving lingering sorrow.

When to end me
Death shall send me
All his terrors to affright me:
Thine eyes' Graces
Gild their faces,
And those terrors shall delight me.

When my dying
Life is flying,
Those sweet airs that often slew me

Shall revive me,
Or reprieve me,
And to many deaths renew me.

THE DEW NO MORE SHALL WEEP.

The dew no more shall weep,
The primrose's pale cheek to deck;
The dew no more shall sleep,
Nuzzled in the lily's neck:
Much rather would it tremble here,
And leave them both to be thy tear.

Not the soft gold which
Steals from the amber-weeping tree,
Makes sorrow half so rich,
As the drops distilled from thee:
Sorrow's best jewels be in these
Caskets, of which Heaven keeps the keys.

When sorrow would be seen
In her bright majesty,
(For she is a queen)
Then is she dressed by none but thee;
Then, and only then, she wears
Her richest pearls;—I mean thy tears.

Not in the evening's eyes
When they red with weeping are,
For the sun that dies,
Sits sorrow with a face so fair:
No where but here doth meet
Sweetness so sad, sadness so sweet.

ABRAHAM COWLEY.

1618—1667.

In 1647 "the melancholy Cowley" published a volume of poems, entitled, "The Mistresse, or severall copies of Love Verses." "Poets," he says in his preface (I quote from the folio edition of 1656), "Poets are scarce thought freemen of their company, without paying some duties, and obliging themselves to be true to love. Sooner, or later, they must all pass through that trial, like some Mohammedan monks, that are bound by their order, once at least in their life, to make a pilgrimage to Mecca." That Cowley himself passed through that trial, or, to parody his own expression, made a pilgrimage to the Mecca of Love, is admitted by most of his biographers, but they tell us nothing of the route which he took, and through what dangers or delights it led him. We only know that he wandered astray in the desert, misled perhaps by some glittering mirage, and never reached the shrine. "In the latter part of his life," says Pope, or Spence for him, "he showed a sort of aversion for women; and would leave the room when they came in: 't was probably from a disappointment in love. He was much in love with his Leonora; who is mentioned at the end of that good ballad on his different mistresses. She was married to Dean Sprat's brother; and Cowley never was in love with anybody after."

THE SPRING.

Though you be absent here, I needs must say
The trees as beauteous are, and flowers as gay,
As ever they were wont to be;
Nay, the birds' rural music too
Is as melodious and free,
As if they sung to pleasure you:
I saw a rose-bud ope this morn, I 'll swear
The blushing morning opened not more fair.

How could it be so fair, and you away?
How could the trees be beauteous, flowers so gay?
Could they remember but last year,
How you did them, they you delight,
The sprouting leaves which saw you here,
And called their fellows to the sight,
Would, looking round for the same sight in vain,
Creep back into their silent barks again.

Where'er you walked, trees were as reverend made,
As when of old gods dwelt in every shade.
Is 't possible they should not know
What loss of honour they sustain,
That thus they smile and flourish now,
And still their former pride retain?
Dull creatures! 't is not without cause that she,
Who fled the god of wit, was made a tree.

In ancient times sure they much wiser were,
When they rejoiced the Thracian verse to hear;
In vain did Nature bid them stay,
When Orpheus had his song begun,
They called their wondering roots away,
And bade them silent to him run.
How would those learnèd trees have followed you!
You would have drawn them, and their poet too.

But who can blame them now, for, since you 're gone,
They 're here the only fair, and shine alone.
You did their natural right invade;
Wherever you did walk or sit,
The thickest boughs could make no shade,
Although the sun had granted it:
The fairest flowers could please no more, near you,
Than painted flowers, set next to them, could do.

Whene'er then you come hither, that shall be
The time, which this to others is, to me.

The little joys which here are now,
The name of punishments do bear;
When by their sight they let us know
How we deprived of greater are.
'T is you the best of seasons with you bring;
This is for beasts, and that for men, the Spring.

CLAD ALL IN WHITE.

Fairest thing that shines below,
Why in this robe dost thou appear?
Wouldst thou a white most perfect show,
Thou must at all no garment wear:
Thou wilt seem much whiter so,
Than winter when 't is clad with snow.

'T is not the linen shows so fair:
Her skin shines through, and makes it bright;
So clouds themselves like suns appear,
When the sun pierces them with light:
So lilies in a glass enclose,
The glass will seem as white as those.

Thou now one heap of beauty art;
Nought outwards, or within is foul;
Condensèd beams make every part;
Thy body 's clothed like thy soul:
Thy soul, which does itself display,
Like a star placed i' th' milky way.

Such robes the saints departed wear,
Woven all with light divine;
Such their exalted bodies are,
And with such full glory shine.
But they regard not mortals' pain:
Men pray, I fear, to both in vain.

Yet seeing thee so gently pure,
My hopes will needs continue still;
Thou wouldst not take this garment, sure,
When thou hadst an intent to kill.
Of peace and yielding who would doubt,
When the white flag he sees hung out?

THE CHRONICLE.

A BALLAD.

Margarita first possessed,
If I remember well, my breast,
Margarita, first of all;
But, when awhile the wanton maid
With my restless heart had played,
Martha took the flying ball.

Martha soon did it resign
To the beauteous Catharine.
Beauteous Catharine gave place
(Though loath and angry she to part
With the possession of my heart)
To Elisa's conquering face.

Elisa till this hour might reign,
Had she not evil counsels ta'en:
Fundamental laws she broke,
And still new favourites she chose,
Till up in arms my passions rose,
And cast away her yoke.

Mary then and gentle Anne
Both to reign at once began;
Alternately they swayed:
And sometimes Mary was the fair,
And sometimes Anne the crown did wear,
And sometimes both I obeyed.

Another Mary then arose,
    And did rigorous laws impose;
    A mighty tyrant, she!
Long, alas! should I have been
Under that iron-sceptred queen,
    Had not Rebecca set me free.

When fair Rebecca set me free,
    'T was then a golden time with me;
    But soon those pleasures fled;
For the gracious princess died,
In her youth and beauty's pride,
    And Judith reignéd in her stead.

One month, three days, and half an hour,
    Judith held the sovereign power;
    Wondrous beautiful her face;
But so small and weak her wit,
That she to govern was unfit,
    And so Susanna took her place.

But, when Isabella came,
    Armed with a resistless flame,
    And th' artillery of her eye;
Whilst she proudly marched about
Greater conquests to find out,
    She beat out Susan, by the by.

But in her place I then obeyed
    Black-eyed Bess, her viceroy-maid,
    To whom ensued a vacancy.
Thousand worse passions then possessed
The interregnum of my breast:
    Bless me from such an anarchy!

Gentle Henrietta then,
    And a third Mary next began;
    Then Joan, and Jane, and Audria,

And then a pretty Thomasine,
And then another Catharine,
And then a long *et cætera.*

But should I now to you relate,
The strength and riches of their state,
The powders, patches, and the pins,
The ribands, jewels, and the rings,
The lace, the paint, and warlike things,
That make up all their magazines:

If I should tell the politic arts
To take and keep men's hearts;
The letters, embassies, and spies,
The frowns, and smiles, and flatteries,
The quarrels, tears, and perjuries,
Numberless, nameless mysteries!

And all the little lime-twigs laid
By Machiavel, the waiting-maid;
I more voluminous should grow
(Chiefly, if I like them should tell
All change of weathers that befel)
Than Holinshed, or Stow.

But I will briefer with them be,
Since few of them were long with me.
An higher and a noble strain,
My present emperess doth claim,
Heleonora, first o' th' name,
Whom God grant long to reign!

ROBERT HERRICK.

1591—1674.

["*Hesperides.*" 1648.]

CHERRY RIPE.

CHERRY ripe, ripe, ripe, I cry,
Full and fair ones; come and buy!
If so be you ask me where
They do grow, I answer, There,
Where my Julia's lips do smile;
There 's the land, or cherry-isle,
Whose plantations fully show
All the year where cherries grow.

THE ROCK OF RUBIES, AND THE QUARRY OF PEARLS.

Some asked me where the rubies grew,
And nothing I did say,
But with my finger pointed to
The lips of Julia.
Some asked how pearls did grow, and where,
Then spoke I to my girl,
To part her lips, and showed them there
The quarrelets of pearl.

THE CAPTIVED BEE, OR THE LITTLE FILCHER.

As Julia once a slumbering lay,
It chanced a bee did fly that way,
After a dew, or dew-like shower,
To tipple freely in a flower.
For some rich flower he took the lip
Of Julia, and began to sip;
But when he felt he sucked from thence
Honey, and in the quintessence,
He drank so much he scarce could stir,
So Julia took the pilferer,
And thus surprised, as filchers use,
He thus began himself t' excuse:
Sweet lady-flower, I never brought
Hither the least one thieving thought:
But taking those rare lips of yours
For some fresh, fragrant, luscious flowers,
I thought I might there take a taste,
Where so much syrup ran at waste.
Besides, know this, I never sting
The flower that gives me nourishing:
But with a kiss, or thanks, do pay
For honey that I bear away.
This said, he laid his little scrip
Of honey 'fore her ladyship;
And told her, as some tears did fall,
That that he took, and that was all.
At which she smiled, and bade him go
And take his bag, but thus much know:
When next he came a pilfering so,
He should from her full lips derive
Honey enough to fill his hive.

TO DAISIES, NOT TO SHUT SO SOON.

Shut not so soon; the dull-eyed night
Has not as yet begun
To make a seizure on the light,
Or to seal up the sun.

No marigolds yet closéd are,
No shadows great appear;
Nor doth the early shepherd's star
Shine like a spangle here.

Stay but till my Julia close
Her life-begetting eye;
And let the whole world then dispose
Itself to live, or die.

THE NIGHT-PIECE, TO JULIA.

Her eyes the glow-worm lend thee,
The shooting stars attend thee;
And the elves also,
Whose little eyes glow
Like the sparks of fire, befriend thee.

No Will-o'-th'-Wisp mislight thee;
Nor snake or slow-worm bite thee;
But on, on thy way,
Not making a stay,
Since ghost there's none to affright thee.

Let not the dark thee cumber;
What though the moon does slumber?
The stars of the night,
Will lend thee their light,
Like tapers clear without number.

Then, Julia, let me woo thee,
Thus, thus to come unto me;
And when I shall meet
Thy silvery feet,
My soul I 'll pour into thee.

UPON JULIA'S HAIR, BUNDLED UP IN A GOLDEN NET.

Tell me, what needs those rich deceits,
These golden toils and trammel-nets,
To take thine hairs, when they are known
Already tame, and all thine own?
'Tis I am wild, and more than hairs
Deserve these meshes and those snares,
So free thy tresses; let them flow
As airs do breathe or winds do blow;
And let such curious net-works be
Less set for them than spread for me.

TO ANTHEA.

Anthea, I am going hence
With some small stock of innocence,
But yet those blesséd gates I see
Withstanding entrance unto me.
To pray for me do thou begin,
The porter then will let me in.

TO ANTHEA.

Now is the time, when all the lights wax dim,
And thou, Anthea, must withdraw from him
Who was thy servant. Dearest, bury me
Under that holy oak, or gospel-tree,
Where, though thou see 'st not, thou may'st think upon
Me, when thou yearly go 'st procession:

Or for mine honour, lay me in that tomb
In which thy sacred relics shall have room;
For my embalming, sweetest, there will be
No spices wanting, when I'm laid by thee.

BEING ONCE BLIND, HIS REQUEST TO BIANCHA.

When age or chance has made me blind,
So that the path I cannot find;
And when my falls and stumblings are
More than the stones i' th' street by far;
Go thou afore, and I shall well
Follow thy perfumes by the smell:
Or be my guide, and I shall be
Led by some light that flows from thee.
Thus held, or led by thee, I shall
In ways confused nor slip nor fall.

TO THE WESTERN WIND.

Sweet western wind, whose luck it is
    Made rival with the air,
To give Perenna's lip a kiss,
    And fan her wanton hair,

Bring me but one, I'll promise thee,
    Instead of common showers,
Thy wings shall be embalmed by me,
    And all beset with flowers.

TO HIS MAID PRUE.

These summer-birds did with thy master stay
The times of warmth, but then they flew away,

Leaving their poet, being now grown old,
Exposed to all the coming winter's cold.
But thou, kind Prue, didst with my fates abide
As well the winter's as the summer's tide:
For which thy love, live with thy master here,
Not two, but all the seasons of the year.

UPON PRUE, HIS MAID.

In this little urn is laid
Prudence Baldwin, once my maid;
From whose happy spark here let
Spring the purple violet.

TO ELECTRA.

I dare not ask a kiss;
    I dare not beg a smile;
Lest having that or this,
    I might grow proud the while.

No, no, the utmost share
    Of my desire shall be,
Only to kiss that air
    That lately kisséd thee.

TO MYRRHA, HARD-HEARTED.

Fold now thine arms, and hang the head,
Like to a lily witheréd:
Next, look thou like a sickly moon,
Or like Jocasta in a swoon.
Then weep, and sigh, and softly go,
Like to a widow drowned in woe:
Or like a virgin full of ruth,
For the lost sweet-heart of her youth:

And all because, fair maid, thou art
Insensible of all my smart;
And of those evil days that be
Now posting on to punish thee.
The gods are easy and condemn
All such as are not soft like them.

UPON THE LOSS OF HIS MISTRESSES.

I have lost, and lately, these
Many dainty mistresses:
Stately Julia, prime of all;
Sappho next, a principal:
Smooth Anthea, for a skin
White, and heaven-like crystalline:
Sweet Electra, and the choice
Myrrha for the lute and voice;
Next Corinna, for her wit,
And the graceful use of it,
With Perilla. All are gone;
Only Herrick 's left alone,
For to number sorrow by
Their departures hence, and die.

RICHARD LOVELACE.

1618—1658.

LUCASTA.

THE life of Lovelace is a melancholy chapter of literary biography, for in whatever light we regard him he possesses a strong claim to our admiration and pity. He figures in English Literature as a poet of the first order, and in the History of his time as an accomplished gentleman and a valiant soldier—the beau ideal of a cavalier: Charles Stewart had no more faithful servant than Richard Lovelace. His attachment to the royal family may be dated from his eighteenth year, when he was made master of arts at Oxford, at the intercession of a great lady belonging to the queen. When he quitted the University he came up to London, and lived at court for some time in great splendour. He served against the Scotch in two expeditions, and returning to England when the hopes of his party were at an end, he retired to his estates in Kent, and stirred up the people of his neighbourhood in behalf of their monarch. He was chosen by the whole body of the county to deliver to the House of Commons a petition for settling the government, and restoring the king to his rights. For presenting this petition he was committed to the Gate House at Westminster, and kept in strict confinement for nearly four months. Here he wrote his famous lyric, "To ALTHEA," which, Southey says, will last as long as the language. He was at length released, on giving bail to the amount of forty thousand pounds, but was restricted from stirring beyond the lines of communication, without a pass from the Speaker. This forced inactivity chafed his proud spirit, and drove him into living extravagantly to keep up the credit of the king. He furnished his two brothers, Frank and William, with men and arms for the royal cause, and sent his third brother, Dudley Posthumous, to Holland to study tactics and fortification. He devoted himself to the king, body and soul, only reserving his heart, which about this time was taken captive by Lucy Sacheverel, the Lucasta of his poems. She was rich and beautiful, we are told, but not so steadfast as she should have been; for when Lovelace, who, after the rendition of the Oxford garrison in 1646, formed a regiment and entered the service of the French king, was wounded at Dunkirk, she engaged herself to another. It is true that Lovelace was reported killed, and that a year or two elapsed before he reappeared; still she should have waited until it was known that he was dead, and his great heart was cold. He returned to England in 1648, to find her married, and to undergo again the horrors of imprisonment; for immediately on their landing, he and his brother, Dudley, were confined in Peter House. He bore up manfully under this double calamity, and busied himself in preparing his poems for the press, but his heart was broken.

"After the murther of Charles I.," says Anthony à Wood, "Lovelace was set at liberty, and having by that time consumed all his estate, grew very melancholy, (which brought him at length into a consumption;) became very poor in body and purse; was the object of charity; went in ragged cloathes, (whereas, when he was in his glory he wore cloth of gold and silver,) and mostly lodged in obscure and dirty places, more befitting the worst of beggars and poorest of servants, &c. He died in a mean lodging in Gunpowder-alley, near Shoe-lane, and was buried at the west end of the Church of S. Bride, alias Bridget, in London, near to the body of his kinsman Will. Lovelace of Grays-Inn, esqr., in sixteen hundred fifty and eight." Aubrey says that he died in a cellar in Long Acre. "Mr. Edm. Wyld had made collections for him, and given him money." "Geo. Petty, haberdasher in Fleet-street, carried XXs to him every Monday morning from Sir —— Many and Charles Cotton esqr., for months, but was never repayd." He also adds that "he was an extraordinary handsome man, but prowd." Poor Lovelace!

His poems were published in 1649, under the title of "LUCASTA: EPODES, ODES, SONNETS, SONGS, etc." They were very popular at the time, and are so still with poets, though not so generally known as they deserve to be, owing to their not being included in any of the popular collections of English poetry. "A man may discern therein," says Edward Phillips, "sometimes those sparks of a Poetic fire, which had they been the main design, and not Parergon in some work of Heroic argument, might happily have blazed out into the perfection of sublime Poesy."

TO LUCASTA.

THE ROSE.

Sweet, serene, sky-like flower,
Haste to adorn her bower:
    From thy long cloudy bed,
    Shoot forth thy damask head.

New-startled blush of Flora!
The grief of pale Aurora,
    Who will contest no more;
    Haste, haste to strew her floor.

Vermilion ball that 's given
From lip to lip in heaven;
    Love's couch's coverlid;
    Haste, haste to make her bed.

Dear offspring of pleased Venus,
And jolly, plump Silenus;
    Haste, haste to deck the hair
    Of th' only, sweetly fair.

See! rosy is her bower,
Her floor is all this flower;
    Her bed a rosy nest
    By a bed of roses pressed.

But early as she dresses,
Why fly you her bright tresses?
    Ah, I have found, I fear:
    Because her cheeks are near.

TO LUCASTA.

GOING BEYOND THE SEAS.

If to be absent were to be
        Away from thee;
    Or that, when I am gone,
    You or I were alone;
Then, my Lucasta, might I crave
Pity from blustering wind, or swallowing wave.

But I 'll not sigh one blast or gale,
        To swell my sail,
    Or pay a tear to 'suage
    The foaming blue-god's rage;
For whether he will let me pass
Or not, I 'm still as happy as I was.

Though seas and land be 'twixt us both,
Our faith and troth,
Like separated souls,
All time and space controls:
Above the highest sphere we meet
Unseen, unknown, and greet as angels greet.

So then we do anticipate
Our after fate,
And are alive i' th' skies,
If thus our lips and eyes
Can speak like spirits unconfined
In heaven, their earthly bodies left behind.

TO ALTHEA, FROM PRISON.

When love with unconfinéd wings
Hovers within my gates,
And my divine Althea brings
To whisper at my grates;
When I lie tangled in her hair,
And fettered with her eye,
The birds that wanton in the air,
Know no such liberty.

When flowing cups run swiftly round
With no allaying Thames,
Our careless heads with roses bound,
Our hearts with loyal flames;
When thirsty grief in wine we steep,
When healths and draughts go free,
Fishes, that tipple in the deep,
Know no such liberty.

When, like committed linnets, I
With shriller throat shall sing
The mercy, sweetness, majesty,
And glories of my king;

When I shall voice aloud how good
He is, how great should be,
Enlargéd winds, that curl the flood,
Know no such liberty.

Stone walls do not a prison make,
Nor iron bars a cage;
Minds innocent and quiet take
That for an heritage:
If I have freedom in my love,
And in my soul am free,
Angels alone, that soar above,
Enjoy such liberty.

SONG.

[The last three stanzas of this spirited lyric being a little too free for quotation, I have omitted them.]

Amarantha, sweet and fair,
Ah! braid no more that shining hair!
As my curious hand or eye,
Hovering round thee, let it fly.

Let it fly as unconfined
As its calm ravisher, the Wind;
Who hath left his darling, th' east,
To wanton o'er that spicy nest.

Every tress must be confessed,
But neatly tangled at the best;
Like a clue of golden thread,
Most excellently ravelléd.

Do not, then, wind up that light
In ribands, and o'ercloud in night,
Like the Sun in 's early ray,
But shake your head, and scatter day!

TO LUCASTA, ON GOING TO THE WARS.

Tell me not, sweet, I am unkind,
That from the nunnery
Of thy chaste breast and quiet mind,
To war and arms I fly.

True, a new mistress now I chase,
The first foe in the field;
And with a stronger faith embrace
A sword, a horse, a shield.

Yet this inconstancy is such
As you, too, shall adore;
I could not love thee, dear, so much,
Loved I not honour more.

THE SCRUTINY.

Why should you say I am forsworn,
Since thine I vowed to be?
Lady, it is already morn,
And 't was last night I swore to thee
That fond impossibility.

Have I not loved thee much, and long,
A tedious twelve hours' space?
I must all other beauties wrong,
And rob thee of a new embrace,
Could I still dote upon thy face.

Not but all joy in thy brown hair
By others may be found;
But I must search the black and fair,
Like skillful mineralists that sound
For treasure in unploughed-up ground.

Then, if when I have loved my round,
Thou prov'st the pleasant she;
With spoils of meaner beauties crowned,
I laden will return to thee,
Even sated with variety.

ELINDA'S GLOVE.

SONNET.

Thou snowy farm with thy five tenements!
Tell thy white mistress here was one
That called to pay his daily rents:
But she a-gathering flowers and hearts is gone,
And thou left void to rude possession.

But grieve not, pretty Ermine cabinet,
Thy alabaster lady will come home;
If not, what tenant then can fit
The slender turnings of thy narrow room,
But must ejected be by his own doom?

Then give me leave to leave my rent with thee:
Five kisses, one unto a place;
For though the lute 's too high for me,
Yet servants, knowing minikin nor base,
Are still allowed to fiddle with the case.

JOHN CLEVELAND.

1613—1658.

["*Poems*" (?) 1651.]

UPON PHILLIS, WALKING IN A MORNING BEFORE SUN-RISING.

THE sluggish morn as yet undressed,
My Phillis brake from out her East,
As if she'd made a match to run
With Venus, Usher to the Sun.
The trees (like yeomen of her guard,
Serving more for pomp than ward,
Banked on each side with loyal duty)
Wave branches to enclose her beauty.
The plants, whose luxury was lopped,
Or age with crutches underpropped,
(Whose wooden carcasses are grown
To be but coffins of their own,)
Revive, and at her general dole
Each receives his ancient soul.
The wingéd choristers began
To chirp their matins; and the fan
Of whistling winds, like organs, played
Unto their voluntaries, made
The wakened earth in odours rise
To be her morning sacrifice.
The flowers, called out of their beds,
Start and raise up their drowsy heads,

And he that for their colour seeks,
May find it vaulting in her cheeks,
Where roses mix no civil war
Between her York and Lancaster.
The marigold, whose courtier's face
Echoes the sun, and doth unlace
Her at his rise, at his full stop
Packs, and shuts up her gaudy shop;
Mistakes her cue, and doth display;
Thus Phillis antedates the day.
  These miracles had cramped the sun,
Who, thinking that his kingdom 's won,
Powders with light his frizzled locks,
To see what saint his lustre mocks.
The trembling leaves through which he played,
Dappling the walk with light and shade,
(Like lattice-windows,) give the spy
Room but to peep with half an eye,
Lest her full orb his sight should dim,
And bid us all good night in him,
Till she would spend a gentle ray,
To force us a new-fashioned day.
  But what religious palsy 's this,
Which makes the boughs divest their bliss,
And that they might her footsteps straw,
Drop their leaves with shivering awe?
Phillis perceives, (and lest her stay
Should wed October unto May,
And, as her beauty caused a Spring,
Devotion might an Autumn bring,)
Withdrew her beams, yet made no night,
But left the sun her curate-light.

PATRICK CAREY.

[" *Trivial Poems and Triolets.*" 1651.]

FAIR beauties! if I do confess
Myself inconstant in my drink,
You ought not to love me the less,
I say but that which most men think:
And (troth) there is less hurtful art
In a light tongue, than a false heart.

Some use to swear that you will find
Nothing but truth within their breasts;
Yet waver more than does the wind,
When in a tempest least it rests;
Nought of my thoughts I'll say to you,
But what you'll find to be most true.

More than I promise I'll perform;
They give you oaths, but keep them not;
You build i' th' air, when as you form
False hopes on vows long since forgot.
Leave, leave them then, and deal with me,
So you will ne'er deceivéd be.

Fairly beforehand I declare,
That when I'm weary, I shall leave;
Fore-warnéd thus, you'll be aware,
Whilst falser men would ye deceive:

Besides, in this I nothing do,
But what I'd swear you will do too.

When of your love I weary grow,
Before I change, I'll tell you on 't;
Do you the same when you are so,
And give me time to think upon 't;
Elsewhere I soon shall place my heart,
Then, kindly we'll shake hands, and part.

THOMAS STANLEY.

1620(?)—1678.

["*Poems.*" 1651.]

THE DEPOSITION.

THOUGH, when I loved thee, thou wert fair,
    Thou art no longer so;
Those glories all the pride they wear
    Unto opinion owe.
Beauties, like stars, in borrowed lustre shine,
And 't was my love that gave thee thine.

The flames that dwelt within thine eye
    Do now with mine expire;
Thy brightest graces fade and die
    At once with my desire.
Love's fires thus mutual influence return;
Thine cease to shine when mine to burn.

Then, proud Celinda, hope no more
    To be implored or wooed;
Since by thy scorn thou dost restore
    The wealth my love bestowed:
And thy despised disdain too late shall find
That none are fair but who are kind!

THE TOMB.

When, cruel fair one, I am slain
By thy disdain,
And, as a trophy of thy scorn,
To some old tomb am borne,
Thy fetters must their power bequeath
To those of Death;
Nor can thy flame immortal burn,
Like monumental fires within an urn:
Thus freed from thy proud empire, I shall prove
There is more liberty in Death than Love.

And when forsaken lovers come
To see my tomb,
Take heed thou mix not with the crowd,
And (as a victor) proud,
To view the spoils thy beauty made,
Press near my shade,
Lest thy too cruel breath or name
Should fan my ashes back into a flame,
And thou, devoured by this revengeful fire,
His sacrifice, who died as thine, expire.

But if cold earth, or marble, must
Conceal my dust,
Whilst hid in some dark ruins, I,
Dumb and forgotten, lie,
The pride of all thy victory
Will sleep with me;
And they who should attest thy glory,
Will, or forget, or not believe this story.
Then to increase thy triumph, let me rest,
Since by thine eye slain, buried in thy breast.

THE EXEQUIES.

Draw near,
You lovers that complain
Of Fortune or Disdain,
And to my ashes lend a tear;
Melt the hard marble with your groans,
And soften the relentless stones,
Whose cold embraces the sad subject hide
Of all Love's cruelties, and Beauty's pride.

No verse,
No epicedium bring,
Nor peaceful requiem sing,
To charm the terrors of my hearse;
No profane slumbers must flow near
The sacred silence that dwells here.
Vast griefs are dumb; softly, O, softly mourn,
Lest you disturb the peace attends my urn.

Yet strew
Upon my dismal grave
Such offerings as you have,
Forsaken cypress, and sad yew;
For kinder flowers can take no birth,
Or growth, from such unhappy earth.
Weep only o'er my dust, and say, Here lies
To Love and Fate an equal sacrifice.

SIR EDWARD SHERBURNE.

1618—1702.

["*Salmacis*," *etc.* 1651.]

CHANGE DEFENDED.

LEAVE, Chloris, leave, prithee no more
With want of love, or lightness charge me:
'Cause thy looks captived me before,
May not another's now enlarge me?

He, whose misguided zeal hath long
Paid homage to some star's pale light,
Better informed, may without wrong,
Leave that t' adore the queen of night.

Then if my heart, which long served thee,
Will to Carintha now incline;
Why termed inconstant should it be,
For bowing 'fore a richer shrine?

Censure that lover 's such, whose will
Inferior objects can entice;
Who changes for the better still,
Makes that a virtue, you call vice.

LOVE ONCE, LOVE EVER.

Shall I hopeless then pursue
    A fair shadow that still flies me?
Shall I still adore, and woo
    A proud heart, that does despise me?
I a constant love may so,
But alas! a fruitless, show.

Shall I by the erring light
    Of two crosser stars still sail?
That do shine, but shine in spite,
    Not to guide, but make me fail?
I a wandering course may steer,
But the harbour ne'er come near.

Whilst these thoughts my soul possess,
    Reason passion would o'ersway;
Bidding me my flames suppress,
    Or divert some other way:
But what reason would pursue,
That my heart runs counter to.

So a pilot, bent to make
    Search for some unfound out land,
Does with him the magnet take,
    Sailing to the unknown strand;
But that (stir which way he will)
To the lovéd north points still.

HENRY KING.

1591—1669.

[" *Poems, Elegies, Paradoxes, and Sonnets.*" 1657.]

THE SURRENDER.

My once dear love, helpless that I no more
Must call thee so, the rich affections' store
That fed our hopes, now lies exhaust and spent,
Like sums of treasure unto bankrupts lent.
We that did nothing study but the way
To love each other, with which thoughts the day
Rose with delight to us, and with them set,
Must learn the hateful art how to forget.
We that did nothing wish, that Heaven could give,
Beyond ourselves, nor did desire to live
Beyond that wish, all these now cancel must,
As if not writ in faith, but words and dust.
Yet witness those clear vows which lovers make;
Witness the chaste desires that never brake
Into unruly hearts; witness that breast
Which in thy bosom anchored his whole rest.
'T is no default in us; I dare acquite
Thy maiden faith, thy purpose fair and white
As thy pure self; cross planets did envy
Us to each other, and Heaven did untie
Faster than vows could bind. O that the stars
When lovers meet, should stand opposed in wars!

Since, then, some higher Destinies command,
Let us not strive, nor labour to withstand
What is past help; the longest date of grief
Can never yield a hope of our relief;
And though we waste ourselves in moist laments,
Tears may drown us, but not our discontents.
Fold back our arms, take home our fruitless loves,
That must new fortunes try; like turtle doves
Dislodgéd from their haunts, we must in tears
Unwind a love knit up in many years.
In this last kiss I here surrender thee
Back to thyself; so thou again art free.
Thou in another, sad as that, re-send
The truest heart that lover e'er did lend.
Now turn from each; so fare our severed hearts
As the divorced soul from her body parts.

THE LEGACY.

My dearest love, when thou and I must part,
And th' icy hand of Death shall seize that heart
Which is all thine, within some spacious will
I'll leave no blanks for legacies to fill:
'Tis my ambition to die one of those
Who but himself hath nothing to dispose.
And since that is already thine, what need
I to re-give it by some newer deed?
Yet take it once again, free circumstance
Does oft the value of mean things advance:
Who thus repeats what he bequeathed before,
Proclaims his bounty richer than his store.
But let me not upon my love bestow
What is not worth the giving. I do owe
Something to dust: my body's pampered care
Hungry corruption and the worm will share.
That mouldering relic which in earth must lie,
Would prove a gift of horror to thine eye;

With this cast rag of my mortality
Let all my faults and errors buried be.
And as my sere-cloth rots, so may kind fate
Those worst acts of my life incinerate.
He shall in story fill a glorious room,
Whose ashes and whose sins sleep in one tomb.
If now to my cold hearse thou deign to bring
Some melting sighs as thy last offering,
My peaceful exequies are crowned, nor shall
I ask more honour at my funeral.
Thou wilt more richly 'balm me with thy tears
Than all the nard fragrant Arabia bears.
And as the Paphian Queen, by her grief's shower,
Brought up her dead love's spirit in a flower,
So by those precious drops rained from thine eyes,
Out of my dust, O may some Virtue rise!
And like thy better Genius thee attend,
Till thou in my dark period shalt end.
Lastly, my constant truth let me commend
To him thou choosest next to be thy friend.
For (witness all things good!) I would not have
Thy youth and beauty married to my grave;
'T would show thou didst repent the style of wife,
Should'st thou relapse into a single life.
They with preposterous grief the world delude,
Who mourn for their lost mates in solitude;
Since widowhood more strongly doth enforce
The much-lamented lot of their divorce.
Themselves then of their losses guilty are,
Who may, yet will not suffer a repair.
Those were Barbarian wives that did invent
Weeping to death at th' husband's monument.
But in more civil rites she doth approve
Her first, who ventures on a second love;
For else it may be thought if she refrain,
She sped so ill she durst not try again.
Up then, my love, and choose some worthier one,
Who may supply my room when I am gone;

So will the stock of our affection thrive,
No less in death, than were I still alive.
And in my urn I shall rejoice, that I
Am both testator thus, and legacy.

THE EXEQUY.

Accept, thou shrine of my dead saint,
Instead of dirges, this complaint;
And for sweet flowers to crown thy hearse,
Receive a strew of weeping verse
From thy grieved friend, whom thou might'st see
Quite melted into tears for thee.
  Dear loss! since thy untimely fate,
My task hath been to meditate
On thee, on thee; thou art the book,
The library whereon I look,
Though almost blind; for thee (loved clay)
I languish out, not live the day,
Using no other exercise
But what I practise with mine eyes:
By which wet glasses I find out,
How lazily Time creeps about
To one that mourns: this, only this,
My exercise and business is:
So I compute the weary hours
With sighs dissolvéd into showers.
  Nor wonder if my time go thus
Backward and most preposterous;
Thou hast benighted me, thy set
This eve of blackness did beget,
Who wast my day, (though overcast
Before thou hadst thy noontide passed,)
And I remember must in tears,
Thou scarce hadst seen so many years
As day tells hours; by thy clear Sun
My love and fortune first did run;

But thou wilt never more appear,
Folded within my hemisphere,
Since both thy light and motion
Like a fled star is fallen and gone,
And 'twixt me and my soul's dear wish
The earth now interposéd is,
Which such a strange eclipse doth make
As ne'er was read in Almanac.
  I could allow thee for a time
To darken me, and my sad clime;
Were it a month, a year, or ten,
I would thy exile live till then,
And all that space my mirth adjourn,
So thou would'st promise to return;
And putting off thy ashy shroud,
At length disperse this sorrow's cloud.
  But woe is me! the longest date
Too narrow is to calculate
These empty hopes; never shall I
Be so much blest as to descry
A glimpse of thee, till that day come
Which shall the earth to cinders doom,
And a fierce fever must calcine
The body of this world like thine,
(My little world!) that fit of fire
Once off, our bodies shall aspire
To our souls' bliss: then we shall rise,
And view ourselves with clearer eyes
In that calm region, where no night
Can hide us from each other's sight.
  Meantime thou hast her, Earth: much good
May my harm do thee! Since it stood
With Heaven's will I might not call
Her longer mine, I give thee all
My short-lived right and interest
In her, whom living I loved best:
With a most free and bounteous grief,
I give thee what I could not keep.

Be kind to her, and, prithee, look
Thou write into thy doom's-day book
Each parcel of this Rarity
Which in thy casket shrined doth lie:
See that thou make thy reckoning straight,
And yield her back again by weight:
For thou must audit on thy trust
Each grain and atom of this dust,
As thou wilt answer Him that lent,
Not gave thee, my dear monument.
So close the ground, and 'bout her shade
Black curtains draw; my bride is laid.
  Sleep on, my love, in thy cold bed
Never to be disquieted!
My last good night! Thou wilt not wake
Till I thy fate shall overtake:
Till age, or grief, or sickness must
Marry my body to that dust
It so much loves, and fill the room
My heart keeps empty in thy tomb.
Stay for me there; I will not fail
To meet thee in that hollow vale.
And think not much of my delay;
I am already on the way,
And follow thee with all the speed
Desire can make, or sorrows breed.
Each minute is a short degree,
And every hour a step towards thee.
At night when I betake to rest,
Next morn I rise nearer my west
Of life, almost by eight hours' sail,
Than when sleep breathed his drowsy gale.
  Thus from the Sun my bottom steers,
And my day's compass downward bears:
Nor labour I to stem the tide
Through which to thee I swiftly glide.
  'Tis true, with shame and grief I yield,
Thou like the van first took'st the field,

And gotten hast the victory,
In thus adventuring to die
Before me, whose more years might crave
A just precedence in the grave.
But hark! my pulse like a soft drum
Beats my approach, tells thee I come;
And slow howe'er my marches be,
I shall at last sit down by thee.
  The thought of this bids me go on,
And wait my dissolution
With hope and comfort. Dear, (forgive
The crime) I am content to live
Divided, with but half a heart,
Till we shall meet, and never part.

SONG.

Dry those fair, those crystal eyes,
Which like growing fountains rise,
To drown their banks: grief's sullen brooks
Would better flow in furrowed looks;
Thy lovely face was never meant
To be the shore of discontent.

Then clear those waterish stars again,
Which else portend a lasting rain;
Lest the clouds which settle there,
Prolong my winter all the year,
And thy example others make
In love with sorrow for thy sake.

SIR ROBERT HOWARD.

1622—1698.

["*Poems.*" (?) 1660.]

TO THE INCONSTANT CYNTHIA.

Tell me once, dear, how it does prove
That I so much forsworn could be?
I never swore always to love,
I only vowed still to love thee:
    And art thou now what thou wert then,
    Unsworn unto by other men?

In thy fair breast, and once fair soul,
I thought my vows were writ alone;
But others' oaths so blurred the scroll,
That I no more could read my own.
    And am I still obliged to pay,
    When you had thrown the bond away?

Nor must we only part in joy;
Our tears as well must be unkind:
Weep you, that could such truth destroy,
And I, that could such falseness find!
    Thus we must unconcerned remain
    In our divided joys and pain.

Yet we may love, but on this different score,
You what I am, I what you were before.

CHARLES SACKVILLE.

EARL OF DORSET.

1637—1706.

SONG.

WRITTEN AT SEA, THE FIRST DUTCH WAR, 1665, THE NIGHT BEFORE AN ENGAGEMENT.

To all you ladies now at land,
We men at sea indite;
But first would have you understand
How hard it is to write;
The Muses now, and Neptune too,
We must implore to write to you.
With a fa la, la, la, la.

For though the Muses should prove kind,
And fill our empty brain;
Yet if rough Neptune rouse the wind,
To wave the azure main,
Our paper, pen, and ink, and we,
Roll up and down our ships at sea.
With a fa la, la, la, la.

Then if we write not by each post,
Think not we are unkind;
Nor yet conclude our ships are lost
By Dutchmen or by wind:

Our tears we 'll send a speedier way;
The tide shall bring them twice a day.
With a fa la, la, la, la.

The King with wonder and surprise,
Will swear the seas grow bold;
Because the tides will higher rise
Than e'er they did of old:
But let him know it is our tears
Brings floods of grief to Whitehall-stairs.
With a fa la, la, la, la.

Should foggy Opdam chance to know
Our sad and dismal story,
The Dutch would scorn so weak a foe,
And quit their fort at Goree;
For what resistance can they find
From men who 've left their hearts behind?
With a fa la, la, la, la.

Let wind and weather do its worst,
Be you to us but kind;
Let Dutchmen vapour, Spaniards curse,
No sorrow shall we find:
'Tis then no matter how things go,
Or who 's our friend, or who 's our foe.
With a fa la, la, la, la.

To pass our tedious hours away,
We throw a merry main;
Or else at serious ombre play;
But why should we in vain,
Each other's ruin thus pursue?
We were undone when we left you.
With a fa la, la, la, la.

But now our fears tempestuous grow,
And cast our hopes away;

Whilst you, regardless of our woe,
    Sit careless at a play:
Perhaps permit some happier man
To kiss your hand, or flirt your fan.
        With a fa la, la, la, la.

When any mournful tune you hear,
    That dies in every note,
As if it sighed with each man's care
    For being so remote:
Think then how often love we've made
To you, when all those tunes were played.
        With a fa la, la, la, la.

In justice you can not refuse
    To think of our distress,
When we, for hopes of honour, lose
    Our certain happiness;
All those designs are but to prove
Ourselves more worthy of your love.
        With a fa la, la, la, la.

And now we've told you all our loves,
    And likewise all our fears,
In hopes this declaration moves
    Some pity for our tears;
Let's hear of no inconstancy,
We have too much of that at sea.
        With a fa la, la, la, la.

SIR CHARLES SEDLEY.

1639—1701.

["*The Mulberry Garden.*" 1668.]

SONG.

Ah Chloris! that I now could sit
As unconcerned, as when
Your infant beauty could beget
No pleasure, nor no pain.

When I the dawn used to admire,
And praised the coming day,
I little thought the growing fire
Must take my rest away.

Your charms in harmless childhood lay
Like metals in the mine:
Age from no face took more away,
Than youth concealed in thine.

But as your charms insensibly
To their perfection pressed,
Fond love as unperceived did fly,
And in my bosom rest.

My passion with your beauty grew,
And Cupid at my heart,

Still, as his mother favoured you,
    Threw a new flaming dart.

Each gloried in their wanton part:
    To make a lover, he
Employed the utmost of his art,
    To make a beauty, she.

Though now I slowly bend to love,
    Uncertain of my fate,
If your fair self my chains approve,
    I shall my freedom hate.

Lovers, like dying men, may well
    At first disordered be;
Since none alive can truly tell
    What fortune they must see.

[*"Miscellaneous Works."* 1702.]

SONG.

Not, Celia, that I juster am,
    Or better than the rest;
For I would change each hour, like them,
    Were not my heart at rest.

But I am tied to very thee,
    By every thought I have:
Thy face I only care to see,
    Thy heart I only crave.

All that in woman is adored,
    In thy dear self I find;
For the whole sex can but afford
    The handsome and the kind.

Why then should I seek farther store,
And still make love anew?
When change itself can give no more,
'T is easy to be true.

SONG.

Phillis, let's shun the common fate,
And let our love ne'er turn to hate.
I'll doat no longer than I can,
Without being called a faithless man.
When we begin to want discourse,
And kindness seems to taste of force,
As freely as we met we'll part,
Each one possessed of their own heart.
Thus, whilst rash fools themselves undo,
We'll game, and give off savers too;
So equally the match we'll make,
Both shall be glad to draw the stake.
A smile of thine shall make my bliss,
I will enjoy thee in a kiss.
If from this height our kindness fall,
We'll bravely scorn to love at all.
If thy affection first decay,
I will the blame on Nature lay.
Alas! what cordial can remove
The hasty fate of dying Love?
Thus we will all the world excel,
In loving, and in parting well.

TO CHLORIS.

Chloris, I can not say your eyes
Did my unwary heart surprise;
Nor will I swear it was your face,
Your shape, or any nameless grace;

For you are so entirely fair,
To love a part injustice were.

No drowning man can know which drop
Of water his last breath did stop:
So when the stars in heaven appear,
And join to make the night look clear,
The light we no one's bounty call,
But the obliging gift of all.

He that does lips or hands adore,
Deserves them only, and no more:
But I love all, and every part,
And nothing less can ease my heart.
Cupid that lover weakly strikes,
Who can express what 't is he likes.

SONG.

Love still has something of the sea,
From whence his mother rose:
No time his slaves from doubt can free,
Nor give their thoughts repose.

They are becalmed in clearest days,
And in rough weather tossed;
They wither under cold delays,
Or are in tempests lost.

One while they seem to touch the port,
Then straight into the main
Some angry wind, in cruel sport,
The vessel drives again.

At first disdain and pride they fear,
Which if they chance to 'scape,
Rivals and falsehood soon appear,
In a more dreadful shape.

By such degrees to joy they come,
  And are so long withstood,
So slowly they receive the sum,
  It hardly does them good.

'Tis cruel to prolong a pain,
  And to defer a joy,
Believe me, gentle Celemene,
  Offends the wingéd boy.

An hundred thousand oaths your fears
  Perhaps would not remove;
And if I gazed a thousand years,
  I could no deeper love.

SONG.

Phillis, men say that all my vows
  Are to thy fortune paid;
Alas! my heart he little knows,
  Who thinks my love a trade.

Were I of all these woods the lord,
  One berry from thy hand
More real pleasure would afford
  Than all my large command.

My humble love has learned to live,
  On what the nicest maid,
Without a conscious blush, may give
  Beneath the myrtle shade.

ANDREW MARVELL.

1620—1678.

[“*Miscellaneous Poems?*” (?) 1681.]

THE GALLERY.

CHLORA, come view my soul, and tell
Whether I have contrived it well;
How all its several lodgings lie,
Composed into one gallery,
And the great arras-hangings, made
Of various faces, by are laid,
That, for all furniture, you 'll find
Only your picture in my mind.
Here thou art painted in the dress
Of an inhuman murtheress,
Examining upon our hearts,
(Thy fertile shop of cruel arts,)
Engines more keen than ever yet
Adorned a tyrant's cabinet,
Of which the most tormenting are,
Black eyes, red lips, and curléd hair.
But, on the other side, thou 'rt drawn
Like to Aurora in the dawn,
When in the east she slumbering lies,
And stretches out her milky thighs,

While all the morning quire does sing,
And manna falls and roses spring,
And, at thy feet, the wooing doves
Sit perfecting their harmless loves.
Like an enchantress here thou show'st,
Vexing thy restless lover's ghost,
And, by a light obscure, dost rave
Over his entrails, in the cave,
Divining thence, with horrid care,
How long thou shalt continue fair,
And (when informed) them throw'st away,
To be the greedy vulture's prey.
But, against that, thou sittest afloat,
Like Venus in her pearly boat;
The halcyons, calming all that 's nigh,
Betwixt the air and water fly;
Or, if some rolling wave appears,
A mass of ambergrease it bears,
Nor blows more wind than what may well
Convoy the perfume to the smell.
These pictures, and a thousand more,
Of thee, my gallery do store,
In all the forms thou canst invent,
Either to please me, or torment;
For thou alone, to people me,
Art grown a numerous colony,
And a collection choicer far
Than or Whitehall's, or Mantua's were.
But of these pictures, and the rest,
That at the entrance likes me best,
Where the same posture and the look
Remains with which I first was took;
A tender shepherdess, whose hair
Hangs loosely playing in the air,
Transplanting flowers from the green hill
To crown her head and bosom fill.

THE PICTURE OF T. C. IN A PROSPECT OF FLOWERS.

See with what simplicity
This nymph begins her golden days!
In the green grass she loves to lie,
And there with her fair aspect tames
The wilder flowers and gives them names,
But only with the roses plays,
And them does tell
What colours best become them, and what smell.

Who can foretell for what high cause
This darling of the gods was born?
Yet this is she whose chaster laws
The wanton Love shall one day fear,
And, under her command severe,
See his bow broke, and ensigns torn.
Happy who can
Appease this virtuous enemy of man!

O then let me in time compound
And parley with those conquering eyes,
Ere they have tried their force to wound;
Ere with their glancing wheels they drive
In triumph over hearts that strive,
And them that yield but more despise,
Let me be laid
Where I may see the glories from some shade.

Meantime, whilst every verdant thing
Itself does at thy beauty charm,
Reform the errors of the spring;
Make that the tulips may have share
Of sweetness, seeing they are fair;
And roses of their thorns disarm;
But most procure
That violets may a longer age endure.

But O, young beauty of the woods,
Whom Nature courts with fruits and flowers,
Gather the flowers, but spare the buds,
Lest Flora, angry at thy crime
To kill her infants in their prime,
Should quickly make the example yours,
And ere we see,
Nip, in the blossom, all our hopes in thee.

THE MOWER TO THE GLOW-WORMS.

Ye living lamps, by whose dear light
The nightingale does sit so late,
And studying all the summer night,
Her matchless songs does meditate;

Ye country comets, that portend
No war nor prince's funeral,
Shining unto no other end
Than to presage the grass's fall;

Ye glow-worms, whose officious flame
To wandering mowers shows the way,
That in the night have lost their aim,
And after foolish fires do stray;

Your courteous lights in vain you waste,
Since Juliana here is come,
For she my mind hath so displaced,
That I shall never find my home.

JOHN WILMOT,

EARL OF ROCHESTER.

1647—1680.

["*Poems on Several Occasions.*" (?) 1680.]

A SONG.

All my past life is mine no more,
The flying hours are gone;
Like transitory dreams given o'er,
Whose images are kept in store
By memory alone.

The time that is to come is not;
How can it then be mine?
The present moment 's all my lot;
And that, as fast as it is got,
Phillis, is only thine.

Then talk not of inconstancy,
False hearts, and broken vows;
If I, by miracle, can be
This live-long minute true to thee,
'Tis all that Heaven allows.

SONG.

Give me leave to rail at you,
I ask nothing but my due;
To call you false, and then to say
You shall not keep my heart a day:
But alas! against my will,
I must be your captive still.
Ah! be kinder then, for I
Cannot change, and would not die.

Kindness has resistless charms,
All besides but weakly move;
Fiercest anger it disarms,
And clips the wings of flying Love.
Beauty does the heart invade,
Kindness only can persuade;
It gilds the lover's servile chain,
And makes the slaves grow pleased again.

CHARLES COTTON.

1630—1687.

[“*Poems on Several Occasions.*” (?) 1689.]

TO CHLORIS.

ODE.

FAREWELL, my sweet, until I come
    Improved in merit, for thy sake,
With characters of honour, home,
    Such as thou canst not then but take.

To loyalty my love must bow,
    My honour, too, calls to the field,
Where, for a lady's busk, I now
    Must keen and sturdy iron wield.

Yet, when I rush into those arms,
    Where death and danger do combine,
I shall less subject be to harms
    Than to those killing eyes of thine.

Since I could live in thy disdain,
    Thou art so far become my fate,
That I by nothing can be slain,
    Until thy sentence speaks my date.

33

But, if I seem to fall in war,
T' excuse the murder you commit,
Be to my memory just, so far,
As in thy heart t' acknowledge it :

That 's all I ask ; which thou must give
To him, that dying, takes a pride
It is for thee ; and would not live
Sole prince of all the world beside.

ESTRENNES.

TO CALISTA.

I reckon the first day I saw those eyes,
Which in a moment made my heart their prize,
To all my whole futurity,
The first day of my first new year :
Since then I first began to be,
And knew why Heaven placed me here ;
For till we love, and love discreetly too,
We nothing are, nor know we what we do.

Love is the soul of life, though that I know
Is called soul too, but yet it is not so.
Not rational at least, until
Beauty, with her diviner light,
Illuminates the groping will,
And shows us how to choose aright ;
And that 's first proved by th' objects it refuses,
And by being constant then to that it chooses.

Days, weeks, months, years, and lustres take
So small time up i' th' lover's almanac,
And can so little love assuage,
That we (in truth) can hardly say,

When we have lived at least an age,
A long one, we have loved a day.
This day to me, so slowly does time move,
Seems but the noon unto my morning love.

Love by swift time, which sickly passions dread,
Is no more measured than 't is limitéd:
That passion, where all others cease,
And with the fuel lose the flame,
Is evermore in its increase,
And yet being love, is still the same;
They err call liking love; true lovers know
He never loved who does not always so.

You, who my last love have, my first love had,
To whom my all of love was, and is paid,
Are only worthy to receive
The richest new year's gift I have,
My love, which I this morning give,
A nobler never monarch gave,
Which each new year I will present anew,
And you'll take care, I hope, it shall be due.

JOHN DRYDEN.

1631—1701.

[*"Miscellany Poems."* (?) 1693.]

SONG.

FAIR, sweet, and young, receive a prize
Reserved for your victorious eyes:
From crowds, whom at your feet you see,
O pity, and distinguish me!
As I from thousand beauties more
Distinguish you, and only you adore.

Your face for conquest was designed,
Your every motion charms my mind;
Angels, when you your silence break,
Forget their hymns, to hear you speak;
But when at once they hear and view,
Are loath to mount, and long to stay with you.

No graces can your form improve,
But all are lost, unless you love;
While that sweet passion you disdain,
Your veil and beauty are in vain:
In pity then prevent my fate,
For after dying all reprieve 's too late.

SONG TO A FAIR YOUNG LADY,

GOING OUT OF THE TOWN IN THE SPRING.

Ask not the cause, why sullen Spring
So long delays her flowers to bear;
Why warbling birds forget to sing,
And winter storms invert the year.
Chloris is gone, and fate provides
To make it Spring where she resides.

Chloris is gone, the cruel fair;
She cast not back a pitying eye;
But left her lover in despair,
To sigh, to languish, and to die:
Ah, how can those fair eyes endure
To give the wounds they will not cure!

Great god of Love, why hast thou made
A face that can all hearts command,
That all religions can invade,
And change the laws of every land?
Where thou hadst placed such power before,
Thou shouldst have made her mercy more.

When Chloris to the temple comes,
Adoring crowds before her fall:
She can restore the dead from tombs,
And every life but mine recall:
I only am by love designed
To be the victim for mankind.

JOHN NORRIS.

1657—1711.

["*Poems and Miscellanies.*" (?) 1717.]

SUPERSTITION.

I CARE not, though it be
By the preciser sort thought popery;
    We poets can a license show
    For everything we do.
Hear, then, my little saint! I'll pray to thee.

If now thy happy mind,
Amidst its various joys, can leisure find
    To attend to anything so low
    As what I say or do,
Regard, and be what thou wast ever—kind.

Let not the blessed above
Engross thee quite, but sometimes hither rove;
    Fain would I thy sweet image see,
    And sit and talk with thee;
Nor is it curiosity, but love.

Ah! what delight 't would be,
Wouldst thou sometimes, by stealth, converse with me.

How should I thy sweet commune prize,
And other joys despise;
Come, then, I ne'er was yet denied by thee.

I would not long detain
Thy soul from bliss, nor keep thee here in pain;
Nor should thy fellow-saints e'er know
Of thy escape below;
Before thou 'rt missed, thou shouldst return again.

Sure Heaven must needs thy love,
As well as other qualities, improve;
Come, then, and recreate my sight
With rays of thy pure light;
'T will cheer my eyes more than the lamps above.

But if Fate 's so severe
As to confine thee to thy blissful sphere,
(And by thy absence I shall know
Whether thy state be so,)
Live happy, and be mindful of me there.

THOMAS PARNELL.

1679—1718.

Miss Anne Minchin was the heroine of these two songs. The first was probably written during Parnell's courtship, the last after she became his wife. He married her in 1705, when he was archdeacon of Clogher, in Ireland. She bore him three children, two sons and a daughter, and died in 1711. "I am heartily sorry for poor Mrs. Parnell's death," Swift wrote, in his Journal to Stella. "She seemed to be an excellent, good-natured young woman, and I believe the poor lad is much afflicted." "The death of his wife," says Goldsmith, "was a loss to him that he was unable to support or recover. From that time he could never venture to court the muse in solitude, where he was sure to find the image of her who inspired his attempts. He began, therefore, to throw himself into every company, and to seek from wine, if not relief, at least insensibility. Those helps that sorrow first called for assistance, habit soon rendered necessary, and he died before his fortieth year, in some measure a martyr to conjugal fidelity."

SONG.

My days have been so wondrous free,
    The little birds that fly
With careless ease from tree to tree,
    Were but as blessed as I.

Ask gliding waters, if a tear
    Of mine increased their stream?
Or ask the flying gales, if e'er
    I lent one sigh to them?

But now my former days retire,
    And I'm by beauty caught,
The tender chains of sweet desire
    Are fixed upon my thought.

Ye nightingales, ye twisting pines!
    Ye swains that haunt the grove!
Ye gentle echoes, breezy winds!
    Ye close retreats of love!

With all of nature, all of art,
    Assist the dear design;
O teach a young, unpractised heart
    To make my Nancy mine!

The very thought of change I hate,
    As much as of despair;
Nor ever covet to be great,
    Unless it be for her.

'T is true, the passion in my mind
    Is mixed with soft distress;
Yet while the fair I love is kind,
    I cannot wish it less.

SONG.

When thy beauty appears,
In its graces and airs,
All bright as an angel new dropped from the sky;
At distance I gaze, and am awed by my fears,
So strangely you dazzle my eye!

But when without art,
Your kind thoughts you impart,
When your love runs in blushes through every vein;
When it darts from your eyes, when it pants in your heart,
Then I know you 're a woman again.

There 's a passion and pride
In our sex, she replied,
And thus (might I gratify both) I would do;
Still an angel appear to each lover beside,
But still be a woman to you.

MATTHEW PRIOR.

1664—1721.

"PRIOR was not a right good man," Pope is made to say in Spence's Anecdotes. "He used to bury himself, for whole days and nights together, with a poor mean creature, and often drank hard. He left most of his effects to the poor woman he kept company with, his Chloe; everybody knows what a wretch she was. I think she had been a little alehouse-keeper's wife." "This celebrated lady," Spence added in a note, "is now married to a cobbler at ****." "Prior had a narrow escape by dying," Arbuthnot wrote to a friend, "for if he had lived he had married a brimstone ——, one Bessy Cox, that keeps an alehouse in Long Acre. Her husband died about a month ago, and Prior has left his estate between his servant, Jonathan Drift, and Bessy Cox. Lewis got drunk with punch with Bess night before last. Do not say where you had this news of Prior. I hope all my mistress' ministers will not behave themselves so. We are to have a bowl of punch at Bessy Cox's. She would fain have put it upon Lewis that she was his Emma. She owned *Flanders Jane* was his Chloe. I know of no security against this dotage in bachelors, but to repent of their misspent time, and marry with speed."

AN ODE.

The merchant, to secure his treasure,
    Conveys it in a borrowed name;
Euphelia serves to grace my measure,
    But Cloe is my real flame.

My softest verse, my darling lyre,
    Upon Euphelia's toilet lay;
When Cloe noted her desire,
    That I should sing, that I should play.

My lyre I tune, my voice I raise,
But with my numbers mix my sighs;
And whilst I sing Euphelia's praise,
I fix my soul on Cloe's eyes.

Fair Cloe blushed: Euphelia frowned:
I sung and gazed: I played and trembled:
And Venus to the Loves around
Remarked, how ill we all dissembled.

TO CLOE WEEPING.

See, while thou weep'st, fair Cloe, see
The world in sympathy with thee.
The cheerful birds no longer sing;
Each droops his head, and hangs his wing.
The clouds have bent their bosoms lower,
And shed their sorrows in a shower.
The brooks beyond their limits flow;
And louder murmurs speak their woe.
The nymphs and swains adopt thy cares;
They heave thy sighs, and weep thy tears.
Fantastic nymph! that grief should move
Thy heart obdurate against Love.
Strange tears! whose power can soften all,
But that dear breast on which they fall.

A SONG.

If wine and music have the power
To ease the sickness of the soul;
Let Phœbus every string explore,
And Bacchus fill the sprightly bowl.
Let them their friendly aid employ,
To make my Cloe's absence light;
And seek for pleasure, to destroy
The sorrows of this live-long night.

But she to-morrow will return;
Venus, be thou to-morrow great;
Thy myrtles strew, thy odours burn,
And meet thy favourite nymph in state.
Kind Goddess, to no other powers
Let us to-morrow's blessings own:
Thy darling Loves shall guide the hours,
And all the day be all thine own.

SONG.

In vain you tell your parting lover,
You wish fair winds may waft him over.
Alas! what winds can happy prove,
That bear me far from what I love?
Alas! what dangers on the main
Can equal those that I sustain,
From slighted vows, and cold disdain?
Be gentle, and in pity choose
To wish the wildest tempests loose:
That, thrown again upon the coast,
Where first my shipwrecked heart was lost,
I may once more repeat my pain;
Once more in dying notes complain
Of slighted vows, and cold disdain.

ALEXANDER POPE.

1688—1744.

THE feminine attachments of Pope fitted into each other like a nest of boxes. He was partial to three women, Teresa and Martha Blount, and Lady Mary Wortley Montagu, but whether this partiality ever deepened into love may be doubted. If it did it was for Martha Blount. She was the daughter of Mr. Lister Blount, of Mapledurham. It is not known with certainty when Pope became acquainted with the Blounts, but it was before 1712, when he addressed an epistle to Martha, probably as early as 1707, when he lived with his parents at Binfield. The manor of Mapledurham at the furthest was only ten miles from Binfield, and it was natural that the families should know each other. In the absence of a stronger reason, the bond of a common faith, at that time a proscribed one in England, would have occasionally brought them together. Be this however as it may, we know that they were acquainted, at an early period of Pope's life, and that Pope himself was a frequent visitor at Mapledurham. The Blount girls were about his own age, Teresa being born in the same year with himself, and Martha two years later. Which of them first attracted him is a matter of conjecture, for their empire over his heart seems to have been a divided one. He wrote letters to both with the greatest impartiality. Many of these letters he afterwards printed, and not always with the original direction. "You are to understand, madam," he says in one of them, "that my passion for your fair self and your sister has been divided with the most wonderful regularity in the world. Even from my infancy, I have been in love with one after the other of you, week by week, and my journey to Bath fell out in the three hundred seventy-sixth week of the reign of my sovereign lady Sylvia. At the present writing hereof it is the three hundred eighty-ninth week of the reign of your most serene majesty, in whose service I was listed some weeks before I beheld your sister." This letter was probably written to Teresa, whose reign on the whole was a troubled one. Having more wit and vivacity than her sister, she was less disposed to bear the captious exactions of her lover. "I must own," he wrote to Martha in 1714, "I have long been shocked at your sister on several accounts, but above all things at her prudery. I am resolved to break with her forever, and therefore tell her I shall take the first opportunity of sending back all her letters." This direful "first opportunity" was a long time coming, for three years later Pope and Teresa were on such good terms that he executed a deed in her favour, giving her forty pounds a year for six years! Before the six years expired there was another difficulty between them—a quarrel, or something of the kind, which was never made up. He ceased to write to her, seldom, if ever, met her, and when he died never mentioned her name in his will. She passed out of his life in 1722. Martha maintained her ascendency over him, though her reign was weakened at one time by Lady Mary Wortley Montagu. Not that Lady Mary ever disputed it with her. She was no usurper of the fair Martha's rights, but an independent sovereign, whom his majesty, Alexander the Great, had invited to share his little kingdom. He met her in London in 1714, or thereabouts, and was charmed with her beauty and wit. Clever and learned, celebrated as a belle from her childhood, she was just the woman to captivate him. She recognized his genius, and with feminine tact allowed him to shine in her company. Her appreciation flattered him, and touched his heart through his vanity. In 1716 she accompanied her husband (for there was a husband in the case, though a dull one) to Constantinople. Pope was the last person she saw in England before her departure. "In what manner did I behave," he wrote, "the last hour I saw you? What degree of concern did I discover, when I felt a misfortune, which I hope you will never feel, that of parting from what one most esteems? For if my parting looked but like that of your common acquaintance, I am the greatest of all hypocrites that ever decency made. I never since pass by the house but with the same sort of melancholy that we feel upon seeing the tomb of a friend, which only serves to put us in mind of what we have lost," etc., etc. She met his raptures sensibly, and thanked him for the obliging concern which he expressed for her. He continued the correspondence warmly, but was not answered in the same spirit. She gossiped about what she saw in her travels, but avoided any allusion to his passion. Her letters were brilliant and entertaining, and must have delighted him as a wit, but they were not satisfactory to him as a lover. After an absence of two years and a half she returned to England with her husband, and took up her abode in London. Pope engaged a house for them in Twickenham, where he was then residing, and the next summer they moved thither, and he was happy. He renewed his intimacy with Lady Mary, who was a frequent visitor at his house. He wrote notes to her, and verses, and got her to sit to Kneller for her portrait for him. They were the best friends in the world. But by and by there came a change. Their friendship cooled, their intimacy ceased; they hated each other. The cause of the rupture was long a mystery, but years afterwards, when they were both in their graves, it came out, that "at some ill-chosen time, when she least expected what romances call a declaration, he made such passionate love to her, as, in spite of her utmost endeavours to be angry and look grave, produced an immoderate fit of laughter; from that moment he became her implacable enemy." After this unfortunate affair with Lady Mary, Pope returned to his old allegiance with Martha Blount, and for the rest of his life was content with her love, or friendship, or whatever it was she gave him. It was whispered about that they were married, or should have been, but both these charges were denied. Their relation was a subject of scandal in Pope's lifetime, and has been frequently discussed since, but to little purpose. There is no proof in the case, especially in favour of a guilty connection between them, but many circumstances against it, not the least of which is the respect with which Martha Blount was regarded by her contemporaries.

The best people of her time—gentlemen and ladies of unimpeachable virtue—considered themselves honoured by her friendship. But the point is not worth discussing. The reader will form what opinion he pleases: mine is a charitable one. I believe that Pope loved Martha Blount when he was young, as much as he could love any one; but that being, for some reason or other, averse to marriage, he subsided from a lover to a friend. He was Martha Blount's friend, and by all odds the best one she ever had. He managed her affairs for her; introduced her into the houses of the great; quarrelled with his friends when they offended her; in short, watched over her and her interests during his life, and at his death left her the bulk of his fortune. She died on the 12th of July, 1763, nineteen years after Pope, in the seventy-fourth year of her age.

The portrait of Martha Blount given here is from a family picture at Mapledurham. This picture, which is said to have been painted by Kneller, represents her and her sister as gathering flowers, and confirms the line of Gay, who describes the pair, as

"The fair-haired Martha, and Teresa brown."

The coronation mentioned in the poem addressed to Teresa, was that of George the First, which took place in September, 1714. I have not been able to fix the date of the birth-day verses.

EPISTLE TO MRS. TERESA BLOUNT,

ON HER LEAVING THE TOWN AFTER THE CORONATION.

As some fond virgin, whom a mother's care
Drags from the town to wholesome country air,
Just when she learns to roll a melting eye,
And hear a spark, yet think no danger nigh:
From the dear man unwilling she must sever,
Yet takes one kiss before she parts forever:
Thus from the world fair Zephalinda flew,
Saw others happy, and with sighs withdrew;
Not that their pleasures caused her discontent;
She sighed not that they stayed, but that she went.
  She went to plain work, and to purling brooks,
Old-fashioned halls, dull aunts, and croaking rooks:
She went from opera, park, assembly, play,
To morning walks, and prayers three times a day;

To part her time 'twixt reading and bohea,
To muse, and spill her solitary tea,
Or o'er cold coffee trifle with the spoon,
Count the slow clock, and dine exact at noon;
Divert her eyes with pictures in the fire,
Hum half a tune, tell stories to the squire;
Up to her godly garret after seven,
There starve and pray, for that 's the way to heaven.
  Some squire, perhaps, you take delight to rack,
Whose game is whisk, whose treat a toast in sack;
Who visits with a gun, presents you birds,
Then gives a smacking buss, and cries—no words;
Or with his hounds comes hallooing from the stable,
Makes love with nods, and knees beneath a table;
Whose laughs are hearty, though his jests are coarse,
And loves you best of all things—but his horse.
  In some fair evening, on your elbow laid,
You dream of triumphs in the rural shade;
In pensive thought recall the fancied scene,
See coronations rise on every green;
Before you pass th' imaginary sights
Of lords, and earls, and dukes, and gartered knights,
While the spread fan o'ershades your closing eyes;
Then give one flirt, and all the vision flies.
Thus vanish sceptres, coronets, and balls,
And leave you in lone woods, or empty walls!
  So when your slave, at some dear idle time,
(Not plagued with headaches, or the want of rhyme,)
Stands in the streets, abstracted from the crew,
And while he seems to study, thinks of you;
Just when his fancy points your sprightly eyes,
Or sees the blush of soft Parthenia rise,
Gay pats my shoulder, and you vanish quite,
Streets, chairs, and coxcombs rush upon my sight;
Vexed to be still in town, I knit my brow,
Look sour, and hum a tune, as you may now.

Martha Blount.

New York: Darby & Jackson.

EPISTLE TO MRS. MARTHA BLOUNT,

ON HER BIRTHDAY.

O be thou blessed with all that heaven can send,
Long health, long youth, long pleasure, and a friend:
Not with those toys the female world admire,
Riches that vex, and vanities that tire.
With added years if life bring nothing new,
But like a sieve let every blessing through,
Some joy still lost, as each vain year runs o'er,
And all we gain some sad reflection more;
Is that a birthday? 't is, alas! too clear
'T is but the funeral of the former year.
  Let joy or ease, let affluence or content,
And the gay conscience of a life well spent,
Calm every thought, inspirit every grace,
Glow in thy heart, and smile upon thy face.
Let day improve on day, and year on year,
Without a pain, a trouble, or a fear:
Till death, unfelt, that tender frame destroy,
In some soft dream, or ecstasy of joy,
Peaceful sleep out the sabbath of the tomb,
And wake to raptures in a life to come.

JOHN BYROM.

1691—1763.

The Phœbe of Byrom's pastoral was Miss Joanna Bentley, daughter of Dr. Richard Bentley, the celebrated master of Trinity College, of which Byrom was a student. He is said to have written the poem, not so much for love of the lady, as from a desire to attract the notice of her father. It was first published in "The Spectator," for October 6th, 1714. Miss Bentley afterwards married Dr. Dennison Cumberland, Bishop of Clonfert, in Ireland: Cumberland, the dramatist, was her son. Byrom married his cousin, Elizabeth, against the wishes of her father, a rich mercer of Manchester, who refused to do anything for the young couple. They were reduced to sad straits, and Byrom was forced for a time to teach short-hand writing for a living.

A PASTORAL.

My time, O ye Muses, was happily spent,
When Phœbe went with me wherever I went,
Ten thousand sweet pleasures I felt in my breast;
Sure never fond shepherd like Colin was blest!
But now she is gone, and has left me behind,
What a marvellous change on a sudden I find!
When things were as fine as could possibly be,
I thought 'twas the Spring; but, alas! it was she.

With such a companion, to tend a few sheep,
To rise up and play, or to lie down and sleep,
I was so good-humoured, so cheerful and gay,
My heart was as light as a feather all day:

But now I so cross, and so peevish am grown,
So strangely uneasy, as never was known.
My fair one is gone, and my joys are all drowned,
And my heart—I am sure it weighs more than a pound!

The fountain that wont to run sweetly along,
And dance to soft murmurs the pebbles among;
Thou know'st, little Cupid, if Phœbe was there,
'T was pleasure to look at, 't was music to hear:
But now she is absent, I walk by its side,
And still, as it murmurs, do nothing but chide;
Must you be so cheerful, while I go in pain?
Peace there with your bubbling, and hear me complain.

My lambkins around me would oftentimes play,
And Phœbe and I were as joyful as they;
How pleasant their sporting, how happy the time,
When Spring, Love, and Beauty, were all in their prime!
But now, in their frolics, when by me they pass,
I fling at their fleeces a handful of grass;
Be still then, I cry, for it makes me quite mad,
To see you so merry while I am so sad.

My dog I was ever well pleased to see
Come wagging his tail to my fair one and me;
And Phœbe was pleased too, and to my dog said,
Come hither, poor fellow; and patted his head.
But now, when he's fawning, I with a sour look
Cry Sirrah! and give him a blow with my crook;
And I'll give him another; for why should not Tray
Be as dull as his master, when Phœbe's away?

When walking with Phœbe, what sights have I seen!
How fair was the flower, how fresh was the green!
What a lovely appearance the trees and the shade,
The cornfields and hedges, and everything made!
But now she has left me, though all are still there,
They none of them now so delightful appear:

'T was naught but the magic, I find, of her eyes,
Made so many beautiful prospects arise.

Sweet music went with us both all the wood through,
The lark, linnet, throstle, and nightingale too;
Winds over us whispered, flocks by us did bleat,
And chirp went the grasshopper under our feet.
But now she is absent, though still they sing on,
The woods are but lonely, the melody 's gone:
Her voice in the concert, as now I have found,
Gave everything else its agreeable sound.

Rose, what is become of thy delicate hue?
And where is the violet's beautiful blue?
Does aught of its sweetness the blossom beguile?
That meadow, those daisies, why do they not smile?
Ah! rivals, I see what it was that you dressed,
And made yourselves fine for—a place in her breast.
You put on your colours to pleasure her eye,
To be plucked by her hand, on her bosom to die.

How slowly Time creeps, till my Phœbe return!
While amidst the soft Zephyr's cool breezes, I burn;
Methinks if I knew whereabouts he would tread,
I could breathe on his wings, and 't would melt down the lead.
Fly swiftly, ye minutes, bring hither my dear,
And rest so much longer for 't when she is here.
Ah, Colin! old Time is full of delay,
Nor will budge one foot faster for all thou canst say.

Will no pitying power, that hears me complain,
Or cure my disquiet, or soften my pain?
To be cured, thou must, Colin, thy passion remove;
But what swain is so silly to live without love?
No, deity, bid the dear nymph to return,
For ne'er was poor shepherd so sadly forlorn.
Ah! what shall I do? I shall die with despair;
Take heed, all ye swains, how ye part with your fair!

NICHOLAS ROWE.

1673—1718.

ROWE and Addison were both suitors for the hand of the countess-dowager of Warwick, and it was on the occasion of her marriage with the latter (Aug. 2, 1716,) that "COLIN'S COMPLAINT" was written. Addison became acquainted with the noble dame by being tutor to her son. "He formed," said Tonson, "the design of getting that lady from the time when he was first taken into the family." His courtship was long and anxious; but as his reputation and influence increased, his courage rose, and she was finally persuaded to marry him, "on terms very much like those on which a Turkish princess is espoused: 'Daughter, I give thee this man for thy slave.'" She remembered her rank on all occasions, and treated poor Addison without ceremony, driving him, I have somewhere read, to the bottle for consolation. He died in 1719, a year after his discomfited rival, Rowe, who took the marriage very much to heart—on paper. Rowe was twice married.

COLIN'S COMPLAINT.

Despairing beside a clear stream,
A shepherd forsaken was laid;
And while a false nymph was his theme,
A willow supported his head.
The wind that blew over the plain,
To his sighs with a sigh did reply;
And the brook, in return to his pain,
Ran mournfully murmuring by.

"Alas, silly swain that I was!"
Thus sadly complaining, he cried,

"When first I beheld that fair face,
'T were better by far I had died.
She talked, and I blessed the dear tongue;
When she smiled, 't was a pleasure too great:
I listened, and cried, when she sung,
Was nightingale ever so sweet?

"How foolish was I to believe
She could doat on so lowly a clown;
Or that her fond heart would not grieve,
To forsake the fine folk of the town!
To think that a beauty so gay,
So kind and so constant would prove;
Or go clad like our maidens in gray,
Or live in a cottage on love!

"What though I have skill to complain,
Though the Muses my temples have crowned;
What though, when they hear my soft strain,
The virgins sit weeping around?
Ah, Colin, thy hopes are in vain,
Thy pipe and thy laurel resign;
Thy false one inclines to a swain
Whose music is sweeter than thine!

"And you, my companions so dear,
Who sorrow to see me betrayed,
Whatever I suffer, forbear,
Forbear to accuse the false maid.
Though through the wide world I should range,
'T is in vain from my fortune to fly;
'T was hers to be false, and to change,
'T is mine to be constant and die.

"If while my hard fate I sustain,
In her breast any pity is found,
Let her come with the nymphs of the plain,
And see me laid low in the ground.

The last humble boon that I crave,
  Is to shade me with cypress and yew;
And when she looks down on my grave,
  Let her own that her shepherd was true.

"Then to her new love let her go,
  And deck her in golden array,
Be finest at every fine show,
  And frolic it all the long day;
While Colin, forgotten and gone,
  No more shall be talked of, or seen,
Unless when, beneath the pale moon,
  His ghost shall glide over the green."

JONATHAN SWIFT.

1667—1745.

Some time between 1681 and '88, when he was a student in the University of Dublin—say about '85, his eighteenth year—Swift fell in love with a Miss Jane Waryng, (Varina,) the sister of one of his chums. She had a little fortune of one hundred pounds a year, but as Swift had no certain means of support, being entirely dependent on the bounty of an uncle, she declined to marry him, until something better should turn up for them. In 1688 or '89 he quitted the University and entered the service of Sir William Temple, as his amanuensis and reader, on a salary of twenty pounds a year. He ate humble pie in the Temple family, at Shene and Moor Park, for four or five years, and then returned to Ireland, and entered into holy orders. He remained in Ireland a little over a year, not at all pleased with the prospect before him, and resigning his living at Kilroot, in favour of a poor clergyman, returned to his servitude at Moor Park. He was now installed as preceptor to two young ladies—Miss Gifford, a niece of Sir William Temple, and Esther Johnson, afterwards celebrated as Stella. The parentage of Stella is a little dubious. By some she is said to have been the daughter of a merchant, who failed in business in London, and died in her infancy; by others, the daughter of Sir William's steward. Others again say that she was a natural daughter of Sir William. The year of her birth is uncertain. Swift makes her thirty-four, in a birth-day poem, for 1718–19, while in another, written for a similar occasion, six years later, she is forty-three. This difference of three years in her age, places her birth in 1681, or '84. I incline to the former year, which makes her about fifteen when she became the pupil of Swift. She could not have been older than that, if indeed she was so old, for he taught her, we are told, the commonest branches of learning. She does not appear to have been a very apt scholar, though her natural parts were good, but she had many things that made up for this deficiency in Swift's eyes. She was young and beautiful, with agreeable manners, and a heart easily impressed; and where these qualities are united in a woman, even though she is a dunce, which Stella was not, she seldom fails to charm. Add to this an admiration such as Stella felt for Swift's genius, and the love and awe with which he inspired her, and she becomes irresistible. Not that Stella was so with Swift, for his singular nature was not amenable to the laws which govern the masses of mankind; still, she had more influence over him than any human being—except Jonathan Swift! She began by admiring him, she ended by loving him. And he loved her too, in his way, though he still kept up his correspondence with his early flame, Varina. He wrote Varina a lover-like letter in April, 1696, while he was teaching Stella to conjugate the verb *Amo*, and urged her to marry him. "I desire nothing of your fortune," he said; "you shall live where and with whom you please till my affairs are settled to your desire; and in the meantime I will push my advancement with all the eagerness and courage imaginable, and do not doubt to succeed." But as Stella advanced deeper in the grammar of love, his passion for Varina cooled. He resided at Moor Park, till the death of Sir William Temple in January, 1699. Sir William left him a small legacy, and a large amount of MSS. The publication of the latter took him to London, where he remained till the close of the year, on the look-out for a good berth in the church; but not finding one, he accepted an offer of Lord Berkeley to become his secretary and chaplain, and accompanied him to Ireland in that capacity. He arrived in Dublin in the beginning of 1700, and after a series of petty disappointments, which need not be related here, obtained the rectory of Agher, and the vicarage of Laracor and Rath-beggin, in the diocese of Meath. These livings, and the prebend of Dunlarin, which was soon after added to them, raised his income to about four hundred pounds a year—enough in all conscience to have justified him in marrying Varina. But a marriage with her did not enter into his calculations, as she was beginning to perceive. She wrote him a letter, and asked him if the change of his feelings towards her was not owing to the thoughts of a new mistress. "I declare," he answered, (May 4th, 1700,) "upon the word of a Christian and a gentleman, it is not: neither had I ever thoughts of being married to any other person but yourself." He inquired if her health, which seems never to have been good, was improved, reminding her that her doctor had declared that marriage would endanger her life. "Are you in a condition to manage domestic affairs with an income of less (perhaps) than £300 a year? Have you such an inclination to my person and humour, as to comply with my desires and way of living, and endeavour to make us both as happy as you can? Will you be ready to engage in those methods I shall direct for the improvement of your mind, so as to make us entertaining company for each other, without being miserable, when we are neither visiting, nor visited?" Will the place where he is be more welcome than cities and courts without him? Will she? etc. If she can answer these questions in the affirmative, he concludes: "I shall be blessed to have you in my arms, without regarding whether your person be beautiful, or your fortune large. Cleanliness in the first, and competency in the other, is all I look for." Poor Varina! She had waited fifteen years only to be insulted at last! Whether Swift's conduct on this occasion was owing to a natural repugnance to marriage, or to the presence of Stella in Ireland, is a matter of conjecture; the latter reason seems to me the true one. Sir William Temple, I have omitted to mention, left Stella, at his death, a legacy of one thousand pounds. This was but a small sum in England, where interest was low and living expensive, but it was quite a fortune in Ireland, so she followed Swift thither, as he had invited her to do, accompanied by her Duenna, so to speak, an old lady named Dingley. They arrived in Ireland about the time that Swift wrote his last letter to Varina, and took a lodging at Trim, a small town near Laracor, a mile or so from Swift's vicarage. From this time till her death, some twenty odd years later, Stella was Swift's neighbour and companion. She saw him constantly during his residence at Laracor, and when he was absent, in England, or elsewhere, she and Mrs. Dingley occupied the vicarage till his return. In 1701, he went to England and engaged in political life. He was a great man in politics—a tower of strength to his friends, a terror to his enemies, and not undistinguished in literature. He knew all the wits and writers of the time, Congreve, Addison, and Steele, and took his place among them unquestioned, especially after the publication of "The Tale of a Tub" in 1704. We get glimpses of his intimacy with them, and the life that he led in London, in his "Journal to Stella." This Journal, which was written in the form of letters and dispatched to Ireland to Stella, is full of what Swift called his "Little Language," an enigmatical style of writing invented by himself for Stella. She figures in it as M. D., while he is *Presto*, and P. D. F. R. It begins—"The Journal," not the Little Language—in September, 1710, and ends in June, 1713. Between these dates a new influence was at work in his life. I allude to Vanessa—Esther Vanhomrigh. She was the daughter of Mr. Bartholomew Vanhomrigh, a Dutch merchant, who had been commissary of stores for King William during the Irish civil wars, and afterwards Muster-Master-General (whatever that may have been), and commissioner of revenue. He died in Vanessa's childhood, leaving an estate of sixteen thousand pounds, and his widow settled in London with her four children, the eldest of whom, Vanessa, was about nineteen when Swift first met her. An entry in the "Journal to Stella"—the earliest I believe on the subject—fixes October 30th, 1710, as the day of their meeting: at any rate, Swift dined with her mother on that day, and we have no reason to think that she was absent. The family resided within five doors of Swift's lodgings, which were in Bury street, St. James's, and he was frequently their guest, as may be seen in his "Journal." He mentioned them to Stella carelessly, as acquaintances he had recently made, but she seemed to have her suspicions that one, at least, was something more. She remembered, perhaps, her own experience at Moor Park, and, knowing the strange nature of Swift, trembled for the consequences of his intimacy with Vanessa, who was eight or ten years her junior. A great deal has been written about Vanessa and her passion for Swift, but most of it is mere conjecture; we know nothing of the matter beyond what Swift tells us in "Cadenus and Vanessa." This poem, which was written at Windsor in the spring of 1713, is a history of the affair, as far as it had then gone. Vanessa began by reading the books of Swift, who seems to have directed her studies and pursuits, and ended, like Stella before her, by loving him. It was some time before he perceived her love, and when he did it was with pain.

> "Cadenus felt within him rise
> Shame, disappointment, guilt, surprise."

He endeavoured to reason her out of her folly, and she endeavoured to reason him into it, and succeeded, so much did her preference flatter his vanity. He could not promise to return her passion—his age and dignity forbade that—

> "But friendship, in its greatest height,
> A constant, rational delight,
> On virtue's basis fixed to last
> When love's allurements long are past,
> Which gently warms, but cannot burn,
> He gladly offers in return."

Such is Swift's history of the affair, and, making allowance for its being in verse, I have no doubt but it is the true one. Vanessa threw herself in his way, and he was not man enough to resist her. It might have been difficult to shake her off, (I should judge it was,) still, he could have done so, I think, had he tried. At any rate he could have told her of his relations with Stella, and told Stella of her relations with him; but he did neither. He seldom mentioned Vanessa in his "JOURNAL TO STELLA," and never, as far as I can learn, mentioned Stella to Vanessa. I cannot understand his duplicity, nor do I believe he understood it himself. It was madness. In the summer of 1713 he returned to Ireland, the Dean of St. Patrick's. His first care, after taking possession of the Deanery, was to provide for Stella and Mrs. Dingley, whom he probably found in Dublin on his arrival. He secured lodgings for them upon Ormond's Quay, on the other side of the Liffy, and fell back into his old relations with Stella. How he contrived to attach her to him, as he did so many years, is a mystery. He does not appear to have held out to her the prospect of a marriage with him; on the contrary, he at one time favoured her marriage with another. This was in 1705 or '6, when one of his clerical friends, the Rev. Dr. Tisdall, made her an offer of his hand. She consulted with Swift, and refused him. He was not quite satisfied with Swift's conduct on that occasion, and wrote him to that effect, but Swift assured him that he had not stood in his light. If he had thought of marriage himself, he would certainly have made his choice, never having seen any person whose conversation he valued like Stella's; this was the utmost he had given way to. If he spoke the truth, of which there is some doubt, Stella was indeed infatuated. They lived apart in Dublin, as they had done at Laracor, and never saw each other, except in the presence of a third person, which person was generally Mrs. Dingley. But to return to Vanessa. Her mother and two brothers died in 1713, and left her and her sister the remainder of the Vanhomrigh property, a portion of which was in Ireland. This, and her love for Swift, determined her to remove thither. He protested, but to no purpose. She would come. She arrived in Dublin in the summer or autumn of 1714, and immediately began to weave her toils. She made Swift visit her, which, to do him justice, he was loth to do, and reproached him with his neglect and indifference. He temporized, as was his wont. The presence of her rival, and the unsettled state of Swift's affections, preyed upon Stella, and her health began to decline. He saw it, and asked his friend, Dr. Ashe, the Bishop of Clogher, to inquire the cause of her melancholy. The answer was what he might have expected: "Her sensibility to his late indifference, and to the discredit which her character had sustained from the dubious and mysterious connection between them." There was but one remedy, the Bishop thought—Marriage. Swift said he had formed two resolutions in regard to matrimony: one, not to marry till he possessed a sufficient fortune, the other, that it should be at a time which gave him a reasonable prospect of seeing his children settled in life. Neither condition had been fulfilled. He had not acquired a competent fortune, and he was nearly fifty. He would marry Stella, however, if she would consent to keep it secret, and to live apart from him, as she was then doing. She consented, and they were privately married by the Bishop, in 1716, in the garden of the Deanery. It was not a merry thing with Swift, that marriage, whatever it may have been with Stella, for he became dejected and melancholy. His friends were struck with his altered appearance, and one of them—the Rev. Patrick Delany—went to Archbishop King to mention his apprehensions: on entering the library, Swift rushed out distractedly, and passed him without speaking. He found the Archbishop in tears. "You have just met," he said, "the most unhappy man upon earth, but on the subject of his wretchedness you must never ask a question." Swift's intercourse with Stella continued as guarded as before his marriage: he never saw her alone. She had but few acquaintances of her own sex, and those were formal and ceremonious: her only friends were men, mostly clergymen, whom Swift had introduced to her. Now and then she dined at the Deanery, on Swift's public days, but never as its mistress: she was only a guest in her husband's house. She impressed all who saw her by the beauty of her countenance, and particularly by her fine dark eyes. "She was very pale, and looked pensive, but not melancholy, and her hair was as black as a raven." Swift tried to moderate the passion of Vanessa, and introduced Dean Winter to her, as a candidate for her hand. She rejected him with disdain. Dr. Price also addressed her, but with no better success. In 1717 she retired to her estate at Marley Abbey, near Celbridge. She continued to write to Swift, who answered her letters, but refrained from seeing her for two or three years. At the end of that time he renewed his visits. She seldom went abroad at Marley Abbey, and saw but little company: her constant amusement was reading or walking in the garden. Her garden was crowded with laurels, and when Swift was expected she used to plant one or two with her own hand against his arrival. She was always melancholy when he was not with her; when he came she was happy. Her favourite seat was a bower, the opening of which commanded a view of the Liffy, and here she and Swift were often seen, sitting together at a rude table, with books and writing materials before them. It was at best but a painful pleasure, and one fine day it came to an end. Vanessa wrote Stella a letter, and asked her the nature of her connection with Swift. She answered that she was his wife, and full of resentment against him for having given any woman the right to put such a question, left her lodgings, and retired to the house of a friend. Vanessa's letter fell into the hands of Swift, who rode to Marley Abbey in a paroxysm of fury: as he entered the room where Vanessa was, she was struck with terror. He flung the letter on the table before her, and, instantly mounting his horse, rode back to Dublin. When she opened his packet, and saw that it contained only her own letter to Stella, she knew that all was over. Her heart was broken. She died in a few weeks, (May, 1723,) leaving her fortune to a Mr. Marshall and Bishop Berkeley. She directed them to publish "CADENUS AND VANESSA," and all the letters that had passed between Swift and herself; but her wishes were not respected regarding the letters, for they were destroyed, though not before many of them had been copied. When Swift heard of her death he fled to the south of Ireland, and shut himself up for two months in utter solitude. Of course Stella forgave him on his return to Dublin. He remained in Ireland till 1726, when he made a visit of pleasure to England. A similar visit in the spring of the next year was interrupted by the illness of Stella. He was staying with Pope at Twickenham when the news reached him. He wrote back word that she was not to be allowed to die at the Deanery, and, quitting Pope on pretence of business in London, started for

Ireland. He arrived at Dublin in October, and found her dying, not in the Deanery, as he had feared, but in her lodgings. A few days before her death she came to see him in a chair. When she reached the Deanery she was so exhausted that it was with difficulty that she was brought into the parlour. She tasted some mulled wine, which he had prepared for her, and feeling faint desired to lie down. She was carried up stairs, and placed on a bed, and Swift sat down beside her and took her hand. Her companion, Mrs. Whiteway, a cousin of Swift's, retired into an adjoining room to give them an opportunity to converse together; but, the door being left ajar to give Stella air, she could not but overhear some of their conversation, though they spoke in whispers. "Well, my dear," she heard Swift say to Stella, "if you wish it, it shall be owned." "It is too late," she answered with a sigh. She died on the 28th of January, 1728.

After her death, and probably after Swift's, one of her raven tresses came into the possession of an antiquary. It was wrapped in paper, and labelled in Swift's handwriting, "*Only a woman's hair.*"

STELLA'S BIRTH DAY.

MARCH 13, 1718–19.

Stella this day is thirty-four,
(We sha'n't dispute a year or more:)
However, Stella, be not troubled,
Although thy size and years are doubled
Since first I saw thee at sixteen,
The brightest virgin on the green;
So little is thy form declined;
Made up so largely in thy mind.
  O, would it please the gods to split
Thy beauty, size, and years, and wit!
No age could furnish out a pair
Of nymphs so graceful, wise, and fair;
With half the lustre of your eyes,
With half your wit, your years, and size.
And then, before it grew too late,
How should I beg of gentle Fate,
(That either nymph might have her swain,)
To split my worship too in twain.

STELLA'S BIRTH DAY.

1719–20.

All travellers at first incline
Where'er they see the fairest sign:
And if they find the chambers neat,
And like the liquor and the meat,
Will call again, and recommend
The Angel Inn to every friend.
What though the painting grows decayed,
The house will never lose its trade:
Nay, though the treacherous tapster, Thomas,
Hangs a new Angel two doors from us,
As fine as daubers' hands can make it,
In hopes that strangers may mistake it,
We think it both a shame and sin
To quit the true old Angel Inn.
  And this is Stella's case in fact,
An angel's face a little cracked,
(Could poets or could painters fix
How angels look at thirty-six:)
This drew us in at first to find
In such a form an angel's mind;
And every virtue now supplies
The fainting rays of Stella's eyes.
See at her levee crowding swains,
Whom Stella freely entertains
With breeding, humour, wit, and sense,
And puts them but to small expense;
Their mind so plentifully fills,
And makes such reasonable bills,
So little gets for what she gives,
We really wonder how she lives!
And had her stock been less, no doubt,
She must have long ago run out.

Then who can think we'll quit the place,
When Doll hangs out a newer face?
Or stop and light at Chloe's head,
With scraps and leavings to be fed?
Then, Chloe, still go on to prate
Of thirty-six and thirty-eight;
Pursue your trade of scandal-picking,
Your hints that Stella is no chicken;
Your innuendoes, when you tell us
That Stella loves to talk with fellows:
And let me warn you to believe
A truth, for which your soul should grieve;
That should you live to see the day
When Stella's locks must all be gray,
When age must print a furrowed trace
On every feature of her face;
Though you, and all your senseless tribe,
Could art, or time, or nature bribe,
To make you look like Beauty's Queen,
And hold forever at fifteen;
No bloom of youth can ever blind
The cracks and wrinkles of your mind:
All men of sense will pass your door,
And crowd to Stella's at four-score.

TO STELLA.

WRITTEN ON THE DAY OF HER BIRTH, MARCH 13, 1723–4, BUT NOT ON THE SUBJECT, WHEN I WAS SICK IN BED.

Tormented with incessant pains,
Can I devise poetic strains?
Time was, when I could yearly pay
My verse to Stella's native day:
But now unable grown to write,
I grieve she ever saw the light.
Ungrateful! since to her I owe

That I these pains can undergo.
She tends me like an humble slave;
And, when indecently I rave,
When out my brutish passions break,
With gall in every word I speak,
She with soft speech my anguish cheers,
Or melts my passions down with tears;
Although 't is easy to descry
She wants assistance more than I;
Yet seems to feel my pains alone,
And is a stoic in her own.
Where, among scholars, can we find
So soft and yet so firm a mind?
All accidents of life conspire
To raise up Stella's virtue higher;
Or else to introduce the rest
Which had been latent in her breast.
Her firmness who could e'er have known,
Had she not evils of her own?
Her kindness who could ever guess,
Had not her friends been in distress?
Whatever base returns you find
From me, dear Stella, still be kind.
In your own heart you'll reap the fruit,
Though I continue still a brute.
But when I once am out of pain,
I promise to be good again;
Meantime, your other juster friends
Shall for my follies make amends;
So may we long continue thus,
Admiring you, you pitying us.

STELLA'S BIRTH DAY.

1724–5.

As, when a beauteous nymph decays,
We say, she's past her dancing days;

So poets lose their feet by time,
And can no longer dance in rhyme.
Your annual bard had rather chose
To celebrate your birth in prose:
Yet merry folks, who want by chance
A pair to make a country dance,
Call the old housekeeper, and get her
To fill a place for want of better:
While Sheridan is off the hooks,
And friend Delany at his books,
That Stella may avoid disgrace,
Once more the Dean supplies their place.
  Beauty and wit, too sad a truth!
Have always been confined to youth;
The god of wit and beauty's queen,
He twenty-one and she fifteen,
No poet ever sweetly sung,
Unless he were, like Phœbus, young;
Nor ever nymph inspired to rhyme,
Unless, like Venus, in her prime.
At fifty-six, if this be true,
Am I a poet fit for you?
Or, at the age of forty-three,
Are you a subject fit for me?
Adieu! bright wit and radiant eyes!
You must be grave, and I be wise.
Our fate in vain we would oppose:
But I'll be still your friend in prose:
Esteem and friendship to express,
Will not require poetic dress;
And if the Muse deny her aid
To have them sung, they may be said.
  But, Stella, say, what evil tongue
Reports you are no longer young?
That Time sits with his scythe to mow
Where erst sat Cupid with his bow;
That half your locks are turned to gray?
I'll ne'er believe a word they say.

'T is true, but let it not be known,
My eyes are somewhat dimmish grown;
For nature, always in the right,
To your decays adapts my sight;
And wrinkles undistinguished pass,
For I 'm ashamed to use a glass:
And, till I see them with these eyes,
Whoever says you have them, lies.
No length of time can make you quit
Honour and virtue, sense and wit;
Thus you may still be young to me,
When I can better hear than see.
O ne'er may Fortune show her spite
To make me deaf, and mend my sight!

ALLAN RAMSAY.

1686—1758.

[" *Tea-Table Miscellany.*" 1724.]

THE LASS OF PATIE'S MILL.

THE lass of Patie's mill,
 So bonny, blyth, and gay,
In spite of all my skill,
 She stole my heart away.
When tedding of the hay,
 Bare-headed on the green,
Love 'midst her locks did play,
 And wanton'd in her een.

Her arms white, round, and smooth,
 Breasts rising in their dawn,
To age it would give youth
 To press 'em with his hand:
Thro' all my spirits ran
 An extasy of bliss,
When I such sweetness fand
 Wrapt in a balmy kiss.

Without the help of art,
 Like flowers which grace the wild,
She did her sweets impart,
 Whene'er she spoke or smil'd.

Her looks they were so mild,
Free from affected pride,
She me to love beguil'd;
I wish'd her for my bride.

O had I all the wealth
Hopeton's high mountains fill,
Insur'd lang life and health,
And pleasure at my will;
I 'd promise and fulfil
That none but bonny she,
The lass of Patie's mill,
Shou'd share the same wi' me.

O'ER THE MOOR TO MAGGIE.

And I'll o'er the moor to Maggy,
Her wit and sweetness call me,
Then to my fair I'll show my mind,
Whatever may befall me:
If she love mirth I'll learn to sing,
Or likes the Nine to follow,
I'll lay my lugs in Pindus' spring,
And invocate Apollo.

If she admire a martial mind,
I'll sheath my limbs in armour;
If to the softer dance inclin'd,
With gayest airs I'll charm her;
If she love grandeur, day and night
I'll plot my nation's glory,
Find favour in my prince's sight,
And shine in future story.

Beauty can wonders work with ease,
Where wit is corresponding,

And bravest men know best to please,
 With complaisance abounding.
My bonny Maggy's love can turn
 Me to what shape she pleases,
If in her breast that flame shall burn,
 Which in my bosom bleezes.

GI'E ME A LASS WITH A LUMP OF LAND.

Gi'e me a lass with a lump of land,
 And we for life shall gang thegither;
Tho' daft or wise, I'll never demand,
 Or black or fair it maks nae whether.
I'm aff with wit, and beauty will fade,
 And blood alane is no worth a shilling;
But she that's rich her market's made,
 For ilka charm about her is killing.

Gi'e me a lass with a lump of land,
 And in my bosom I'll hug my treasure;
Gin I had anes her gear in my hand,
 Shou'd love turn dowf, it will find pleasure.
Laugh on wha likes, but there's my hand,
 I hate with poortith, tho' bonny to meddle;
Unless they bring cash, or a lump of land,
 They'se never get me to dance to their fiddle.

There's meikle good love in bands and bags,
 And siller and gowd's a sweet complexion;
But beauty, and wit, and virtue in rags,
 Have tint the art of gaining affection.
Love tips his arrows with woods and parks,
 And castles, and riggs, and moors, and meadows;
And naithing can catch our modern sparks,
 But well-tocher'd lasses, or jointur'd widows.

JAMES THOMSON.

1700—1748.

[" *Orpheus Caledonius.*" 1725.]

TO FORTUNE.

FOREVER, Fortune, wilt thou prove
An unrelenting foe to love,
And, when we meet a mutual heart,
Come in between, and bid us part:

Bid us sigh on from day to day,
And wish, and wish the soul away;
Till youth and genial years are flown,
And all the love of life is gone?

But busy, busy still art thou,
To bind the loveless joyless vow,
The heart from pleasure to delude,
And join the gentle to the rude.

For pomp, and noise, and senseless show,
To make us Nature's joys forego,
Beneath a gay dominion groan,
And put the golden fetter on!

For once, O Fortune, hear my prayer,
And I absolve thy future care;
All other blessings I resign,
Make but the dear Amanda mine.

TO HER I LOVE.

Tell me, thou soul of her I love,
    Ah! tell me, whither art thou fled;
To what delightful world above,
    Appointed for the happy dead?

Or dost thou, free, at pleasure, roam,
    And sometimes share thy lover's woe;
Where, void of thee, his cheerless home
    Can now, alas! no comfort know?

O if thou hover'st round my walk,
    While, under every well-known tree,
I to thy fancied shadow talk,
    And every tear is full of thee:

Should then the weary eye of grief,
    Beside some sympathetic stream,
In slumber find a short relief,
    O visit then my soothing dream!

HENRY CAREY.

—1748.

"A vulgar error having long prevailed among many persons, who imagine Sally Salisbury the subject of this ballad, the Author begs leave to undeceive and assure them it has not the least allusion to her, he being a stranger to her very name at the time this Song was composed. For as innocence and virtue were ever the boundaries to his Muse, so in this little poem he had no other view than to set forth the beauty of a chaste and disinterested passion, even in the lowest class of human life. The real occasion was this: a Shoemaker's 'Prentice making holiday with his Sweetheart, treated her with a sight of Bedlam, the puppet-shews, the flying-chairs, and all the elegancies of Moorfields: from whence proceeding to the Farthing-pye-house, he gave her a collation of buns, cheese-cakes, gammon of bacon, stuff'd beef, and bottled ale; through all which scenes the Author dodg'd them (charm'd with the simplicity of their courtship) from whence he drew this little sketch of nature; but being then young and obscure, he was very much ridiculed by some of his acquaintance for this performance; which nevertheless made its way into the polite world, and amply recompensed him by the applause of the divine Addison, who was pleased (more than once) to mention it with approbation."—Carey's Poems, *3d edition*, 1729.

SALLY IN OUR ALLEY.

Of all the girls that are so smart,
There 's none like pretty Sally;
She is the darling of my heart,
And she lives in our alley.
There is no lady in the land
Is half so sweet as Sally;
She is the darling of my heart,
And she lives in our alley.

Her father he makes cabbage nets,
And through the streets does cry 'em;
Her mother she sells laces long,
To such as please to buy 'em:
But sure such folks could ne'er beget
So sweet a girl as Sally;
She is the darling of my heart,
And she lives in our alley.

When she is by, I leave my work,
I love her so sincerely;
My master comes like any Turk,
And bangs me most severely:
But let him bang his belly full,
I 'll bear it all for Sally:
She is the darling of my heart,
And she lives in our alley.

Of all the days that 's in the week,
I dearly love but one day,
And that 's the day that comes betwixt
The Saturday and Monday.
For then I 'm dressed in all my best,
To walk abroad with Sally;
She is the darling of my heart,
And she lives in our alley.

My master carries me to church,
And often am I blamed,
Because I leave him in the lurch
As soon as text is named;
I leave the church in sermon-time,
And slink away to Sally;
She is the darling of my heart,
And she lives in our alley.

When Christmas comes about again,
O then I shall have money;

I 'll hoard it up, and, box and all,
I 'll give it to my honey:
I would it were ten thousand pound,
I 'd give it all to Sally;
She is the darling of my heart,
And she lives in our alley.

My master, and the neighbours all,
Make game of me and Sally;
And (but for her) I 'd better be
A slave and row a galley;
But when my seven long years are out,
O then I 'll marry Sally:
O then we 'll wed, and then we 'll bed,
But not in our alley.

CHARLES HAMILTON.

LORD BINNING.

—1732.

THE SHEPHERD'S COMPLAINT.

Did ever swain a nymph adore,
 As I ungrateful Nanny do?
Was ever shepherd's heart so sore?
 Was ever broken heart so true?
My eyes are swelled with tears; but she
Has never shed a tear for me.

If Nanny called, did Robin stay,
 Or linger when she bid me run?
She only had the word to say,
 And all she asked was quickly done:
I always thought on her, but she
Would ne'er bestow a thought on me.

To let her cows my clover taste,
 Have I not rose by break of day?
When did her heifers ever fast,
 If Robin in his yard had hay?
Though to my fields they welcome were,
I never welcome was to her.

If Nanny ever lost a sheep,
I cheerfully did give her two:
Did not her lambs in safety sleep
Within my folds in frost and snow?
Have they not there from cold been free?
But Nanny still is cold to me.

Whene'er I climbed our orchard trees,
The ripest fruit was kept for Nan;
O how those hands that drowned her bees
Were stung—I'll ne'er forget the pain!
Sweet were the combs, as sweet could be;
But Nanny ne'er looked sweet on me.

If Nanny to the well did come,
'T was I that did her pitchers fill;
Full as they were, I brought them home;
Her corn I carried to the mill.
My back did bear her sacks; but she
Would never bear the sight of me.

To Nanny's poultry oats I gave,
I'm sure they always had the best;
Within this week her pigeons have
Eat up a peck of peas at least;
Her little pigeons kiss; but she
Would never take a kiss from me.

Must Robin always Nanny woo,
And Nanny still on Robin frown?
Alas, poor wretch! what shall I do,
If Nanny does not love me soon?
If no relief to me she'll bring,
I'll hang me on her apron string.

WILLIAM SHENSTONE.

1714—1763.

Shenstone was in love twice, if so lazy a fellow as he was, can be said to have been in love. His first innamorata was a Miss Graves, sister of one of his college friends, Mr. Richard Graves, author of "The Spiritual Quixote," and other works. He became acquainted with her in 1735, and had a sort of Platonic feeling towards her for several years. A parting from her on one occasion was the cause of his commencing the "Pastoral Ballad." In 1743 he went to Cheltenham, where he met a Miss C—— (how provoking these blanks are!) and his bosom, as the novelists of that day would have said, was for the second time awakened to the tender passion. He grew melancholy and poetical, as was his wont, and, on parting from his charmer, re-wrote the Ballad, and divided it into four parts, as it now stands. He also wrote a number of songs, in which she figured as Delia. She seems never to have known of his passion, at least from him. "Marriage was not once the subject of our conversation," he says, in one of his letters, "nor even love." But it was just as well so, if we may credit Mr. Graves, who hints, in his "Recollections of Shenstone," that the lady would never have married a man of the poet's means, because she had a sister who had married a baronet!

The "Pastoral Ballad" was modelled after "The Despairing Shepherd" of Rowe, which Shenstone admired greatly. It was very popular in its time, and is still, with old-fashioned readers.

A PASTORAL BALLAD.

IN FOUR PARTS.

1743.

I. Absence.

Ye shepherds, so cheerful and gay,
    Whose flocks never carelessly roam;
Should Corydon's happen to stray,
    O call the poor wanderers home!

Allow me to muse and to sigh,
    Nor talk of the change that ye find;
None once was so watchful as I;
    I have left my dear Phyllis behind.

Now I know what it is to have strove
    With the torture of doubt and desire;
What it is to admire and to love,
    And to leave her we love and admire.
Ah! lead forth my flock in the morn,
    And the damps of each evening repel;
Alas! I am faint and forlorn;
    I have bade my dear Phyllis farewell.

Since Phyllis vouchsafed me a look,
    I never once dreamed of my vine;
May I lose both my pipe and my crook,
    If I knew of a kid that was mine.
I prized every hour that went by,
    Beyond all that had pleased me before;
But now they are past, and I sigh,
    And I grieve that I prized them no more.

But why do I languish in vain?
    Why wander thus pensively here?
O why did I come from the plain,
    Where I fed on the smiles of my dear?
They tell me, my favourite maid,
    The pride of that valley, is flown;
Alas! where with her I have strayed,
    I could wander with pleasure alone.

When forced the fair nymph to forego,
    What anguish I felt at my heart:
Yet I thought—but it might not be so—
    'Twas with pain that she saw me depart.
She gazed as I slowly withdrew,
    My path I could hardly discern;

So sweetly she bade me adieu,
    I thought that she bade me return.

The pilgrim that journeys all day
    To visit some far distant shrine,
If he bear but a relic away,
    Is happy, nor heard to repine.
Thus widely removed from the fair,
    Where my vows, my devotion, I owe;
Soft Hope is the relic I bear,
    And my solace wherever I go.

II. Hope.

My banks they are furnished with bees,
    Whose murmur invites one to sleep;
My grottoes are shaded with trees,
    And my hills are white over with sheep.
I seldom have met with a loss,
    Such health do my fountains bestow;
My fountains, all bordered with moss,
    Where the harebells and violets grow.

Not a pine in my grove is there seen,
    But with tendrils of woodbine is bound;
Not a beech's more beautiful green,
    But a sweetbriar entwines it around.
Not my fields, in the prime of the year,
    More charms than my cattle unfold;
Not a brook that is limpid and clear,
    But it glitters with fishes of gold.

One would think she might like to retire
    To the bower I have laboured to rear;
Not a shrub that I heard her admire,
    But I hasted and planted it there.
O how sudden the jessamine strove
    With the lilac to render it gay!

Already it calls for my love
    To prune the wild branches away.

From the plains, from the woodlands and groves,
    What strains of wild melody flow!
How the nightingales warble their loves,
    From thickets of roses that blow!
And when her bright form shall appear,
    Each bird shall harmoniously join
In a concert so soft and so clear,
    As she may not be fond to resign.

I have found out a gift for my fair;
    I have found where the wood-pigeons breed;
But let me that plunder forbear,
    She will say 't was a barbarous deed.
For he ne'er could be true, she averred,
    Who could rob a poor bird of its young;
And I loved her the more when I heard
    Such tenderness fall from her tongue.

I have heard her with sweetness unfold
    How that pity was due to a dove;
That it ever attended the bold,
    And she called it the sister of Love.
But her words such a pleasure convey,
    So much I her accents adore,
Let her speak, and whatever she say,
    Methinks I should love her the more.

Can a bosom so gentle remain
    Unmoved when her Corydon sighs?
Will a nymph that is fond of the plain,
    These plains and this valley despise?
Dear regions of silence and shade!
    Soft scenes of contentment and ease!
Where I could have pleasingly strayed,
    If aught in her absence could please.

But where does my Phyllida stray,
And where are her grots and her bowers?
Are the groves and the valleys as gay,
And the shepherds as gentle as ours?
The groves may perhaps be as fair,
And the face of the valleys as fine;
The swains may in manners compare,
But their love is not equal to mine.

III. Solicitude.

Why will you my passion reprove?
Why term it a folly to grieve,
Ere I show you the charms of my love?
She is fairer than you can believe.
With her mien she enamours the brave,
With her wit she engages the free,
With her modesty pleases the grave;
She is every way pleasing to me.

O you that have been of her train,
Come join in my amorous lays;
I could lay down my life for the swain,
That will sing but a song in her praise.
When he sings, may the nymphs of the town
Come trooping, and listen the while;
Nay, on him let not Phyllida frown,
But I cannot allow her to smile.

For when Paridel tries in the dance
Any favour with Phyllis to find,
O how, with one trivial glance,
Might she ruin the peace of my mind!
In ringlets he dresses his hair,
And his crook is bestudded around;
And his pipe—O my Phyllis, beware
Of a magic there is in the sound.

'T is his with mock passion to glow,
  'T is his in smooth tales to unfold
How her face is as bright as the snow,
  And her bosom, be sure, is as cold.
How the nightingales labour the strain
  With the notes of his charmer to vie;
How they vary their accents in vain,
  Repine at her triumphs, and die.

To the grove or the garden he strays,
  And pillages every sweet;
Then suiting the wreath to his lays,
  He throws it at Phyllis's feet.
"O Phyllis," he whispers, "more fair,
  More sweet, than the jessamine's flower!
What are pinks in a morn to compare?
  What is eglantine after a shower?

"Then the lily no longer is white,
  Then the rose is deprived of its bloom,
Then the violets die with despite,
  And the woodbines give up their perfume."
Thus glide the soft numbers along,
  And he fancies no shepherd his peer;
Yet I never should envy the song,
  Were not Phyllis to lend it an ear.

Let his crook be with hyacinths bound,
  So Phyllis the trophy despise:
Let his forehead with laurels be crowned,
  So they shine not in Phyllis's eyes.
The language that flows from the heart,
  Is a stranger to Paridel's tongue:
Yet may she beware of his art,
  Or sure I must envy the song.

IV. Disappointment.

Ye shepherds, give ear to my lay,
    And take no more heed of my sheep:
They have nothing to do but to stray;
    I have nothing to do but to weep.
Yet do not my folly reprove;
    She was fair, and my passion begun;
She smiled, and I could not but love;
    She is faithless, and I am undone.

Perhaps I was void of all thought:
    Perhaps it was plain to foresee,
That a nymph so complete would be sought
    By a swain more engaging than me.
Ah! love every hope can inspire;
    It banishes wisdom the while;
And the lip of the nymph we admire
    Seems forever adorned with a smile.

She is faithless, and I am undone;
    Ye that witness the woes I endure,
Let reason instruct you to shun
    What it can not instruct you to cure.
Beware how you loiter in vain
    Amid nymphs of a higher degree:
It is not for me to explain
    How fair and how fickle they be.

Alas! from the day that we met,
    What hope of an end to my woes,
When I cannot endure to forget
    The glance that undid my repose?
Yet time may diminish the pain:
    The flower, and the shrub, and the tree
Which I reared for her pleasure in vain,
    In time may have comfort for me.

The sweets of a dew-sprinkled rose,
    The sound of a murmuring stream,
The peace which from solitude flows,
    Henceforth shall be Corydon's theme.
High transports are shown to the sight,
    But we 're not to find them our own;
Fate never bestowed such delight,
    As I with my Phyllis had known.

O ye woods, spread your branches apace,
    To your deepest recesses I fly;
I would hide with the beasts of the chase,
    I would vanish from every eye.
Yet my reed shall resound through the grove
    With the same sad complaint it begun;
How she smiled, and I could not but love,
    Was faithless, and I am undone!

LORD LYTTLETON.

1709—1773.

Lord Lyttleton courted Lucy Fortescue, daughter of Hugh Fortescue, Esq., a country gentleman of Devonshire. She was in her twenty-second year, and was beautiful and accomplished; he was eight or nine years older, and was extremely plain, "of a feeble, ill-compacted frame, and a meagre, sallow countenance." His manners, however, were elegant, and his talents above mediocrity, and, as a woman seldom thinks of the person of her lover, he succeeded in winning the affections of Miss Fortescue, and they were married in 1741. They lived an ideal life for four or five years, surrounded by books and friends, and devoted to each other. Two children were born to them, and Lady Lyttleton was confined with a third, when she sickened and died. "I believe," her husband wrote to his father, two days before her death, "I believe God supports me above my own strength, for the sake of my friends who are concerned for me, and in return for the resignation with which I endeavor to submit to his will. If it please Him, in his infinite mercy, to restore my dear wife to me, I shall most thankfully acknowledge his goodness; if not, I shall most humbly endure his chastisement, which I have too much deserved." Lady Lyttleton died on the 19th of January, 1747, and was buried at Over-Arley, in Staffordshire. Her disconsolate husband erected a monument to her in the chancel of the church at Hagley, and solaced himself, Johnson sneeringly remarks, by writing a long monody on her memory.

Lord Lyttleton married again in 1749. His second wife was Elizabeth Rich, daughter of Sir Robert Rich, an intimate and dear friend of his Lucy. The experiment is said to have been an unhappy one, and to have added bitterness to his regrets.

AN IRREGULAR ODE,

WRITTEN AT WICKHAM. 1746.

Ye sylvan scenes, with artless beauty gay,
Ye gentle shades of Wickham, say,

What is the charm that each successive year,
Which sees me with my Lucy here,
Can thus to my transported heart
A sense of joy unfelt before impart?

Is it glad Summer's balmy breath, that blows
From the fair jasmine and the blushing rose?
Her balmy breath, and all her blooming store
Of rural bliss, was here before:
Oft have I met her on the verdant side
Of Norwood Hill, and in the yellow meads
Where Pan the dancing Graces leads,
Arrayed in all her flowery pride.
No sweeter fragrance now the gardens yield,
No brighter colours paint th' enamelled field.

Is it to Love these new delights I owe?
Four times has the revolving Sun
His annual circle through the zodiac run,
Since all that Love's indulgent power
On favoured mortals can bestow,
Was given to me in this auspicious bower.

Here first my Lucy, sweet in virgin charms,
Was yielded to my longing arms;
And round our nuptial bed,
Hovering with purple wings, th' Idalian boy
Shook from his radiant torch the blissful fire
Of innocent desires,
While Venus scattered myrtles o'er her head.
Whence then this strange increase of joy?
He, only he, can tell, who, matched like me,
(If such another happy man there be,)
Has by his own experience tried
How much The Wife is dearer than The Bride.

MARK AKENSIDE.

1721—1770.

SONG.

The shape alone let others prize,
    The features of the fair;
I look for spirit in her eyes,
    And meaning in her air.

A damask cheek, an ivory arm,
    Shall ne'er my wishes win;
Give me an animated form,
    That speaks a mind within.

A face where awful honour shines,
    Where sense and sweetness move,
And angel innocence refines
    The tenderness of love.

These are the soul of beauty's frame,
    Without whose vital aid,
Unfinished all her features seem,
    And all her roses dead.

But ah! where both their charms unite,
    How perfect is the view,
With every image of delight,
    With graces ever new:

Of power to charm the greatest woe,
The wildest rage control,
Diffusing mildness o'er the brow,
And rapture through the soul.

Their power but faintly to express
All language must despair;
But go, behold Arpasia's face,
And read it perfect there.

NATHANIEL COTTON.

1721—1788.

[*"A Collection of Poems by Several Hands."* 1763.]

THE FIRESIDE.

DEAR Chloe, while the busy crowd,
The vain, the wealthy, and the proud,
    In folly's maze advance;
Though singularity and pride
Be called our choice, we 'll step aside,
    Nor join the giddy dance.

From the gay world we 'll oft retire
To our own family and fire,
    Where love our hours employs;
No noisy neighbour enters here,
No intermeddling stranger near,
    To spoil our heartfelt joys.

If solid happiness we prize,
Within our breast this jewel lies,
    And they are fools who roam;
The world hath nothing to bestow,
From our own selves our bliss must flow,
    And that dear hut our home.

Of rest was Noah's dove bereft,
When with impatient wing she left
That safe retreat, the ark;
Giving her vain excursions o'er,
The disappointed bird once more
Explored the sacred bark.

Though fools spurn Hymen's gentle powers,
We, who improve his golden hours,
By sweet experience know,
That marriage, rightly understood,
Gives to the tender and the good
A paradise below.

Our babes shall richer comfort bring;
If tutored right they 'll prove a spring
Whence pleasures ever rise;
We 'll form their minds, with studious care,
To all that 's manly, good, and fair,
And train them for the skies.

While they our wisest hours engage,
They 'll joy our youth, support our age,
And crown our hoary hairs;
They 'll grow in virtue every day,
And thus our fondest loves repay,
And recompense our cares.

No borrowed joys, they 're all our own,
While to the world we live unknown,
Or by the world forgot:
Monarchs, we envy not your state,
We look with pity on the great,
And bless our humble lot.

Our portion is not large, indeed;
But then how little do we need!
For nature's calls are few.

In this the art of living lies,
To want no more than may suffice,
    And make that little do.

We'll therefore relish with content,
Whate'er kind Providence has sent,
    Nor aim beyond our power:
For, if our stock be very small,
'Tis prudence to enjoy it all,
    Nor lose the present hour.

To be resigned when ills betide,
Patient when favours are denied,
    And pleased with favours given;
Dear Chloe, this is wisdom's part;
This is that incense of the heart,
    Whose fragrance smells to heaven.

We'll ask no long-protracted treat,
Since winter-life is seldom sweet;
    But, when our feast is o'er,
Grateful from table we'll arise,
Nor grudge our sons, with envious eyes,
    The relics of our store.

Thus, hand in hand, through life we'll go;
Its checkered paths of joy and woe
    With cautious steps we'll tread:
Quit its vain scenes without a tear,
Without a trouble, or a fear,
    And mingle with the dead:

While conscience, like a faithful friend,
Shall through the gloomy vale attend,
    And cheer our dying breath;
Shall, when all other comforts cease,
Like a kind angel whisper peace,
    And smooth the bed of death.

ROBERT BURNS.

1759—1796.

The loves and heroines of Burns, were as numberless, and some, it is whispered, as light,

"As the gay motes that people the sun-beams."

I shall not attempt to write their history, which might easily be extended to a volume, but content myself with a brief sketch of two or three of the most prominent, beginning with Bonnie Jean. Jean Armour, afterwards Mrs. Burns, was the daughter of a master-mason who resided in Mauchline. The Burns family removed thither, or to speak with more exactness, removed to the farm of Mossgiel, in the parish of Mauchline, in March, 1784. In April the acquaintance of Burns and Jean commenced. "There was a race at Mauchline in the end of April," says Mr. Chambers in his excellent biography of the poet, "and there it was customary for the young men, with little ceremony, to invite such girls as they liked off the street into a humble dancing-hall, where a fiddler had taken up his station to give them music. The payment of a penny for a dance was held by the minstrel as guerdon sufficient. Burns and Jean happened to be in the same dance, but not as partners, when some confusion and a little merriment was excited by his dog tracking his footsteps through the room. He playfully remarked to his partner that 'he wished he could get any of the lasses to like him as well as his dog did.' A short while after, he passed through the Mauchline washing-green, where Jean, who had overheard his remark, was bleaching clothes. His dog running over the clothes, the young maiden desired him to call it off, and this led them into conversation. Archly referring to what passed at the dance, she asked if he had yet got any of the lasses to like him as well as his dog? From that time their intimacy commenced." We know nothing of their courtship, which was doubtless like that of most rural lovers, except that it gave birth to one or two songs of no great merit, and ended in disgrace to Jean, who found herself, in the winter of 1786, in the way that ladies wish to be, who love their lords. It was a dark day with Burns, for the farm which he and his brother Gilbert had taken at Mossgiel, had proved a failure; but he made Jean all the reparation he could at the time by acknowledging her as his wife. He gave her a document in writing, sufficient, according to the Scottish laws, to constitute an irregular though valid marriage. This, he hoped, would satisfy Jean's father, but it had the contrary effect, for instead of mending the matter it made it worse in his eyes. Burns came forward and proposed to emigrate to the West Indies to better his fortune, and when he should have accomplished that, to return, and claim Jean as his wife. He was even willing to become a common labourer, in order to maintain her and her expected child. Mr. Armour rejected all his proposals, and declared that he would annul the marriage, such as it was. He compelled Jean to give him her marriage certificate, which he placed in the hands of a lawyer, and made her believe that he was her only friend. She clung to him in her weakness, to the surprise of Burns, who was filled with indignation. He now determined to emigrate, and agreed with a Mr. Douglas to go out to Jamaica as a book-keeper on his estate; and, not having money to pay his passage, printed proposals for publishing his poems by subscription. This was in the beginning of April, 1786. Between that time and the middle of May a new character appeared on the scene. It was Highland Mary. A great deal of obscurity hangs over her, owing to Burns' reserve and mystification concerning this episode of his life, but the researches of his editors have discovered a few facts, which will serve for landmarks to guide us through the mist. Her name was Mary Campbell. She was of Highland parentage, from the neighbourhood of Dunoon, on the Firth of Clyde. Her father was a sailor in a revenue cutter, the station of which was at Campbelton in Kintyre, where his family then resided. Nothing is known of Mary before her affair with Burns, except that she had lived for several years in the family of a clergyman in Arran, and afterwards as a servant in Ayrshire. If she could be traced in Ayrshire before the autumn of 1785, at which time she was a nursemaid in the family of Mr. Gavin Hamilton, in Mauchline, I have no doubt but we should find her somewhere in the neighbourhood of Lochlea, when the Burns family was residing there. I prefer to think that she was an early flame of Burns, as he himself declared—an old love whose acquaintance he renewed after the estrangement of Jean, rather than that he met her after he knew Jean, and courted her and Jean at the same time. It is more creditable to him as a man, and till there is a stronger reason to believe it false than any I have yet seen, it shall be an article in my creed. But be the facts what they may, Burns now turned to Mary Campbell, and found her willing to marry him. It was agreed between them that she should give up her place, and go home for a short time to her friends in the Highlands, in order to arrange her marriage with Burns. They had a farewell meeting on the second Sunday in May (the 14th of the month), in a sequestered spot on the banks of the Ayr. It would be pleasant to know what passed on that occasion—to read the sacred volume of their hearts, illuminated with the light of love, and stained with the tears of parting, but it cannot be: the volume is closed forever, and they are gone. All that remains is tradition, and a leaf or two from the Book of Song, written from memory years after, when Mary was in Heaven, and Burns the husband of Jean. They brought their Bibles to the place of meeting, and exchanged them reverently. Mary's copy was small and plain, Robert's was large and elegant, and in two volumes. On a blank leaf of the first he had written the text, "*And ye shall not swear by my name falsely. I am the Lord;*" and on the second, "*Thou shalt not forswear thyself, but shalt perform unto the Lord thine oath.*" "Their adieu was performed with all those simple and striking ceremonials which rustic sentiment has devised to prolong tender emotions, and to impose awe. The lovers stood on each side of a small purling brook—they laved their hands in the limpid stream—and holding a Bible between them, pronounced their vows to be faithful to each other." They parted at the gloaming, never to meet again! Burns returned to Mossgiel and Mary to the Highlands. She spent the summer at Campbelton with her family, and in the early part of the autumn accepted a situation which had been procured for her in Glasgow. Her term of service was to commence at Martinmas (11th of November). She started from Campbelton about the first of October, with her father, and her younger brother Robert, who was on the eve of learning the trade of a ship-carpenter with a relative in Greenock. This relative, whose name was Peter Macpherson, gave the lad a feast on his being admitted into the craft, and Mary served the company. They made a night of it, and in the morning Master Robert was not able to go to his work. When Macpherson came home to breakfast, he asked what had kept him from the yard, and Mary replied that he had probably taken a little too much after supper. "It is just as well, then, in case of the worst," said Macpherson, "that I have agreed to purchase that lair in the kirk-yard," referring to a burying-place which he had recently secured for his family. Mary attended upon her brother in his illness, which lasted several days, and as he was beginning to recover, was taken sick herself. Her friends believed that she was suffering from the cast of an evil eye, and advised her father to go to a cross-burn, and select seven smooth stones, and boil them in new milk, and then give her the milk to drink. This superstitious prescription was followed, but without effect, for her sickness proved to be a malignant fever, which soon carried her off. She was buried in the lair of which Macpherson had jestingly spoken. He had purchased it just in time. Her death took place about the middle of October, five months after her parting with Burns in the woods of Ayr. It must have seemed a long time to him, whatever it did to her, for it was crowded with incidents, some of them painful enough. He had visited the Armours to see Jean, "not from the least view of reconciliation," he wrote to a friend, "but merely to ask for her health," but was forbidden the house by her mother, and not very well received by Jean herself. He had tried to forget her, and had run into all kinds of dissipation and riots, (I am quoting his own words,) mason-meetings, drinking-matches, and other mischiefs, to drive her out of his head, but all in vain. He had submitted to the censure of the church, by standing in his pew before the congregation for five successive Sundays, receiving, on the last, a rebuke from the minister, after which he was declared a bachelor. He had skulked from Mauchline to avoid being thrown into jail at the instance of Mr. Armour, who threatened to prosecute him to obtain a guarantee for the maintenance of Jean's expected child. He had published his poems, and the noise they were making through the country was soon to be heard in Edinburgh. Jean had given birth to twins, (September 3d,) and one of them, a boy, was now at Mossgiel, to gladden and grieve him. Joy and sorrow, shame and glory, had been pressed into his cup until it was full to overflowing. It ran over with the last bitter drop—the death of Mary Campbell. He was at Mossgiel, one day, in the midst of his family, brooding over his prospects, and perhaps humming a tune to the monotonous whir of the old spinning-wheel which his sister was turning, when a letter containing the intelligence of her death was handed in to him. He went to the window and opened it: a look of agony came into his face as he read it: he folded it up when he had finished, and went out without speaking a word. A month later he was in Edinburgh—the wonder and glory of his nation! His triumphant career in Edinburgh—a career without a parallel in the history of poets—is too well known to need a description here, so I shall pass over it, and come to his next love-affair—the curious episode of Clarinda. Her name was Agnes M'Lehose, and she was the wife of Mr. James M'Lehose, a gentleman of a roving disposition, who had as good as abandoned her and his children, to seek his fortune in the West Indies. Burns met her for the first time at a tea-party, at the house of a mutual friend, in the beginning of December, 1787. They were so much pleased with each other—she with his genius, and he with her voluptuous beauty—that a second party was proposed, to come off at her own house on the ensuing Saturday evening. Burns accepted the proposal with avidity, having acquired on the sudden a mighty relish for tea, but the night before the drinking was to have taken place, he was overset by a drunken coachman, and carried to his lodgings with a bruised knee. He wrote Mrs. M'Lehose a letter, stating the circumstance, and expressing his regret, and paid her some high-flown compliments which tickled her amazingly. She answered in the same strain, and inclosed him a poem which she had written. They kept up a brisk fire of small notes, charged with friendship and flattery. The fifth discharge of Burns brought down the colours of his "sweet enemy," but he gallantly destroyed his own, and they hoisted a new set, and continued their loving encounter, masked as Sylvander and Clarinda. They met a second time shortly after the New Year, and exchanged confidences, Clarinda giving Sylvander a history of her past life and troubles, and receiving his own in return. It is not easy to see what they proposed to themselves as the end of all this meeting and letter-writing; it could not have been marriage, for the husband of Mrs. M'Lehose was living, while Jean had a new claim upon Burns; neither does it seem to have been that looser tie, which society sometimes forgives in poets—at least I acquit Clarinda of all guilty intentions. She was young and unfortunate—the abandoned wife of a man whom she could not love—a creature of sentiment and sensibility—the ardent admirer of Burns, whose fiery temperament she sympathized with—in short, a passionate and imprudent woman. She set her cap at Burns, as the saying is, without thinking of the consequences, and he encouraged her, rake that he was: always the slave of the moment, he gave himself up to the passion she inspired with an energy that startled her. She was for esteem and friendship—a Platonic attachment; his tropical nature demanded a warmer return. The correspondence that passed between them was printed, when the grave had closed over both, and a precious batch of nonsense it was: it is impossible to read it without a smile. Burns must have laughed to himself when he penned a paragraph like this: "You have a heart formed—gloriously formed—for all the most refined luxuries of love: why was that heart ever wrung? Oh, Clarinda! shall we not meet in a state, some yet unknown state of being, where the lavish hand of plenty shall minister to the highest wish of benevolence, and where the chill north wind of prudence shall never blow over the flowery fields of enjoyment?" He fooled her to the top of her bent. Their intimacy lasted till he departed from Edinburgh, when it may be said to have terminated, though several letters passed between them afterwards. He started from Edinburgh on the 18th of February, 1788, and arrived at

Mossgiel on the 24th. It was time that he came, not only for his own sake as a man, but also for that of Jean, who had been turned out of doors by her father. There were many reasons why he should return to her, and not the least of these was a second pair of twins, who were born shortly after his arrival. In April he acknowledged her as his wife. His marriage made Clarinda furious, though I do not see why it should have done so. *She* could not marry him, and to keep him from marrying another was beyond her power, as no one should have known better than herself. She entered into her flirtation, or passion, or whatever the reader pleases to call it, with her eyes open, and ought to have foreseen the end. It might have been worse, much worse—for her. She never forgave Burns for deserting her, though she continued to correspond with him at intervals during his life, and after his death preserved his letters with jealous veneration. She died in 1841, at the age of eighty-two.

MY NANIE, O.

The heroine of this song, which was written about 1780, was a farmer's daughter, named Agnes Fleming. She lived near Lochlea, when Burns resided there, and afterwards in the family of Mr. Gavin Hamilton, at Mauchline. She is said to have been anything but handsome, though her figure and carriage were good.

Behind yon hills where Stinsiar flows
'Mang moors and mosses many, O,
The wintry sun the day has closed,
And I'll awa to Nanie, O.

The westlin wind blaws loud and shrill;
The night's baith mirk and rainy, O:
But I'll get my plaid, and out I'll steal,
And owre the hills to Nanie, O.

My Nanie's charming, sweet, and young;
Nae artfu' wiles to win ye, O:
May ill befa' the flattering tongue
That wad beguile my Nanie, O!

Her face is fair, her heart is true,
As spotless as she's bonnie, O:
The opening gowan, wet wi' dew,
Nae purer is than Nanie, O.

A country lad is my degree,
And few there be that ken me, O;
But what care I how few they be?
I'm welcome aye to Nanie, O.

My riches a's my penny-fee,
And I maun guide it cannie, O;
But warl's gear ne'er troubles me,
My thoughts are a' my Nanie, O.

Our auld guidman delights to view
His sheep and kye thrive bonnie, O;
But I'm as blithe that hauds his pleugh,
And has nae care but Nanie, O.

Come weel, come woe, I care nae by,
I'll tak what Heaven will send me, O;
Nae ither care in life have I,
But live and love my Nanie, O.

MARY MORRISON.

The heroine of this beautiful song is not known with certainty, but the weight of evidence is in favor of Ellison Begbie, the daughter of a farmer in the parish of Galston. She was a servant in a family on the banks of the Cessnock, about two miles from Lochlea, where Burns resided when he wrote the song (1783, or '84), and is known to have been one of his sweethearts at that time. She was not at all beautiful, though much run after by the young men of the neighbourhood. She was the heroine of Burns' song, "*On Cessnock Banks there lives a lass.*"

O, Mary, at thy window be,
It is the wished, the trysted hour!
Those smiles and glances let me see,
That make the miser's treasure poor:
How blithely wad I bide the stoure,
A weary slave frae sun to sun,
Could I the rich reward secure,
The lovely Mary Morrison.

Yestreen when to the trembling string,
The dance gaed through the lighted ha',
To thee my fancy took its wing,
I sat, but neither heard nor saw.
Though this was fair, and that was braw,
And yon the toast of a' the town,
I sighed, and said amang them a',
'Ye are na Mary Morrison.'

O, Mary, canst thou wreck his peace,
Wha for thy sake wad gladly die?
Or canst thou break that heart of his,
Whase only faut is loving thee?
If love for love thou wilt na gie,
At least be pity to me shown;
A thought ungentle canna be
The thought o' Mary Morrison.

RIGS O' BARLEY.

The heroine of this song was Anne Rankine (afterwards Mrs. Anne Mirry), the youngest daughter of Mr. John Rankine, a farmer in the neighbourhood of Lochlea. She met Burns at the house of her father, (to whom, by the way, Burns addressed a poetical epistle,) and was much amused on his first visit by his making a circuit around the parlour, to avoid treading on a small carpet in the centre of the floor! After the publication of the "Rigs o' Barley," she told him she had not expected to be celebrated by him in print. "O, ay," he answered, "I was just wanting to give you a cast among the lave." She was a tall, masculine-looking woman, and for the greater part of her life, which was a long one, she kept a house of entertainment in Cumnock.

It was upon a Lammas night,
When corn rigs are bonnie,
Beneath the moon's unclouded light,
I held awa to Annie:
The time flew by wi' tentless heed,
Till 'tween the late and early,
Wi' sma' persuasion she agreed
To see me through the barley.

The sky was blue, the wind was still,
The moon was shining clearly;
I set her down wi' right good will
Amang the rigs o' barley;
I ken't her heart was a' my ain,
I loved her most sincerely;
I kissed her owre and owre again,
Amang the rigs o' barley.

I locked her in my fond embrace;
Her heart was beating rarely:
My blessings on that happy place,
Amang the rigs o' barley!
But by the moon and stars so bright,
That shone that hour so clearly!
She aye shall bless that happy night,
Amang the rigs o' barley.

I hae been blithe wi' comrades dear;
I hae been merry drinkin';
I hae been joyfu' gath'rin' gear;
I hae been happy thinkin':
But a' the pleasures e'er I saw,
Though three times doubled fairly,
That happy night was worth them a',
Amang the rigs o' barley.

CHORUS.

Corn rigs, and barley rigs,
And corn rigs are bonnie:
I'll ne'er forget that happy night
Amang the rigs wi' Annie.

SONG.

Will ye go to the Indies, my Mary,
And leave auld Scotia's shore?

Will ye go to the Indies, my Mary,
    Across the Atlantic's roar?

O sweet grows the lime and the orange,
    And the apple on the pine;
But a' the charms o' the Indies
    Can never equal thine.

I hae sworn by the Heavens to my Mary,
    I hae sworn by the Heavens to be true;
And sae may the Heavens forget me,
    When I forget my vow!

O plight me your faith, my Mary,
    And plight me your lily-white hand;
O plight me your faith, my Mary,
    Before I leave Scotia's strand.

We hae plighted our troth, my Mary,
    In mutual affection to join;
And curst be the cause that shall part us!
    The hour and the moment o' time!

I LOVE MY JEAN.

This song, and the one that follows, were written in the summer of 1788, at Ellisland, where Burns was building a house. They were addressed to Mrs. Burns, who remained at Mauchline. "N. B.," said the poet in a note to the first—"It was in the honeymoon."

Of a' the airts the wind can blaw,
    I dearly like the west,
For there the bonnie lassie lives,
    The lassie I loe best:
There wild woods grow, and rivers row,
    And mony a hill between;
But day and night, my fancy's flight
    Is ever wi' my Jean.

I see her in the dewy flowers,
    I see her sweet and fair:
I hear her in the tunefu' birds,
    I hear her charm the air:
There 's not a bonnie flower that springs
    By fountain, shaw, or green:
There 's not a bonnie bird that sings,
    But minds me of my Jean.

O, WERE I ON PARNASSUS' HILL.

O, were I on Parnassus' hill!
Or had of Helicon my fill;
That I might catch poetic skill,
    To sing how dear I love thee.
But Nith maun be my muse's well,
My muse maun be thy bonnie sel';
On Corsincon I 'll glower and spell,
    And write how dear I love thee.

Then come, sweet muse, inspire my lay!
For a' the lee-lang simmer's day
I couldna sing, I couldna say,
    How much, how dear I love thee.
I see thee dancing o'er the green,
Thy waist sae jimp, thy limbs sae clean,
Thy tempting lips, thy roguish een—
    By heaven and earth I love thee!

By night, by day, a-field, at hame,
The thoughts of thee my breast inflame;
And aye I muse and sing thy name,
    I only live to love thee.
Though I were doomed to wander on
Beyond the sea, beyond the sun,
Till my last weary sand was run;
    Till then, and then I 'd love thee.

TO MARY IN HEAVEN.

This touching poem was written in October, 1789, on the third anniversary of Highland Mary's death. Burns spent the day in the harvest field, apparently in excellent spirits: "but as the twilight deepened," (I am quoting the account of Mrs. Burns, from Lockhart's Life of the poet,) "he appeared to grow 'very sad about something,' and at length wandered out into the barn-yard, to which his wife, in her anxiety for his health, followed him, entreating him, in vain, to observe that frost had set in, and to return to his fireside. On being again and again requested to do so, he always promised compliance, but still remained where he was, striding up and down slowly, and contemplating the sky, which was singularly clear and starry. At last Mrs. Burns found him stretched on a heap of straw, with his eyes fixed on a beautiful planet, 'that shone like another moon,' and prevailed on him to come in. He immediately, on entering the house, called for his desk, and wrote, exactly as they now stand, with all the ease of one copying from memory, these sublime and pathetic verses."

Thou ling'ring star, with less'ning ray,
    That lov'st to greet the early morn,
Again thou usher'st in the day
    My Mary from my soul was torn.
O Mary! dear departed shade!
    Where is thy place of blissful rest?
See'st thou thy lover lowly laid?
    Hear'st thou the groans that rend his breast?

That sacred hour can I forget?
    Can I forget the hallowed grove,
Where by the winding Ayr we met,
    To live one day of parting love?
Eternity will not efface
    Those records dear of transports past;
Thy image at our last embrace,
    Ah! little thought we 't was our last!

Ayr, gurgling, kissed his pebbled shore,
    O'erhung with wild woods, thickening green;
The fragrant birch, and hawthorn hoar,
    Twined am'rous round the raptured scene;

The flowers sprang wanton to be prest,
    The birds sang love on every spray;
Till too, too soon, the glowing west
    Proclaim'd the speed of wingéd day.

Still o'er these scenes my mem'ry wakes,
    And fondly broods with miser care;
Time but th' impression deeper makes,
    As streams their channels deeper wear.
My Mary, dear departed shade!
    Where is thy place of blissful rest?
See'st thou thy lover lowly laid?
    Hear'st thou the groans that rend his breast?

SONG.

This passionate song, which Scott said was worth a thousand romances, was addressed to Mrs. M'Lehose, when she was on the eve of a voyage to the West Indies. It was written in December, 1791.

Ae fond kiss, and then we sever!
Ae fareweel, and then forever!
Deep in heart-wrung tears I 'll pledge thee,
Warring sighs and groans I 'll wage thee.

Who shall say that Fortune grieves him,
While the star of hope she leaves him?
Me, nae cheerful twinkle lights me;
Dark despair around benights me.

I 'll ne'er blame my partial fancy,
Naething could resist my Nancy:
But to see her was to love her;
Love but her, and love forever.

Had we never loved sae kindly,
Had we never loved sae blindly,
Never met—or never parted,
We had ne'er been broken hearted.

Fare thee weel, thou first and fairest!
Fare thee weel, thou best and dearest!
Thine be ilka joy and treasure,
Peace, Enjoyment, Love and Pleasure!

Ae fond kiss, and then we sever!
Ae farewell, alas! forever!
Deep in heart-wrung tears I'll pledge thee,
Warring sighs and groans I'll wage thee.

BONNIE LESLEY.

The young lady in whose praise this song was written, was Miss Leslie Baillie, (afterwards Mrs. Cumming, of Logie,) a neighbour of Burns' friend, Mrs. Dunlop. "Mr. B., with his two daughters," he wrote to that lady, on the 22d of August, 1792, "accompanied by Mr. H. of G., passing through Dumfries a few days ago, on their way to England, did me the honour of calling on me; on which I took my horse—though, God knows, I could ill spare the time—and accompanied them fourteen or fifteen miles, and dined and spent the day with them. 'T was about nine, I think, when I left them, and, riding home, I composed the following ballad, of which you will probably think you have a dear bargain, as it will cost you another groat of postage. You must know there is an old ballad beginning with—

'My bonnie Lizzie Baillie,
I'll rowe thee in my plaidie,' etc.

So I parodied it as follows, which is literally the first copy, 'unanointed, unannealed,' as Hamlet says."

O saw ye bonnie Lesley,
    As she gaed o'er the Border?
She's gane, like Alexander,
    To spread her conquests farther.

To see her is to love her,
    And love but her forever;
For nature made her what she is,
    And never made anither!

Highland Mary.

New York. Derby & Jackson

Thou art a queen, fair Lesley,
    Thy subjects we, before thee;
Thou art divine, fair Lesley,
    The hearts o' men adore thee.

The deil he couldna scaith thee,
    Or aught that wad belang thee;
He'd look into thy bonnie face
    And say, 'I canna wrang thee!'

The powers aboon will tent thee;
    Misfortune sha' na steer thee;
Thou'rt like themselves sae lovely,
    That ill they'll ne'er let near thee.

Return again, fair Lesley,
    Return to Caledonie!
That we may brag, we hae a lass
    There's nane again sae bonnie.

HIGHLAND MARY.

14th November, 1792.

Ye banks, and braes, and streams around
    The castle o' Montgomery,
Green be your woods, and fair your flowers,
    Your waters never drumlie!
There simmer first unfauld her robes,
    And there the langest tarry;
For there I took the last fareweel
    O' my sweet Highland Mary.

How sweetly bloomed the gay green birk,
    How rich the hawthorn's blossom,
As underneath their fragrant shade
    I clasped her to my bosom!

The golden hours, on angel wings,
Flew o'er me and my dearie;
For dear to me as light and life,
Was my sweet Highland Mary.

Wi' many a vow, and locked embrace,
Our parting was fu' tender;
And, pledging aft to meet again,
We torn oursels asunder:
But O, fell death's untimely frost,
That nipt my flower sae early!
Now green 's the sod, and cauld 's the clay,
That wraps my Highland Mary!

O pale, pale now, those rosy lips,
I aft hae kissed sae fondly!
And closed for aye the sparkling glance
That dwelt on me sae kindly:
And mouldering now in silent dust
That heart that loed me dearly;
But still within my bosom's core
Shall live my Highland Mary.

WILLIAM LISLE BOWLES.

1762—1850.

Bowles made his appearance in the world of letters in 1789, by publishing a small collection of sonnets, most of which hinted of a disappointment in love. The object of his affections is said to have been a niece of Sir Samuel Romilly, whose rejection of his suit set him wandering about the Continent and writing poetry. He seems to have been quite unhappy, in a quiet way; but he finally consoled himself with a wife, for in 1797 he married Magdalene Wake, daughter of the Rev. Charles Wake, prebendary of Westminster.

Bowles' sonnets were the delight and inspiration of Coleridge in his youth. "As my school finances," he says, "did not permit me to purchase copies, I made, within less than a year and a half, more than forty transcriptions."

IN MEMORIAM.

How blessed with thee the path could I have trod
Of quiet life, above cold want's hard fate,
(And little wishing more,) nor of the great
Envious, or their proud name; but it pleased God
To take thee to his mercy: thou didst go
In youth and beauty to thy cold death-bed;
Even whilst on dreams of bliss we fondly fed,
Of years to come of comfort! Be it so.
Ere this I have felt sorrow; and even now,
Though sometimes the unbidden tear will start,
And half unman the miserable heart,
The cold dew I shall wipe from my sad brow,
And say, since hopes of bliss on earth are vain,
Best friend, farewell, till we do meet again!

APPROACH OF SUMMER.

How shall I meet thee, Summer, wont to fill
    My heart with gladness, when thy pleasant tide
    First came, and on the Coomb's romantic side
Was heard the distant cuckoo's hollow bill!
Fresh flowers shall fringe the margin of the stream,
    As with the songs of joyance and of hope
    The hedge-rows shall ring loud, and on the slope
The poplars sparkle in the passing beam;
The shrubs and laurels that I loved to tend,
    Thinking their May-tide fragrance would delight,
With many a peaceful charm, thee, my poor friend,
    Shall put forth their green shoots, and cheer the sight!
But I shall mark their hues with sadder eyes,
And weep the more for one who in the cold earth lies!

ABSENCE. OCT. 26, 1791.

How shall I cheat the heavy hours, of thee
    Deprived, of thy kind looks and converse sweet,
    Now that the waving grove the dark storms beat,
And wintry winds sad sounding o'er the lea,
Scatter the sallow leaf! I would believe
    Thou, at this hour, with tearful tenderness
    Dost muse on absent images, and press
In thought my hand, and say: O do not grieve,
    Friend of my heart, at wayward fortune's power:
    One day we shall be happy, and each hour
Of pain forget, cheered by the summer ray.
    These thoughts beguile my sorrow for thy loss,
    And, as the aged pines their dark heads toss,
Oft steal the sense of solitude away.
    So am I sadly soothed, yet do I cast
    A wishful glance upon the seasons past,
And think how different was the happy tide,
When thou, with looks of love, wert smiling by my side.

WILLIAM COWPER.

1731—1800.

In 1749, Cowper entered the office of Mr. Chapman, a solicitor in Southampton Row, with whom he remained three years. His ostensible object was studying law, but his real business was giggling with his fellow clerk, Thurlow, afterwards Lord Chancellor, and making love to his cousin, Theodora Jane, a daughter of his uncle, Ashley Cowper. This young lady and her sister Harriet, the Lady Hesketh of the poet's correspondence, were in the habit of visiting their young kinsman in his chambers, and making giggle with him and his companion. At what stage of their acquaintance the unfledged barrister was first attracted to his fair cousin, we are not told, but it was probably at an early one, for young gentlemen of his age and temperament—he was a melancholy youth of eighteen—are ready to fall in love at the shortest notice. Be this as it may, he loved his cousin, and her influence over him was soon perceptible; he lost his natural bashfulness, spruced up his dress, and endeavoured to shine in conversation. When his uncle became aware of his attachment, he objected to it, basing his objection at first on Cowper's want of means. "If you marry William Cowper, what will you do?" he asked his daughter. "Do?" she answered, "why, wash all day, and ride on the great dog at night." The episode growing serious, he refused his consent, on the ground that marriage was improper between persons so nearly related. Cowper tried to overcome the objection, and continued to meet his cousin; but when he found that she deemed it her duty to obey her father, whose will was unalterable, their interviews ceased, and they never met again. Years afterwards, when his intimacy with Lady Hesketh was renewed, he said to her, "I still look back to the memory of your sister and regret her; but how strange it is, if we were to meet now we should not know each other." It is possible that they might not have known each other then, but it would not have been because his cousin had forgotten him, for she never forgot him. She kept for many a long year the poems that he wrote her in his early days, and only parted with them when she was an old woman, to one who would keep them more securely than she could do. Whether the sight of them reminded her too vividly of her youth, or Cowper's insanity and death affected her too painfully, she never told; but she sent them to a friend with directions not to open them until she was dead. She died unmarried in 1824, and they were published for the first time in 1825. I have glanced through them

—there are some twelve or fourteen in all—and found nothing that seemed worth quoting. They are like most of the love-poems of the last century—imitative, conventional, passionless, written from the head rather than the heart. A lock of hair is begged in one; in another a quarrel is spoken of, and happily as a thing that is past. And these trifles, poor Theodora, are all that remain of thy love! It is sad to think of.

Thirteen years of melancholy, despair, and madness passed, and Cowper found a home at Huntingdon with the Unwins. The family consisted of the Rev. William Unwin, his wife Mary, and a son and daughter: "The most agreeable people imaginable," Cowper wrote to his friend, Joseph Hill, in 1765. "They treat me more like a near relation than a stranger, and their house is always open to me. The old gentleman carries me to Cambridge in his chaise. He is a man of learning and sense, and as simple as Parson Adams. His wife has a very uncommon understanding, has read much to excellent purpose, and is more polite than a duchess." In June, 1767, Mr. Unwin was killed by a fall from his horse. A few months later his widow removed to Olney, and Cowper accompanied her. The connection between the poet and this lady has frequently been commented upon by his biographers, who cannot quite make up their minds whether he loved her, or not. The relation was a subject of gossip at the time, some going so far as to say that he was married to her, which he flatly denied. It is said by one of his biographers that he intended to marry her, and repeatedly declared that if he entered into a church again, it would be for the purpose of making her his wife. Southey scouts the idea, and insists upon it that the relation was a friendly one, and nothing more. My own opinion is that Cowper loved Mrs. Unwin, or fancied that he did so, but was prevented from marrying her by the return of his madness, or her disinclination to enter again into the bonds of matrimony, or some other reason equally valid. But this is mere conjecture. It is enough for us to know that they were not married, and that the tie which bound them together, whatever it may have been, was an innocent and happy one. They were probably necessary to each other. At any rate, Mrs. Unwin was necessary to Cowper, especially in his hours of despondency and gloom. She watched him with the skill of a physician, and the tenderness of a mother, and it was to her that he owed some of the brightest years of his life. She incited him to write, suggesting to him the subjects of some of his most admired poems. During his nineteen years' residence at Olney with her, he dawned upon the world as a poet, by the publication of his first volume of poems, wrote "The Task," and translated the greater part of Homer. In November, 1786, they removed to Weston, where Mrs. Unwin was struck with paralysis, and where, in the autumn of 1793, Cowper wrote the poem which I have quoted. Hayley visited them at this place, and perceived the approach of the storm which finally wrecked the poet's intellect. "There was something indescribable," he says, "in his appearance, which led me to apprehend that, without some signal event in his favour to reanimate his spirits, they would gradually sink into hopeless dejection. The state of his aged, infirm companion afforded additional ground for increasing solicitude. Her cheerful and beneficent spirit could hardly resist her own accumulated maladies, so far as to preserve ability sufficient to watch over the tender health of him, whom she had watched and guarded so long." In 1796, they removed to East Dereham, in Norfolk, where, on the 17th of December, Mrs. Unwin died, in the seventy-second year of her age. Cowper, who was in one of his fits of insanity, was aware that her dissolution was expected, and when the servant opened his window, on the morning of the day she died, he said to her, "Sally, is there life above stairs?" He visited her bedside that morning as usual, and returning to his room, desired his relative, Mr. Johnson, to read to him. The book was Miss Burney's "CAMILLA." Mr. Johnson read a few pages, when he was beckoned from the room, and informed that all was over. When he returned, Cowper did not ask why he had been called out, so he told him that Mrs. Unwin had breathed her last. It did not seem to move him, and the reading proceeded as before. A few hours later he said that he was sure she was not dead, but would come to life in the grave, and be suffocated on his account. As he seemed to wish to see her, Mr. Johnson led him into her chamber. At first he fancied that he saw her stir, but on looking more closely he saw that she was indeed dead, and flung himself to the other side of the room with a passionate burst of feeling. He soon grew calm, and when he had descended the stairs, asked for a glass of wine, and from that moment never mentioned her name, nor spoke of her again.

TO MARY.

The twentieth year is well nigh past
Since first our sky was overcast;
Ah, would that this might be the last!
My Mary!

Thy spirits have a fainter flow,
I see thee daily weaker grow;
'Twas my distress that brought thee low,
My Mary!

Thy needles, once a shining store,
For my sake restless heretofore,
Now rust disused, and shine no more;
My Mary!

For though thou gladly wouldst fulfil
The same kind office for me still,
Thy sight now seconds not thy will,
My Mary!

But well thou play'dst the housewife's part,
And all thy threads with magic art
Have wound themselves about this heart,
My Mary!

Thy indistinct expressions seem
Like language uttered in a dream;
Yet me they charm, whate'er the theme,
My Mary!

Thy silver locks, once auburn bright,
Are still more lovely in my sight
Than golden beams of orient light,
My Mary!

For could I view nor them, nor thee,
What sight worth seeing could I see?
The sun would rise in vain for me,
My Mary!

Partakers of thy sad decline,
Thy hands their little force resign;
Yet gently pressed, press gently mine,
My Mary!

Such feebleness of limbs thou provest,
That now at every step thou movest
Upheld by two; yet still thou lovest,
My Mary!

And still to love, though pressed with ill,
In wintry age to feel no chill,
With me is to be lovely still,
My Mary!

But ah! by constant heed I know,
How oft the sadness that I show
Transforms thy smiles to looks of woe,
My Mary!

And should my future lot be cast
With much resemblance of the past,
Thy worn-out heart will break at last,
My Mary!

THOMAS CAMPBELL.

1777—1844.

THE Caroline of this poem was the daughter of a clergyman of Inverary, whom Campbell met at Sunipol, in the Isle of Mull, in the summer of 1795. She was on a visit at the house of one of his relatives, with whom he was then lodging, and being about his own age, young, beautiful, and accomplished, he fell to admiring her, and writing verses in her praise. They spent the summer together pleasantly, and parted early in autumn, each with a memorial of their meeting, she with the manuscript of some of his poems, and he with her image in his fancy. They met again at Inverary in the following summer, but nothing came of it, except the second part of Campbell's poem, which was written at that time. He devoted himself to poetry, and she was shortly after married to a certain Thomas W——, Esq., of Sterling.

CAROLINE.

PART I.

I'll bid the hyacinth to blow,
I'll teach my grotto green to be;
And sing my true love, all below
The holly bower and myrtle tree.

There all his wild-wood sweets to bring,
The sweet South wind shall wander by,
And with the music of his wing
Delight my rustling canopy.

Come to my close and clustering bower,
Thou spirit of a milder clime,

Fresh with the dews of fruit and flower,
    Of mountain heath, and moory thyme.

With all thy rural echoes come,
    Sweet comrade of the rosy day,
Wafting the wild bee's gentle hum,
    Or cuckoo's plaintive roundelay.

Where'er thy morning breath has played,
    Whatever isles of ocean fanned,
Come to my blossom-woven shade,
    Thou wandering wind of fairy-land.

For sure from some enchanted isle,
    Where Heaven and Love their sabbath hold,
Where pure and happy spirits smile,
    Of beauty's fairest, brightest mould:

From some green Eden of the deep,
    Where Pleasure's sigh alone is heaved,
Where tears of rapture lovers weep,
    Endeared, undoubting, undeceived:

From some sweet Paradise afar,
    Thy music wanders, distant, lost,
Where Nature lights her leading star,
    And love is never, never crossed.

O gentle gale of Eden bowers,
    If back thy rosy feet should roam,
To revel with the cloudless Hours
    In Nature's more propitious home,

Name to thy loved Elysian groves,
    That o'er enchanted spirits twine,
A fairer form than Cherub loves,
    And let the name be Caroline.

CAROLINE.

PART II.

TO THE EVENING STAR.

Gem of the crimson-coloured Even,
Companion of retiring Day,
Why at the closing gates of Heaven,
Belovéd star, dost thou delay?

So fair thy pensile beauty burns,
When soft the tear of twilight flows;
So due thy plighted love returns,
To chambers brighter than the rose:

To Peace, to Pleasure, and to Love,
So kind a star thou seem'st to be,
Sure some enamoured orb above
Descends and burns to meet with thee.

Thine is the breathing, blushing hour,
When all unheavenly passions fly,
Chased by the soul-subduing power
Of Love's delicious witchery.

O sacred to the fall of day,
Queen of propitious stars, appear,
And early rise, and long delay,
When Caroline herself is here!

Shine on her chosen green resort,
Whose trees the sunward summit crown,
And wanton flowers, that well may court
An angel's feet to tread them down.

Shine on her sweetly-scented road,
    Thou star of evening's purple dome,
That lead'st the nightingale abroad,
    And guid'st the pilgrim to his home.

Shine where my charmer's sweeter breath
    Embalms the soft exhaling dew,
Where dying winds a sigh bequeath,
    To kiss the cheek of rosy hue.

Where winnowed by the gentle air,
    Her silken tresses darkly flow,
And fall upon her brow so fair,
    Like shadows on the mountain snow.

Thus, ever thus, at day's decline,
    In converse sweet, to wander far,
O bring with thee my Caroline,
    And thou shalt be my Ruling Star.

SONG.

Withdraw not yet those lips and fingers,
    Whose touch to mine is rapture's spell;
Life's joy for us a moment lingers,
    And death seems in the word—Farewell.
The hour that bids us part and go,
It sounds not yet, O no, no, no!

Time, whilst I gaze upon thy sweetness,
    Flies like a courser nigh the goal;
To-morrow where shall be his fleetness,
    When thou art parted from my soul?
Our hearts shall beat, our tears shall flow,
But not together, no, no, no!

CHARLES LAMB.

1775—1834.

There were two tragedies in the life of Charles Lamb, neither of which were known in his life-time, except to his dearest friends—the insanity of his sister, and his disappointment in love. We know all about the first, now that the actors have gone—we understand the shadow on his gentle spirit, now that the curtain has fallen—but the last has forever escaped us, melting away like a vapour, or the ghost of a dream at daybreak. We only know that he was in love, in 1795 or '6, and that he suppressed his love, like the brave good man that he was, for the sake of his unfortunate sister, who needed all his care. He affected to consider it a folly, when it was past, and went on his way as if it had never been. Why should he regret it? He had his desk at the India House by day, and at night a cosy fireside and his beloved books. He had Coleridge, whom he revered and loved, and many a night they spent together in the little smoky room at the Salutation and Cat, beguiling the cares of life with poetry. He had Mary too, so cheery and companionable, when she was well, so wretched when she was ill—when she felt her insanity coming on! No, he never regretted it!

Dear Charles Lamb! many a man has been sainted ere now, for not a tythe of thy virtues.

Methinks how dainty sweet it were, reclined
Beneath the vast outstretching branches high
Of some old wood, in careless sort to lie,
Nor of the busier scene we left behind
Aught envying. And O, Anna, mild-eyed maid!
Belovéd! I were well content to play
With thy free tresses all a summer's day,
Losing the time beneath the greenwood shade.
Or we might sit and tell some tender tale
Of faithful vows repaid by cruel scorn,

A tale of true love, or of friend forgot;
And I would teach thee, lady, how to rail
In gentle sort on those who practise not
Or love or pity, though of woman born.

Was it some sweet device of fairy
That mocked my steps with many a lonely glade,
And fancied wanderings with a fair-haired maid?
Have these things been? Or what rare witchery,
Impregning with delights the charméd air,
Enlighted up the semblance of a smile
In those fine eyes? Methought they spake the while
Soft soothing things, which might enforce despair
To drop the murdering knife, and let go by
His foul resolve. And does the lonely glade
Still court the footsteps of the fair-haired maid?
Still in her locks the gales of summer sigh?
While I, forlorn, do wander reckless where,
And 'mid my wanderings meet no Anna there.

When last I roved these winding wood-walks green,
Green winding walks, and shady pathways sweet,
Ofttimes would Anna seek the silent scene,
Shrouding her beauties in the lone retreat.
No more I hear her footsteps in the shade:
Her image only in these pleasant ways
Meets me self-wandering, where in happier days
I held free converse with the fair-haired maid.
I passed the little cottage which she loved,
The cottage which did once my all contain;
It spake of days which ne'er must come again,
Spake to my heart, and much my heart was moved.
"Now fair befall thee, gentle maid!" said I,
And from the cottage turned me with a sigh.

WILLIAM GIFFORD.

1756–1826.

["*Baviad and Mæviad.*" 1797.]

THE GRAVE OF ANNA.

I WISH I was where Anna lies,
    For I am sick of lingering here;
And every hour affection cries,
    Go and partake her humble bier.

I wish I could! For when she died,
    I lost my all; and life has proved
Since that sad hour a dreary void;
    A waste unlovely and unloved.

But who, when I am turned to clay,
    Shall duly to her grave repair,
And pluck the ragged moss away,
    And weeds that have no business there?

And who with pious hand shall bring
    The flowers she cherished, snowdrops cold,
And violets that unheeded spring,
    To scatter o'er her hallowed mould?

And who, while memory loves to dwell
Upon her name forever dear,
Shall feel his heart with passion swell,
And pour the bitter, bitter tear?

I did it; and would fate allow
Should visit still, should still deplore;
But health and strength have left me now,
And I, alas! can weep no more.

Take then, sweet maid, this simple strain,
The last I offer at thy shrine;
Thy grave must then undecked remain,
And all thy memory fade with mine.

And can thy soft persuasive look,
Thy voice that might with music vie,
Thy air that every gazer took,
Thy matchless eloquence of eye;

Thy spirits frolicsome as good,
Thy courage by no ills dismayed,
Thy patience by no wrongs subdued,
Thy gay good-humour, can they fade?

Perhaps: but sorrow dims my eye;
Cold turf, which I no more must view,
Dear name, which I no more must sigh,
A long, a last, a sad adieu!

Genevieve.

New York: Derby & Jackson.

SAMUEL TAYLOR COLERIDGE.

1772—1834.

LOVE.

ALL thoughts, all passions, all delights,
Whatever stirs this mortal frame,
All are but ministers of Love,
        And feed his sacred flame.

Oft in my waking dreams do I
Live o'er again that happy hour,
When midway on the mount I lay
        Beside the ruined tower.

The moonshine, stealing o'er the scene,
Had blended with the lights of eve;
And she was there, my hope, my joy,
        My own dear Genevieve!

She leaned against the arméd man,
The statue of the arméd knight;
She stood and listened to my lay,
        Amid the lingering light.

Few sorrows hath she of her own,
My hope, my joy, my Genevieve!
She loves me best, whene'er I sing,
        The songs that make her grieve.

I played a soft and doleful air,
I sang an old and moving story;
An old rude song, that suited well
That ruin wild and hoary.

She listened with a flitting blush,
With downcast eyes and modest grace;
For well she knew I could not choose
But gaze upon her face.

I told her of the Knight that wore
Upon his shield a burning brand;
And that for ten long years he wooed
The Lady of the Land.

I told her how he pined: and ah!
The deep, the low, the pleading tone
With which I sang another's love,
Interpreted my own.

She listened with a flitting blush,
With downcast eyes and modest grace;
And she forgave me that I gazed
Too fondly on her face!

But when I told the cruel scorn
That crazed that bold and lovely Knight,
And that he crossed the mountain-woods,
Nor rested day nor night;

That sometimes from the savage den,
And sometimes from the darksome shade,
And sometimes starting up at once
In green and sunny glade,

There came and looked him in the face
An angel beautiful and bright;
And that he knew it was a Fiend,
This miserable Knight!

And that, unknowing what he did,
He leaped amid a murderous band,
And saved from outrage worse than death
The Lady of the Land;

And how she wept, and clasped his knees;
And how she tended him in vain,
And ever strove to expiate
The scorn that crazed his brain;

And that she nursed him in a cave;
And how his madness went away,
When on the yellow forest-leaves
A dying man he lay;

His dying words—but when I reached
That tenderest strain of all the ditty,
My faltering voice and pausing harp
Disturbed her soul with pity!

All impulses of soul and sense
Had thrilled my guileless Genevieve;
The music and the doleful tale,
The rich and balmy eve;

And hopes, and fears that kindle hope,
An undistinguishable throng,
And gentle wishes long subdued,
Subdued and cherished long!

She wept with pity and delight,
She blushed with love, and virgin shame;
And like the murmur of a dream,
I heard her breathe my name!

Her bosom heaved, she stepped aside,
As conscious of my look she stept,
Then suddenly, with timorous eye,
She fled to me and wept.

She half inclosed me with her arms,
She pressed me with a meek embrace;
And, bending back her head, looked up,
And gazed upon my face.

'Twas partly love, and partly fear,
And partly 't was a bashful art,
That I might rather feel, than see,
The swelling of her heart.

I calmed her fears, and she was calm,
And told her love with virgin pride;
And so I won my Genevieve,
My bright and beauteous Bride.

1797.

SOMETHING CHILDISH, BUT VERY NATURAL.

WRITTEN IN GERMANY.

If I had but two little wings,
And were a little feathery bird,
To you I'd fly, my dear!
But thoughts like these are idle things,
And I stay here.

But in my sleep to you I fly:
I'm always with you in my sleep!
The world is all one's own.
But then one wakes, and where am I?
All, all alone.

Sleep stays not, though a monarch bids;
So I love to wake ere break of day:
For though my sleep be gone,
Yet while 'tis dark, one shuts one's lids,
And still dreams on.

1798–9.

WILLIAM WORDSWORTH.

1770—1850.

STRANGE fits of passion have I known:
And I will dare to tell,
But in the Lover's ear alone,
What once to me befell.

When she I loved looked every day
Fresh as a rose in June,
I to her cottage bent my way,
Beneath an evening moon.

Upon the moon I fixed my eye,
All over the wide lea;
With quickening pace my horse drew nigh
Those paths so dear to me.

And now we reached the orchard-plot;
And, as we climbed the hill,
The sinking moon to Lucy's cot
Came near, and nearer still.

In one of those sweet dreams I slept,
Kind Nature's gentlest boon!
And all the while my eyes I kept
On the descending moon.

My horse moved on; hoof after hoof
He raised, and never stopped:
When down behind the cottage roof,
At once, the bright moon dropped.

What fond and wayward thoughts will slide
Into a Lover's head!
"O mercy!" to myself I cried,
"If Lucy should be dead!"

1799.

She dwelt among the untrodden ways
Beside the springs of Dove,
A maid whom there were none to praise,
And very few to love:

A violet by a mossy stone,
Half hidden from the eye;
Fair as a star, when only one
Is shining in the sky.

She lived unknown, and few could know
When Lucy ceased to be;
But she is in her grave, and O,
The difference is to me!

1799.

I travelled among unknown men,
In lands beyond the sea;
Nor, England! did I know till then
What love I bore to thee.

'T is past, that melancholy dream!
Nor will I quit thy shore
A second time; for still I seem
To love thee more and more.

Among thy mountains did I feel
    The joy of my desire;
And she I cherished turned her wheel
    Beside an English fire.

Thy mornings showed, thy nights concealed,
    The bowers where Lucy played;
And thine too is the last green field
    That Lucy's eyes surveyed.

1799.

She was a Phantom of delight
When first she gleamed upon my sight;
A lovely Apparition, sent
To be a moment's ornament;
Her eyes as stars of Twilight fair;
Like Twilight's, too, her dusky hair;
But all things else about her drawn
From May-time and the cheerful Dawn;
A dancing Shape, an Image gay,
To haunt, to startle, and waylay.

I saw her upon nearer view,
A Spirit, yet a Woman too!
Her household motions light and free,
And steps of virgin liberty;
A countenance in which did meet
Sweet records, promises as sweet;
A Creature not too bright or good
For human nature's daily food;
For transient sorrows, simple wiles,
Praise, blame, love, kisses, tears, and smiles.

And now I see with eye serene
The very pulse of the machine;
A Being breathing thoughtful breath,
A Traveller between life and death;

The reason firm, the temperate will,
Endurance, foresight, strength, and skill;
A perfect Woman, nobly planned,
To warn, to comfort, and command;
And yet a Spirit still, and bright
With something of angelic light.

1804.

A COMPLAINT.

There is a change,—and I am poor;
Your love hath been, nor long ago,
A fountain at my fond heart's door,
Whose only business was to flow;
And flow it did; not taking heed
Of its own bounty, or my need.

What happy moments did I count!
Blessed was I then all bliss above!
Now, for that consecrated fount
Of murmuring, sparkling, living love,
What have I? Shall I dare to tell?
A comfortless and hidden well.

A well of love,—it may be deep,
I trust it is,—and never dry:
What matter, if the waters sleep
In silence and obscurity?
Such change, and at the very door
Of my fond heart, hath made me poor.

1806.

JAMES MONTGOMERY.

1771–1854.

HANNAH.

AT fond sixteen my roving heart
Was pierced by Love's delightful dart;
Keen transport throbbed through every vein,
I never felt so sweet a pain!

Where circling woods embowered the glade,
I met the dear romantic maid:
I stole her hand—it shrunk—but no;
I would not let my captive go.

With all the fervency of youth,
While passion told the tale of truth,
I marked my Hannah's downcast eye;
'Twas kind, but beautifully shy:

Not with a warmer, purer ray,
The sun, enamoured, wooes young May;
Nor May, with softer maiden grace,
Turns from the sun her blushing face.

But, swifter than the frighted dove,
Fled the gay morning of my love;
Ah! that so bright a morn, so soon
Should vanish in so dark a noon!

The angel of Affliction rose,
And in his grasp a thousand woes;
He poured his vial on my head,
And all the heaven of rapture fled.

Yet, in the glory of my pride
I stood, and all his wrath defied!
I stood, though whirlwinds shook my brain,
And lightnings cleft my soul in twain.

I shunned my nymph; and knew not why
I durst not meet her gentle eye;
I shunned her, for I could not bear
To marry her to my despair.

Yet, sick at heart with hope delayed,
Oft the dear image of that maid
Glanced, like the rainbow, o'er my mind,
And promised happiness behind.

The storm blew o'er, and in my breast
The halcyon Peace rebuilt her nest:
The storm blew o'er, and clear and mild
The sea of Youth and Pleasure smiled.

'T was on the merry morn of May,
To Hannah's cot I took my way:
My eager hopes were on the wing,
Like swallows sporting in the Spring.

Then as I climbed the mountains o'er,
I lived my wooing days once more;
And fancy sketched my marriage lot,
My wife, my children, and my cot.

I saw the village steeple rise,
My soul sprang, sparkling, in my eyes:
The rural bells rang sweet and clear,
My fond heart listened in mine ear.

I reached the hamlet: all was gay;
I love a rustic holiday:
I met a wedding, stepped aside;
It passed—my Hannah was the bride!

There is a grief that cannot feel;
It leaves a wound that will not heal;
My heart grew cold, it felt not then:
When shall it cease to feel again?

1801.

ROBERT BLOOMFIELD.

1766—1823.

["*Rural Tales, Ballads and Songs.*" 1802.]

ROSY HANNAH.

A spring, o'erhung with many a flower,
The gray sand dancing in its bed,
Embanked beneath a hawthorn bower,
Sent forth its waters near my head:
A rosy lass approached my view;
I caught her blue eye's modest beam:
The stranger nodded "How-d' ye-do?"
And leaped across the infant stream.

The water heedless passed away:
With me her glowing image stayed:
I strove, from that auspicious day,
To meet and bless the lovely maid.
I met her where beneath our feet
Through downy moss the wild thyme grew;
Nor moss elastic, flowers though sweet,
Matched Hannah's cheek of rosy hue.

I met her where the dark woods wave,
And shaded verdure skirts the plain;
And when the pale moon rising gave
New glories to her rising train.

From her sweet cot upon the moor,
Our plighted vows to heaven are flown:
Truth made me welcome at her door,
And rosy Hannah is my own.

["*Remains.*" 1824.]

TO HIS WIFE.

I rise, dear Mary, from the soundest rest,
A wandering, way-worn, musing, singing guest.
I claim the privilege of hill and plain;
Mine are the woods, and all that they contain;
The unpolluted gale, which sweeps the glade;
All the cool blessings of the solemn shade;
Health, and the flow of happiness sincere;
Yet there's one wish—I wish that thou wert here;
Free from the trammels of domestic care,
With me these dear autumnal sweets to share;
To share my heart's ungovernable joy,
And keep the birthday of our poor lame boy.
Ah! that's a tender string! Yet since I find
That scenes like these can soothe the harassed mind,
Trust me, 't would set thy jaded spirits free
To wander thus through vales and woods with me.
Thou know'st how much I love to steal away
From noise, from uproar, and the blaze of day;
With double transport would my heart rebound
To lead thee where the clustering nuts are found;
No toilsome efforts would our task demand,
For the brown treasure stoops to meet the hand.
Round the tall hazel beds of moss appear
In green swards nibbled by the forest deer,
Sun, and alternate shade; while o'er our heads
The cawing rook his glossy pinions spreads:
The noisy jay, his wild-woods dashing through;
The ring-dove's chorus, and the rustling bough;

The far-resounding gate; the kite's shrill scream;
The distant ploughman's halloo to his team.
This is the chorus to my soul so dear;
It would delight thee too, wert thou but here:
For we might talk of home, and muse o'er days
Of sad distress, and Heaven's mysterious ways;
Our checkered fortunes with a smile retrace,
And build new hopes upon our infant race:
Pour our thanksgivings forth, and weep the while;
Or pray for blessings on our native isle.
But vain the wish! Mary, thy sighs forbear,
Nor grudge the pleasures which thou canst not share:
Make home delightful, kindly wish for me,
And I'll leave hills, and dales, and woods for thee.

WHITTLEBURY FOREST, *Sept.* 16, 1804.

ALLAN CUNNINGHAM.

1784—1842.

["*Remains of Nithsdale and Galloway Song.*" 1810.]

BONNIE LADY ANN.

THERE 's kames o' honey 'tween my luve's lips,
  An' gold amang her hair,
Her breasts are lapt in a holie veil,
  Nae mortal een look there.
What lips dare kiss, or what hand dare touch,
  Or what arm o' luve dare span,
The honey lips, the creamy palm,
  Or the waist o' Lady Ann!

She kisses the lips o' her bonnie red rose,
  Wat wi' the blobs o' dew;
But nae gentle lip, nor semple lip,
  Maun touch her Lady mou.
But a broider'd belt, wi' a buckle o' gold,
  Her jimpy waist maun span;
O she 's an armfu' fit for heaven,
  My bonnie Lady Ann!

Her bower casement is latticed wi' flowers,
  Tied up wi' silver thread,
An' comely sits she in the midst,
  Men's longing een to feed.

She waves the ringlets frae her cheek,
Wi' her milky, milky han',
An' her cheeks seem touch'd wi' the finger o' God,
My bonnie Lady Ann!

The morning cloud is tassell'd wi' gold,
Like my luve's broider'd cap,
An' on the mantle which my luve wears
Is monie a golden drap.
Her bonnie eebrow 's a holie arch
Cast by no earthlie han';
An' the breath o' Heaven 's atween the lips
O' my bonnie Lady Ann!

I am her father's gardener lad,
An' poor, poor is my fa';
My auld mither gets my sair-won fee,
Wi' fatherless bairnies twa.
My een are bauld, they dwall on a place
Where I darena mint my han';
But I water, and tend, and kiss the flowers
O' my bonnie Lady Ann.

THE POET'S BRIDAL-DAY SONG.

"This rural beauty, who caused such terrible devastation, and who, it is said, first made a poet of her lover, became afterwards his wife; and in her matronly character, she inspired that beautiful little effusion of conjugal tenderness, 'The Poet's Bridal Song.' When first published, it was almost universally copied, and committed to memory; and Allan Cunningham may not only boast that he has woven a wreath to 'grace his Jean,'

'While rivers flow and woods are green,'

but that he has given the sweet wife, seated among her children in sedate and matronly loveliness, an interest even beyond that which belongs to the young girl he has described with raven locks and cheeks of cream, driving rustic admirers to despair, or lingering with her love at eve,

'Amid the falling dew
When looks were fond, and words were few!'

Such is the charm of affection, and truth, and moral feeling, carried straight into the heart by poetry!"

MRS. JAMESON'S LOVES OF THE POETS.

O, my love's like the steadfast sun,
Or streams that deepen as they run;
Nor hoary hairs, nor forty years,
Nor moments between sighs and tears,
Nor nights of thought, nor days of pain,
Nor dreams of glory dreamed in vain,
Nor mirth, nor sweetest song which flows
To sober joys and soften woes,
Can make my heart or fancy flee
One moment, my sweet wife, from thee.

Even while I muse, I see thee sit
In maiden bloom and matron wit,
Fair, gentle as when first I sued,
Ye seem, but of sedater mood;
Yet my heart leaps as fond for thee
As when, beneath Arbigland tree,
We stayed and wooed, and thought the moon
Set on the sea an hour too soon;
Or lingered 'mid the falling dew,
When looks were fond and words were few.

Though I see smiling at thy feet
Five sons and ae fair daughter sweet;
And time, and care, and birth-time woes
Have dimmed thine eye, and touched thy rose,
To thee, and thoughts of thee, belong
All that charms me of tale or song;
When words come down like dews unsought,
With gleams of deep enthusiast thought,
And fancy in her heaven flies free,
They come, my love, they come from thee.

O, when more thought we gave of old
To silver than some give to gold;

'T was sweet to sit and ponder o'er
What things should deck our humble bower!
'T was sweet to pull in hope with thee
The golden fruit from Fortune's tree;
And sweeter still to choose and twine
A garland for these locks of thine,
A song-wreath which may grace my Jean,
While rivers flow and woods are green.

At times there come, as come there ought,
Grave moments of sedater thought,
When Fortune frowns, nor lends our night
One gleam of her inconstant light;
And Hope, that decks the peasant's bower,
Shines like the rainbow through the shower,
O, then I see, while seated nigh,
A mother's heart shine in thine eye,
And proud resolve and purpose meek,
Speak of thee more than words can speak:
I think this wedded wife of mine
The best of all that's not divine.

JAMES HOGG.

1772—1835.

GANG TO THE BRAKENS WI' ME.

I 'LL sing of yon glen of red heather,
An' a dear thing that ca's it her hame,
Wha 's a' made o' love-life thegither,
Frae the tie o' the shoe to the kaime;
Love beckons in every sweet motion,
Commanding due homage to gie;
But the shrine o' my dearest devotion
Is the bend o' her bonny eebree.

I fleech'd an' I pray'd the dear lassie
To gang to the brakens wi' me;
But, though neither lordly nor saucy,
Her answer was, "Laith wad I be!
I neither hae father nor mither,
Sage counsel or caution to gie;
An' prudence has whisper'd me never
To gang to the brakens wi' thee."

Dear lassie, how can ye upbraid me,
An' try your ain love to beguile?
For ye are the richest young lady
That ever gaed o'er the kirk-stile.
Your smile, that is blither than ony,
The bend o' your cheerfu' eebree,

An' the sweet blinks o' love there sae bonny,
Are five hunder thousand to me!

She turn'd her around, an' said, smiling,
While the tear in her blue eye shone clear,
"You 're welcome, kind sir, to your mailing,
For, O, you hae valued it dear:
Gae make out the lease, do not linger,
Let the parson indorse the decree;
And then, for a wave o' your finger,
I 'll gang to the brakens wi' thee!"

There 's joy in the bright blooming feature,
When love lurks in every young line;
There 's joy in the beauties of nature,
There 's joy in the dance and the wine:
But there 's a delight will ne'er perish,
'Mang pleasures all fleeting an' vain,
And that is to love and to cherish
The fond little heart that 's our ain!

PERCY BYSSHE SHELLEY.

1792—1822.

"SHELLEY, like Byron, knew early what it was to love—almost all great poets have. It was in the summer of this year (1809) that he became acquainted with our cousin, Harriet Grove. Living in distant counties, they then met for the first time, since they had been children, at Field-place, where she was on a visit. She was born, I think, in the same year with himself.

'She was like him in lineaments—her eyes,
Her hair, her features, they said were like to his,
But softened all and tempered into beauty.'

After so long an interval, I still remember Miss Grove; and when I call to mind all the women I have ever seen, I know of none that surpassed, or that could compete with her. She was like one of Shakspeare's women—like some Madonna of Raphael. Shelley, in a fragment written many years after, seems to have had her in his mind's eye, when he writes:

'They were two cousins, almost like to twins,
Except that from the catalogue of sins
Nature had razed their love, which could not be,
But in dissevering their nativity;
And so they grew together like two flowers
Upon one stem, which the same beams and showers
Lull or awaken in the purple prime.'

Young as they were, it is not likely that they had entered into a formal engagement with each other, or that their parents looked upon their attachment, if it were mentioned, as any other than an intimacy natural to such near relations, or the mere fancy of a moment; and after they parted, though they corresponded regularly, there was nothing in the circumstance that called for observation. Shelley's love, however, had taken deep root, as proved by the dedication to Queen Mab, written in the following year."

MEDWIN'S LIFE OF SHELLEY.

TO HARRIET.

Whose is the love that, gleaming through the world,
Wards off the poisonous arrow of its scorn?
    Whose is the warm and partial praise,
    Virtue's most sweet reward?

Beneath whose looks did my reviving soul
Riper in truth and virtuous daring grow?
    Whose eyes have I gazed fondly on,
    And loved mankind the more?

Harriet! on thine: thou wert my purer mind;
Thou wert the inspiration of my song;
    Thine are those early wilding flowers,
    Though garlanded by me.

Then press into thy breast this pledge of love,
And know, though time may change and years may roll,
    Each floweret gathered in my heart,
    It consecrates to thine.

TO MARY.

This poem—the dedication to "The Revolt of Islam"—was written in the autumn of 1817, at Marlow, in Buckinghamshire. It is addressed to Mrs. Shelley, *née* Mary Godwin, the daughter of William Godwin and Mary Wolstonecroft. Shelley met her in London about the time of his separation from his first wife, Harriet Westbrooke, and believing that he had found his soul's affinity, persuaded her to elope with him to the Continent. They started from Dover on the 28th of July, 1814, and crossing over to France in a small boat, proceeded to Neufchatel in Switzerland, where they remained a few days, and then returned to England. They lived together till the suicide of Shelley's wife, in November, 1816, when they were made man and wife according to the usages of the church. Their after history—Shelley's melancholy death by drowning in the Bay of Spezia, and Mrs. Shelley's successful literary career—is too well known to need recapitulation in this place.

So now my summer-task is ended, Mary,
And I return to thee, mine own heart's home;
As to his Queen some victor Knight of Faëry,
Earning bright spoils for her enchanted dome;
Nor thou disdain, that ere my fame become
A star among the stars of mortal night,
If it indeed may cleave its natal gloom,
Its doubtful promise thus I would unite
With thy belovéd name, thou Child of love and light.

The toil which stole from thee so many an hour
Is ended—and the fruit is at thy feet!
No longer where the woods to frame a bower
With interlacéd branches mix and meet,
Or where the sound like many voices sweet,
Water-falls leap among wild islands green,
Which framed for my lone boat a lone retreat
Of moss-grown trees and weeds, shall I be seen:
But beside thee, where still my heart has ever been.

Thoughts of great deeds were mine, dear Friend, when first
The clouds which wrap this world from youth did pass.
I do remember well the hour which burst
My spirit's sleep: A fresh May-dawn it was,
When I walked forth upon the glittering grass,
And wept, I knew not why: until there rose
From the near school-room, voices, that, alas!
Were but one echo from a world of woes,
The harsh and grating strife of tyrants and their foes.

And then I clasped my hands and looked around,
But none was near to mock my streaming eyes,
Which poured their warm drops on the sunny ground,
So without shame, I spake: "I will be wise,
And just, and free, and mild, if in me lies
Such power, for I grow weary to behold
The selfish and the mean still tyrannize

Without reproach or check." I then controlled
My tears, my heart grew calm, and I was meek and bold.

And from that hour did I with earnest thought
Heap knowledge from forbidden mines of lore;
Yet nothing that my tyrants knew or taught
I cared to learn, but from that secret store
Wrought linkéd armour for my soul, before
It might walk forth to war among mankind;
Thus power and hope were strengthened more and more
Within me, till there came upon my mind
A sense of loneliness, a thirst with which I pined.

Alas, that love should be a blight and snare
To those who seek all sympathies in one!
Such once I sought in vain; then black despair,
The shadow of a starless night, was thrown
Over the world in which I moved alone;
Yet never found I one not false to me,
Hard hearts, and cold, like weights of icy stone,
Which crushed and withered mine, that could not be
Aught but a lifeless clog, until revived by thee.

Thou Friend, whose presence on my wintry heart
Fell, like bright Spring upon some herbless plain,
How beautiful and calm and free thou wert
In thy young wisdom, when the mortal chain
Of Custom thou didst burst and rend in twain,
And walked as free as light the clouds among,
Which many an envious slave then breathed in vain
From his dim dungeon, and my spirit sprung
To meet thee from the woes which had begirt it long.

No more alone through the world's wilderness,
Although I trod the paths of high intent,
I journeyed now: no more companionless,
Where solitude is like despair, I went.
There is the wisdom of a stern content

When Poverty can blight the just and good,
When Infamy dares mock the innocent,
And cherished friends turn with the multitude
To trample: this was ours, and we unshaken stood!

Now has descended a serener hour,
And with inconstant fortune, friends return;
Though suffering leaves the knowledge and the power
Which says: Let scorn be not repaid with scorn.
And from thy side two gentle babes are born
To fill our home with smiles, and thus are we
Most fortunate beneath life's beaming morn:
And these delights, and thou, have been to me
The parents of the Song I consecrate to thee.

Is it, that now my inexperienced fingers
But strike the prelude of a loftier strain?
Or, must the lyre on which my spirit lingers
Soon pause in silence, ne'er to sound again,
Though it might shake the Anarch Custom's reign,
And charm the minds of men to Truth's own sway,
Holier than was Amphion's? I would fain
Reply in hope, but I am worn away,
And Death and Love are yet contending for their prey.

And what art thou? I know, but dare not speak:
Time may interpret to his silent years.
Yet in the paleness of thy thoughtful cheek,
And in the light thine ample forehead wears,
And in thy sweetest smiles, and in thy tears,
And in thy gentle speech, a prophecy
Is whispered, to subdue my fondest fears:
And through thine eyes, even in thy soul I see
A lamp of vestal fire burning internally.

They say that thou wert, lovely from thy birth,
Of glorious parents thou aspiring Child:
I wonder not, for One then left this earth

Whose life was like a setting planet mild,
Which clothed thee in the radiance undefiled
Of its departing glory; still her fame
Shines on thee, through the tempests dark and wild
Which shake these latter days; and thou canst claim
The shelter, from thy Sire, of an immortal name.

One voice came forth from many a mighty spirit,
Which was the echo of three thousand years;
And the tumultuous world stood mute to hear it,
As some lone man who in a desert hears
The music of his home: unwonted fears
Fell on the pale oppressors of our race,
And Faith, and Custom, and low-thoughted cares,
Like thunder-stricken dragons, for a space
Left the torn human heart, their food and dwelling-place.

Truth's deathless voice pauses among mankind!
If there must be no response to my cry,
If men must rise and stamp with fury blind
On his pure name who loves them,—thou and I,
Sweet Friend! can look from our tranquillity
Like lamps into the world's tempestuous night,
Two tranquil stars, while clouds are passing by
Which wrap them from the foundering seaman's sight,
That burn from year to year with unextinguished light.

LOVE'S PHILOSOPHY.

The fountains mingle with the river,
And the rivers with the ocean;
The winds of heaven mix forever
With a sweet emotion;
Nothing in the world is single;
All things by a law divine
In one another's being mingle—
Why not I with thine?

See, the mountains kiss high heaven,
    And the waves clasp one another;
No sister flower would be forgiven,
    If it disdained its brother:
And the sunlight clasps the earth,
    And the moonbeams kiss the sea;
What are all these kissings worth,
    If thou kiss not me?

1820

TO ———.

Music, when soft voices die,
Vibrates in the memory;
Odours, when sweet violets sicken,
Live within the sense they quicken.

Rose leaves, when the rose is dead,
Are heaped for the belovéd's bed;
And so thy thoughts, when thou art gone,
Love itself shall slumber on.

1821.

LINES TO AN INDIAN AIR.

I arise from dreams of thee
In the first sweet sleep of night,
When the winds are breathing low,
And the stars are shining bright.
I arise from dreams of thee,
And a spirit in my feet
Has led me—who knows how?
To thy chamber window, sweet!

The wandering airs they faint
On the dark, the silent stream;
The champak odours fail,
Like sweet thoughts in a dream;

The nightingale's complaint,
It dies upon her heart,
As I must die on thine,
O belovéd as thou art!

O, lift me from the grass!
I die, I faint, I fail!
Let thy love in kisses rain
On my lips and eyelids pale.
My cheek is cold and white, alas!
My heart beats loud and fast;
O, press it close to thine again,
Where it will break at last.

1821.

TO ———.

One word is too often profaned
For me to profane it;
One feeling too falsely disdained
For thee to disdain it.
One hope is too like despair
For prudence to smother,
And pity from thee more dear
Than that from another.

I can give not what men call love,
But wilt thou accept not
The worship the heart lifts above,
And the Heavens reject not:
The desire of the moth for the star,
Of the night for the morrow,
The devotion to something afar
From the sphere of our sorrow?

1821.

LORD BYRON.

1788—1824.

MARY CHAWORTH.

Byron spent the summer vacation of 1803 at Newstead Abbey, not as its master, for he was only in his sixteenth year, but as the guest of Lord Grey de Ruthen, who was then its tenant. His ostensible motive for sojourning there, was a romantic attachment to his ancestral home, but his real motive was his attachment to Mary Chaworth, whom he had met in London, sometime before, and who now resided at Annesley, in the neighborhood of Newstead. She belonged to a family which had been at variance with his own, one of his ancestors, a grand-uncle, having slain one of its members in a duel. The feud was not forgotten by Byron, though it seems to have been by the Chaworths, (at any rate, it was not remembered to *his* disadvan tage,) and on his first visits to the family, he used to return to Newstead to sleep, being afraid, he said, of the family pictures at Annesley. He fancied "they had taken a grudge to him on account of the duel, and would come down from their frames at night to haunt him." Poor fellow! he was soon haunted by something more substantial—the image of Mary Chaworth. His time at Annesley, says Moore, was mostly passed in riding with Miss Chaworth and her cousin—sitting in idle reverie, as was his custom, pulling at a handkerchief, or in firing at a door which opens upon the terrace, and which still, I believe, bears the marks of his shots. But his chief delight was in sitting to hear Miss Chaworth play; and the pretty Welsh air, 'Mary Anne,' was (partly, of course, on account of the name) his especial favourite. During all this time he had the pain of knowing that the heart of her he loved was devoted to another; that, as he himself expresses it–

> "Her sighs were not for him; to her he was
> Even as a brother, but no more."

Neither is it, indeed, probable, had her affections been disengaged, that Lord Byron would, at this time, have been selected as the object of them. A seniority of two years gives to a girl, "on the eve of womanhood," an advance into life, with which the boy keeps no proportionate pace. Miss Chaworth looked upon Byron as a mere schoolboy. He was in his manners, too, at that period, rough and odd, and (as I have heard from more than one quarter) by no means popular among girls of his own age. If at any moment, however, he had flattered himself with the hope of being loved by her, a circumstance mentioned in his Memoranda, as one of the most painful of those humiliations to which the defect in his foot had exposed him, must have let the truth in, with dreadful certainty, upon his heart. He either was told of, or heard, Miss Chaworth saying to her maid, "Do you think I could care anything for that lame boy?" This speech, as he himself described it, was like a shot through his heart. Though late at night when he heard it, he instantly darted out of the house, and scarcely knowing whither he ran, never stopped until he found himself at Newstead.

With the summer holidays ended this dream of his youth. He saw Miss Chaworth once more in the succeeding year, and took his last farewell of her (as he himself used to relate) on that hill near Annesley, which, in his poem of "The Dream," he describes so happily as "crowned with a peculiar diadem." No one, he declared, could have told how *much* he felt—for his countenance was calm, and his feelings restrained. "The next time I see you," said he, in parting with her, "I suppose you will be Mrs. Chaworth;" (her husband was to take her family name,) and her answer was, "I hope so."

In the following year, 1805, Miss Chaworth was married to his successful rival, Mr. John Musters; and a person who was present when the first intelligence of the event was communicated to him, thus describes the manner in which he received it: "I was present when he first heard of the marriage. His mother said, 'Byron, I have some news for you.' 'Well, what is it?' 'Take out your handkerchief first, for you will want it.' 'Nonsense.' 'Take out your handkerchief, I say.' He did so, to humour her. 'Miss Chaworth is married.' An expression, very peculiar, impossible to describe, passed over his pale face, and he hurried his handkerchief into his pocket, saying, with an affected air of coldness and nonchalance, 'Is that all?' 'Why, I expected you would have been plunged in grief!' He made no reply, and soon began to talk about something else."

Of the after life of Mary Chaworth I know nothing, but I have somewhere read that she was unhappy in her marriage, as Byron hints in "The Dream." She was in a feeble state of health for several years previous to her death, which took place at Wiverton Hall, in February 1832, in consequence of the alarm and danger to which she had been exposed during the sack of Colwick Hall by a party of rioters from Nottingham.

LADY BYRON.

In September, 1814, Byron proposed to Miss Isabella Milbanke, the only daughter of Sir Ralph Milbanke, of Seaham, in the county of Durham. He became acquainted with her about two years before, and by the advice of his friend, Lady Melbourne, offered himself as her suitor. His proposal was not accepted, but Miss Milbanke assured him of her regard and friendship, and expressed a wish that he should write to her. They corresponded with each other till the summer of 1814, when a friend of Byron's, who stood high in his affections and confidence, observing his unsettled state as a bachelor, advised him seriously to marry ; and after much discussion he consented. The next point for consideration was, who was to be the object of his choice; and while his friend mentioned one lady, he himself named Miss Milbanke. To this, however, his adviser strongly objected, remarking to him, that Miss Milbanke had at present no fortune, and that his embarrassed affairs would not allow him to marry without one; that she was, moreover, a learned lady, which would not at all suit him. In consequence of these representations, he agreed that his friend should write a proposal for him to the other lady named, which was accordingly done; and an answer, containing a refusal, arrived as they were, one morning, sitting together. "You see," said Byron, "that, after all, Miss Milbanke is to be the person; I will write to her." He accordingly wrote on the moment, and, as soon as he had finished, his friend, remonstrating still strongly against his choice, took up the letter, but on reading it over, observed, "Well, really, this is a very pretty letter; it is a pity it should not go. I never read a prettier one." "Then it *shall* go," said Byron, and, on so saying, sealed and sent off, on the instant, this fiat of his fate. This time Miss Milbanke accepted him. They were married at Seaham, on the 2d of January, 1815. The sensations of Byron on the occasion were anything but enviable. He described himself, in his "MEMOIR," as waking, on the morning of his marriage, with the most melancholy reflections, on seeing his wedding suit spread out before him. In the same mood he wandered about the grounds alone, till he was summoned for the ceremony, and joined, for the first time on that day, his bride and her family. He knelt down and repeated the words after the clergyman; but a mist was before his eyes, his thoughts were elsewhere; and he was awakened by the congratulations of the bystanders, to find that he was—married. The same morning the wedded pair left Seaham for Halnaby, another seat of Sir Ralph Milbanke, in the same county. When about to depart, Byron said to the bride, "Miss Milbanke, are you ready?"—a mistake, which the lady's confidential attendant pronounced to be a "bad omen." If the omen was bad, the marriage was worse—a mistake and evil to both, though why it was so is a mystery, which none of Byron's biographers have penetrated It lasted a little more than a year, and ended abruptly by the lady's abandoning her lord. She left London at the latter end of January, 1816, on a visit to her father's house in Leicestershire, and Byron was, in a short time after, to follow her. They parted in the utmost kindness, she wrote him a letter, full of playfulness and affection, on the road; and, immediately on her arrival at Kirkby Mallory, her father wrote to acquaint Byron that she would return to him no more! At the time when he had to stand this unexpected shock, his pecuniary embarrassments, which had been gathering around him during the whole of the last year (there having been no less than eight or nine executions in his house within that period), had arrived at their utmost; and at a moment when, to use his own strong expressions, he was "standing alone on his hearth, with his household gods shivered around him," he was also doomed to receive the startling intelligence, that the wife who had just parted with him in kindness, had parted with him—forever!

The cause, or causes, which led Lady Byron to this singular separation, are not known. Various reasons were assigned for it at the time by Byron's friends, and surmises of all sorts were rife in the minds of his enemies, who were glad of such an opportunity to poison the mind of the public against him, but the true cause was known to neither. Byron himself would not, or could not name it. Perhaps it was, as he said, "too simple to be easily found out."

THE COUNTESS GUICCIOLI.

Byron met the Countess of Guiccioli for the first time at an evening party in Venice in the beginning of April, 1819. He had seen her before, in the previous autumn, shortly after her marriage to Count Guiccioli, but being averse to making new acquaintances, was not introduced to her then; and even now he only suffered an introduction from a desire to please his hostess. He made a profound impression on the heart of the susceptible young Italian girl, and from that evening they met daily as long as she remained in Venice. She departed for Ravenna about the middle of April, stopping on her way at the various palaces of her husband, and writing from each the most passionate letters to Byron. She reached Ravenna in an alarming state of illness, which was increased by the death of her mother; symptoms of consumption began to show themselves, and threatened to hurry her to the grave; she seemed, in short, to be dying, nor could anything revive her but an assurance from Byron that he would soon visit her. He arrived at Ravenna about the 10th of June, and was waited upon by Count Guiccioli, who seems, from the first, to have been the most obliging of husbands. The next day he visited the Countess, who was overjoyed to see him again, and soon began to recover. By the end of August she was able to accompany her husband to his Romagnese estates. Byron remained behind at Bologna, and every day during her absence he used to go to her house, at his usual hour of calling upon her, and sit awhile in her apartments, reading and writing in her books. He would then descend into her garden, and pass whole hours in musing. His meditations were not always of the most agreeable character, for one day when he stood there looking into a fountain in a state of unconscious reverie, the thought of the misery that he might bring upon her, affected him so deeply that he burst into an agony of tears. On one of these occasions he wrote this note on the last page of her copy of "CORINNE:"

"MY DEAR TERESA: I have read this book in your garden; my love, you were absent, or else I could not have read it. It is a favourite book of yours, and the writer was a friend of mine. You will not understand these English words, and *others* will not understand them, which is the reason I have not scrawled them in Italian. But you will recognize the handwriting of him who passionately loved you, and you will divine that, over a book which was yours, he could only think of love. In that word, beautiful in all languages, but most so in yours—*Amor mio*—is comprised my existence here and hereafter. I feel I exist here, and I fear that I shall exist hereafter, to *what* purpose you will decide; my destiny rests with you, and you are a woman, eighteen years of age, and two out of a convent. I wish that you had stayed there, with all my heart, or, at least, that I had never met you in your married state.

"But all this is too late. I love you, and you love me, at least you *say so*, and *act* as if you *did* so, which last is a great consolation in all events. But *I* more than love you, and cannot cease to love you.

"Think of me, sometimes, when the Alps and the ocean divide us—but they never will, unless you *wish* it. "BYRON.

"BOLOGNA, *August* 25, 1819."

The Countess rejoined Byron at Bologna in September, and not being able to return to Ravenna with the Count, for her health was still delicate, he permitted her to go to Venice with Byron. The Venetian physicians ordering her to try the country air, she accompanied Byron to his villa at La Mira, where she remained till November, when her husband came for her. He was, or affected to be, much scandalized by her conduct, and insisted upon her signing certain conditions, regulating her life, morals, etc., and especially her affair with Byron, with whom she was forbidden to communicate in future. She set out for Ravenna, and Byron returned to Venice very much out of spirits, and was on the point of starting for England, when accounts reached him that she was again alarmingly ill. Her separation from him preyed upon her so deeply that her relatives, and even her husband, entreated him to hasten to her. He was soon by her side, the Count being polite enough to rent him a suite of apartments in the Palazzo Guiccioli! They lived together like a happy family till the spring of 1820, when the Count took it into his head to get rid of Byron. The Countess, of course, objected, and a family quarrel was the consequence. He appealed to her relatives, but instead of taking his part, they were furious against him; her father even went so far as to challenge him to mortal combat. "I have given her the best advice," Byron wrote to Moore, on the 24th of May, "viz., to stay with him, pointing out the state of a separated woman, (for the priests won't let lovers live openly together, unless the husband sanctions it,) and making the most exquisite moral reflections, but to no purpose. She says, 'I will stay with him, if he will let you remain with me. It is hard that I should be the only woman in Romagna who is not to have her Amico; but, if not, I will not live with him; and as for the consequences, love, etc., etc., etc.'—you know how females reason on such occasions." "The separation business still continues," he wrote again on the 1st of June, "and all the world are implicated, including priests and cardinals. The public opinion is furious against *him*, because he ought to have cut the matter short *at first*, and not waited twelve months to begin." "The Pope has pronounced *their separation*," he continued on the 13th of July. "The decree came yesterday from Babylon; it was *she* and *her* friends who demanded it, on the grounds of her husband's (the noble Count Cavalier's) extraordinary usage. *He* opposed it with all his might, because of the alimony, which has been assigned, with all her goods, chattels, carriage, etc., to be restored by him. . . . . She returns to her father's house, and I can only see her under great restrictions—such is the custom of the country."

For the subsequent history of the Countess and her noble lover, I refer the reader to Moore's Life of Byron, to which I am indebted for the substance, and in many places the language, of this triple-note. He can trace their whereabouts for himself, and make whatever reflections he pleases: I have none to offer him. I can only say with the Abbot, in "MANFRED:"

> "This should have been a noble creature; he
> Hath all the energy which would have made
> A goodly frame of glorious elements,
> Had they been wisely mingled; as it is,
> It is an awful chaos—light and darkness—
> And mind and dust—and passions and pure thoughts,
> Mixed, and contending without end or order."

MAID OF ATHENS.

Byron arrived at Athens on the 25th of December, 1809, and took lodgings at the house of Theodora Macri, the widow of the English vice-consul. She had three daughters, the eldest of whom, Theresa, was Byron's favourite, and the subject of these charming verses, which were written early in March, 1810, when he was on the point of starting for Constantinople. She married a Scotchman named Black, and is still living at Athens, a hale and handsome old woman.

I have printed the Greek refrain in English characters, for the benefit of the general reader. It means, "*My life, I love you!*"

Maid of Athens, ere we part,
Give, O give me back my heart!
Or, since that has left my breast,
Keep it now, and take the rest!
Hear my vow before I go,
Zoë mou, sas agapo.

By those tresses unconfined,
Wooed by each Ægean wind;
By those lids whose jetty fringe
Kiss thy soft cheeks' blooming tinge;
By those wild eyes like the roe,
Zoë mou, sas agapo.

By that lip I long to taste;
By that zone-encircled waist;

Maid of Athens.

[illegible] & Jackson

By all the token-flowers that tell
What words can never speak so well;
By love's alternate joy and woe,
Zoë mou, sas agapo.

Maid of Athens! I am gone:
Think of me, sweet! when alone.
Though I fly to Istambol,
Athens holds my heart and soul:
Can I cease to love thee? No!
Zoë mou, sas agapo.

TO THYRZA.

Thyrza was a real person, though some of Byron's biographers have doubted the fact. "I have again been shocked with a *death*," he wrote to his friend, Mr. Dallas, on the 11th of October, 1811, "and have lost one very dear to me in happier times; but 'I have almost forgot the taste of grief,' and 'supped full of horrors' till I have become callous, nor have I a tear left for an event which, five years ago, would have bowed down my head to the earth." "I thank you," Mr. Dallas answered on the 27th, "for your confidential communication at the bottom of the stanza which so much delighted me. How truly do I wish that the being to whom that verse now belongs had lived, and lived yours! What your obligations to her would have been in that case is inconceivable."

Without a stone to mark the spot,
And say, what Truth might well have said,
By all, save one, perchance forgot,
Ah! wherefore art thou lowly laid?

By many a shore and many a sea
Divided, yet beloved in vain;
The past, the future fled to thee,
To bid us meet—no, ne'er again!

Could this have been—a word, a look,
That softly said, "We part in peace,"
Had taught my bosom how to brook,
With fainter sighs, thy soul's release.

And didst thou not, since Death for thee
 Prepared a light and pangless dart,
Once long for him thou ne'er shalt see,
 Who held, and holds thee in his heart?

O, who like him had watched thee here?
 Or sadly marked thy glazing eye,
In that dread hour ere death appear,
 When silent sorrow fears to sigh,

Till all was past! But when no more
 'T was thine to reck of human woe,
Affection's heart-drops, gushing o'er,
 Had flowed as fast as now they flow.

Shall they not flow, when many a day
 In these, to me, deserted towers,
Ere called but for a time away,
 Affection's mingling tears were ours?

Ours too the glance none saw beside;
 The smile none else might understand;
The whispered thought of hearts allied,
 The pressure of the thrilling hand;

The kiss, so guiltless and refined,
 That Love each warmer wish forbore;
Those eyes proclaimed so pure a mind,
 Even passion blushed to plead for more;

The tone, that taught me to rejoice,
 When prone, unlike thee, to repine;
The song, celestial from thy voice,
 But sweet to me from none but thine;

The pledge we wore—I wear it still,
 But where is thine? Ah! where art thou?
Oft have I borne the weight of ill,
 But never bent beneath till now!

Well hast thou left in life's best bloom
    The cup of woe for me to drain.
If rest alone be in the tomb,
    I would not wish thee here again.

But if in worlds more blest than this
    Thy virtues seek a fitter sphere,
Impart some portion of thy bliss,
    To wean me from mine anguish here.

Teach me, too early taught by thee,
    To bear, forgiving and forgiven:
On earth thy love was such to me,
    It fain would form my hope in heaven!

NEWSTEAD ABBEY, *Oct.* 11, 1811.

FARE THEE WELL.

"*Alas! they had been friends in youth;*
But whispering tongues can poison truth;
And constancy lives in realms above;
And life is thorny; and youth is vain;
And to be wroth with one we love,
Doth work like madness in the brain;
* * * * * *
But never either found another
To free the hollow heart from paining;
They stood aloof, the scars remaining,
Like cliffs, which had been rent asunder;
A dreary sea now flows between;
But neither heat, nor frost, nor thunder,
Shall wholly do away, I ween,
The marks of that which once hath been."

COLERIDGE'S CHRISTABEL.

Fare thee well! and if forever,
    Still forever, fare thee well:
Even though unforgiving, never
    'Gainst thee shall my heart rebel.

Would that breast were bared before thee,
    Where thy head so oft hath lain,

While that placid sleep came o'er thee
    Which thou ne'er canst know again:

Would that breast, by thee glanced over,
    Every inmost thought could show!
Then thou wouldst at last discover
    'T was not well to spurn it so.

Though the world for this commend thee,
    Though it smile upon the blow,
Even its praises must offend thee,
    Founded on another's woe:

Though my many faults defaced me,
    Could no other arm be found,
Than the one which once embraced me,
    To inflict a cureless wound?

Yet, O yet, thyself deceive not;
    Love may sink by slow decay,
But by sudden wrench, believe not
    Hearts can thus be torn away:

Still thine own its life retaineth,
    Still must mine, though bleeding, beat;
And the undying thought which paineth
    Is—that we no more may meet.

There are words of deeper sorrow
    Than the wail above the dead;
Both shall live, but every morrow
    Wake us from a widowed bed.

And when thou wouldst solace gather,
    When our child's first accents flow,
Wilt thou teach her to say "Father!"
    Though his care she must forego?

When her little hands shall press thee,
When her lip to thine is pressed,
Think of him whose prayer shall bless thee,
Think of him thy love had blessed!

Should her lineaments resemble
Those thou never more may'st see,
Then thy heart will softly tremble
With a pulse yet true to me.

All my faults perchance thou knowest,
All my madness none can know;
All my hopes, where'er thou goest,
Wither, yet with *thee* they go.

Every feeling hath been shaken;
Pride, which not a world could bow,
Bows to thee, by thee forsaken,
Even my soul forsakes me now:

But 'tis done; all words are idle;
Words from me are vainer still;
But the thoughts we cannot bridle
Force their way without the will.

Fare thee well! thus disunited,
Torn from every nearer tie,
Seared in heart, and lone, and blighted,
More than this I scarce can die.

LONDON, *March* 17, 1816.

THE DREAM.

I.

Our life is twofold: Sleep hath its own world,
A boundary between the things misnamed
Death and existence: Sleep hath its own world,
And a wide realm of wild reality,

And dreams in their development have breath,
And tears, and torture, and the touch of joy;
They leave a weight upon our waking thoughts,
They take a weight from off our waking toils,
They do divide our being; they become
A portion of ourselves as of our time,
And look like heralds of eternity;
They pass like spirits of the past; they speak
Like sibyls of the future; they have power,
The tyranny of pleasure and of pain;
They make us what we were not, what they will,
And shake us with the vision that 's gone by,
The dread of vanished shadows—Are they so?
Is not the past all shadow? What are they?
Creations of the mind? The mind can make
Substance, and people planets of its own
With beings brighter than have been, and give
A breath to forms which can outlive all flesh.
I would recall a vision which I dreamed,
Perchance in sleep; for in itself a thought,
A slumbering thought, is capable of years,
And curdles a long life into one hour.

II.

I saw two beings in the hues of youth,
Standing upon a hill, a gentle hill,
Green, and of mild declivity, the last
As 't were the cape of a long ridge of such,
Save that there was no sea to lave its base,
But a most living landscape, and the wave
Of woods and cornfields, and the abodes of men
Scattered at intervals, and wreathing smoke
Arising from such rustic roofs: the hill
Was crowned with a peculiar diadem
Of trees, in circular array, so fixed,
Not by the sport of nature, but of man:
These two, a maiden and a youth, were there
Gazing—the one on all that was beneath,
Fair as herself—but the boy gazed on her;

And both were young, and one was beautiful:
And both were young, yet not alike in youth.
As the sweet moon on the horizon's verge,
The maid was on the eve of womanhood;
The boy had fewer summers, but his heart
Had far outgrown his years, and to his eye
There was but one belovéd face on earth,
And that was shining on him; he had looked
Upon it till it could not pass away;
He had no breath, no being, but in hers:
She was his voice; he did not speak to her,
But trembled on her words; she was his sight,
For his eye followed hers, and saw with hers,
Which coloured all his objects: he had ceased
To live within himself; she was his life,
The ocean to the river of his thoughts,
Which terminated all: upon a tone,
A touch of hers, his blood would ebb and flow,
And his cheek change tempestuously—his heart
Unknowing of its cause of agony.
But she in these fond feelings had no share:
Her sighs were not for him; to her he was
Even as a brother, but no more; 't was much,
For brotherless she was, save in the name
Her infant friendship had bestowed on him;
Herself the solitary scion left
Of a time-honoured race. It was a name
Which pleased him, and which pleased him not—and why?
Time taught him a deep answer, when she loved
Another; even *now* she loved another,
And on the summit of that hill she stood
Looking afar if yet her lover's steed
Kept pace with her expectancy, and flew.

III.

A change came o'er the spirit of my dream.
There was an ancient mansion, and before
Its walls there was a steed caparisoned:

Within an antique Oratory stood
The Boy of whom I spake; he was alone,
And pale, and pacing to and fro: anon
He sat him down, and seized a pen, and traced
Words which I could not guess of; then he leaned
His bowed head on his hands, and shook as 't were
With a convulsion; then arose again,
And with his teeth and quivering hands did tear
What he had written, but he shed no tears.
And he did calm himself, and fix his brow
Into a kind of quiet: as he paused,
The Lady of his love re-entered there;
She was serene and smiling then, and yet
She knew she was by him beloved, she knew,
For quickly comes such knowledge, that his heart
Was darkened with her shadow, and she saw
That he was wretched, but she saw not all.
He rose, and with a cold and gentle grasp
He took her hand; a moment o'er his face
A tablet of unutterable thoughts
Was traced, and then it faded, as it came;
He dropped the hand he held, and with slow steps
Retired, but not as bidding her adieu,
For they did part with mutual smiles: he passed
From out the massy gate of that old Hall,
And mounting on his steed he went his way;
And ne'er repassed that hoary threshold more.

IV.

A change came o'er the spirit of my dream.
The Boy was sprung to manhood: in the wilds
Of fiery climes he made himself a home,
And his Soul drank their sunbeams: he was girt
With strange and dusky aspects; he was not
Himself like what he had been; on the sea
And on the shore he was a wanderer.
There was a mass of many images
Crowded like waves upon me, but he was

A part of all; and in the last he lay
Reposing from the noontide sultriness,
Couched among fallen columns, in the shade
Of ruined walls that had survived the names
Of those who reared them; by his sleeping side
Stood camels grazing, and some goodly steeds
Were fastened near a fountain; and a man
Clad in a flowing garb did watch the while,
While many of his tribe slumbered around:
And they were canopied by the blue sky,
So cloudless, clear, and purely beautiful,
That God alone was to be seen in Heaven.

V.

A change came o'er the spirit of my dream.
The Lady of his love was wed with One
Who did not love her better: in her home,
A thousand leagues from his, her native home,
She dwelt, begirt with growing Infancy,
Daughters and sons of Beauty—but behold!
Upon her face there was the tint of grief,
The settled shadow of an inward strife,
And an unquiet drooping of the eye,
As if its lid were charged with unshed tears.
What could her grief be? she had all she loved,
And he who had so loved her was not there
To trouble with bad hopes, or evil wish,
Or ill-repressed affliction, her pure thoughts.
What could her grief be? she had loved him not,
Nor given him cause to deem himself beloved,
Nor could he be a part of that which preyed
Upon her mind—a spectre of the past.

VI.

A change came o'er the spirit of my dream.
The Wanderer was returned. I saw him stand
Before an Altar, with a gentle bride;
Her face was fair, but was not that which made

The Starlight of his Boyhood; as he stood
Even at the altar, o'er his brow there came
The selfsame aspect, and the quivering shock
That in the antique Oratory shook
His bosom in its solitude; and then,
As in that hour, a moment o'er his face
A tablet of unutterable thoughts
Was traced, and then it faded as it came,
And he stood calm and quiet, and he spoke
The fitting vows, but heard not his own words,
And all things reeled around him; he could see
Not that which was, nor that which should have been,
But the old mansion, and the accustomed hall,
And the remembered chambers, and the place,
The day, the hour, the sunshine, and the shade,
All things pertaining to that place and hour,
And her who was his destiny, came back
And thrust themselves between him and the light:
What business had they there at such a time?

VII.

A change came o'er the spirit of my dream.
The Lady of his love—O, she was changed,
As by the sickness of the soul; her mind
Had wandered from its dwelling, and her eyes,
They had not their own lustre, but the look
Which is not of the earth; she was become
The queen of a fantastic realm; her thoughts
Were combinations of disjointed things;
And forms impalpable and unperceived
Of others' sight familiar were to hers.
And this the world calls frenzy; but the wise
Have a far deeper madness, and the glance
Of melancholy is a fearful gift;
What is it but the telescope of truth?
Which strips the distance of its fantasies,
And brings life near in utter nakedness,
Making the cold reality too real!

VIII.

A change came o'er the spirit of my dream.
The Wanderer was alone as heretofore,
The beings which surrounded him were gone,
Or were at war with him; he was a mark
For blight and desolation, compassed round
With Hatred and Contention; Pain was mixed
In all which was served up to him, until,
Like to the Pontic monarch of old days,
He fed on poisons, and they had no power,
But were a kind of nutriment; he lived
Through that which had been death to many men,
And made him friends of mountains: with the stars
And the quick Spirit of the Universe
He held his dialogues, and they did teach
To him the magic of their mysteries;
To him the book of Night was opened wide,
And voices from the deep abyss revealed
A marvel and a secret. Be it so.

IX.

My dream was past; it had no further change.
It was of a strange order, that the doom
Of these two creatures should be thus traced out
Almost like a reality; the one
To end in madness, both in misery.

DIODATI, *July*, 1816.

STANZAS TO THE PO.

River, that rollest by the ancient walls,
    Where dwells the lady of my love, when she
Walks by thy brink, and there perchance recalls
    A faint and fleeting memory of me;

What if thy deep and ample stream should be
    A mirror of my heart, where she may read

The thousand thoughts I now betray to thee,
Wild as thy wave, and headlong as thy speed!

What do I say, a mirror of my heart?
Are not thy waters sweeping, dark and strong?
Such as my feelings were and are, thou art:
And such as thou art were my passions long.

Time may have somewhat tamed them, not for ever;
Thou overflow'st thy banks, and not for aye
Thy bosom overboils, congenial river!
Thy floods subside, and mine have sunk away,

But left long wrecks behind, and now again,
Borne in our old unchanged career, we move;
Thou tendest wildly onward to the main,
And I—to loving *one* I should not love.

The current I behold will sweep beneath
Her native walls, and murmur at her feet;
Her eyes will look on thee, when she shall breathe
The twilight air, unharmed by summer's heat.

She will look on thee; I have looked on thee,
Full of that thought: and, from that moment, ne'er
Thy waters could I dream of, name, or see
Without the inseparable sigh for her!

Her bright eyes will be imaged by thy stream,
Yes! they will meet the wave I gaze on now:
Mine can not witness, even in a dream,
That happy wave repass me in its flow!

The wave that bears my tears returns no more:
Will she return by whom that wave shall sweep?
Both tread thy banks, both wander on thy shore,
I by thy source, she by the dark-blue deep.

But that which keepeth us apart is not
Distance, nor depth of wave, nor space of earth,
But the distraction of a various lot,
As various as the climates of our birth.

A stranger loves the lady of the land,
Born far beyond the mountains, but his blood
Is all meridian, as if never fanned
By the black wind that chills the polar flood.

My blood is all meridian; were it not,
I had not left my clime, nor should I be,
In spite of tortures, ne'er to be forgot,
A slave again of love, at least of thee.

'T is vain to struggle—let me perish young;
Live as I lived, and love as I have loved;
To dust if I return, from dust I sprung,
And then, at least, my heart can ne'er be moved.

ON THE PO, *April*, 1819.

LORD THURLOW.

[*"Poems on Several Occasions."* 1813.]

SINCE all I see, (and all I see is fair,)
But springs from Jove, who is the source of all,
And so of kindred with Olympus' air,
But images what thence divine we call;
No fear there is, that, when my thread is spun,
My golden thread, for love appoints it so,
My heart with this soft passion should have done,
Which ending, in Olympus would be woe:
For since this beauty is but type of thee,
And Nature but the mirror of thy love,
Which oft the Angels may descend to see,
And find well pictured from their bliss above,
Thy memory in that immortal air,
All sights will keep, as in it's budding, fair.

Thy love is to my heart a boundless store
Of soft affection, which to love is near,
And those, that I have never prized before,
For thy dear sake are now to me most dear;
Thy kindred, and thy friends, whose matchless worth,
As lost in darkness, were to me unknown,
By pure example light my path on Earth,
And by their virtues my defects are shown:
Then may I so improve the boundless grace,
Which from the marble air to me is sent,

That in my soul pure honour may have place,
    And virtue her neglected stores augment:
For perfect in thyself thou art I see,
But yet more perfect in thy company.

I think you are the prophet of the Spring,
Or Spring doth on your gentle feet attend,
For ever do I note the Zephyr's wing,
When towards me your precious feet you bend:
The air is then impregnate with delight,
And Nature does her brightest sweets display,
But ah! too soon you wander from my sight,
And sorrow must usurp upon my day:
And yet the thought, that I have seen you then,
Supports me, till the morrow shall appear,
Again to seek you in the walks of men,
That are the star and Phœbus of my sphere:
So do I live in all vicissitude
Of joy and grief, of evil and of good.

I called you, and too well these names you grace,
The World's divine, and merest paragon,
The violet, to whom all plants are base,
The star, that is but joy to look upon:
And are you not without compare the gem,
That kings would in their thronéd pride possess,
To sparkle in the blazing diadem,
And the fair eyes of their true subjects bless?
Your title, and your style must be as great,
As is th' excelling beauty of your cheek,
Nor can I without fault one word abate,
Since all is less, than can your glory speak;
For let Olympus with your face compare,
And men shall own, that you are only fair.

THOMAS MOORE.

1779—1852.

["*Irish Melodies.*" 1813–14.]

BELIEVE ME, IF ALL THOSE ENDEARING YOUNG CHARMS.

Believe me, if all those endearing young charms,
Which I gaze on so fondly to-day,
Were to change by to-morrow, and fleet in my arms,
Like fairy-gifts fading away,
Thou wouldst still be adored, as this moment thou art,
Let thy loveliness fade as it will,
And around the dear ruin each wish of my heart
Would entwine itself verdantly still.

It is not while beauty and youth are thine own,
And thy cheeks unprofaned by a tear,
That the fervour and faith of a soul can be known,
To which time will but make thee more dear;
No, the heart that has truly loved never forgets,
But as truly loves on to the close,
As the sun-flower turns on her god, when he sets,
The same look which she turned when he rose.

I SAW THY FORM IN YOUTHFUL PRIME.

I saw thy form in youthful prime,
Nor thought that pale decay

Would steal before the steps of Time,
    And waste its bloom away, Mary!
Yet still thy features wore that light,
    Which fleets not with the breath;
And life ne'er looked more truly bright
    Than in thy smile of death, Mary!

As streams that run o'er golden mines,
    Yet humbly, calmly glide,
Nor seem to know the wealth that shines
    Within their gentle tide, Mary!
So veiled beneath the simplest guise,
    Thy radiant genius shone,
And that, which charmed all other eyes,
    Seemed worthless in thy own, Mary!

If souls could always dwell above,
    Thou ne'er hadst left that sphere;
Or could we keep the souls we love,
    We ne'er had lost thee here, Mary!
Though many a gifted mind we meet,
    Though fairest forms we see,
To live with them is far less sweet
    Than to remember thee, Mary!

LESBIA HATH A BEAMING EYE.

Lesbia hath a beaming eye,
    But no one knows for whom it beameth;
Right and left its arrows fly,
    But what they aim at no one dreameth.
Sweeter 't is to gaze upon
    My Nora's lid that seldom rises;
Few its looks, but every one,
    Like unexpected light, surprises!
        O, my Nora Creina, dear,

My gentle, bashful Nora Creina,
Beauty lies
In many eyes,
But Love in yours, my Nora Creina.

Lesbia wears a robe of gold,
But all so close the nymph hath laced it,
Not a charm of beauty's mould
Presumes to stay where Nature placed it.
O, my Nora's gown for me,
That floats as wild as mountain breezes,
Leaving every beauty free
To sink or swell as Heaven pleases.
Yes, my Nora Creina dear,
My simple, graceful Nora Creina,
Nature's dress
Is loveliness,
The dress *you* wear, my Nora Creina.

Lesbia hath a wit refined,
But, when its points are gleaming round us,
Who can tell if they 're designed
To dazzle merely, or to wound us?
Pillowed on my Nora's heart
In safer slumbers Love reposes;
Bed of peace! whose roughest part
Is but the crumpling of the roses.
O, my Nora Creina, dear,
My mild, my artless Nora Creina!
Wit, though bright,
Hath no such light,
As warms your eyes, my Nora Creina.

SIR WALTER SCOTT.

1771—1832.

["*Albyn's Anthology.*" 1816.]

NORA'S VOW.

HEAR what Highland Nora said,
"The Earlie's son I will not wed,
Should all the race of nature die,
And none be left but he and I.
For all the gold, for all the gear,
And all the lands both far and near,
That ever valour lost or won,
I would not wed the Earlie's son."

"A maiden's vows," old Callum spoke,
"Are lightly made, and lightly broke;
The heather on the mountain's height
Begins to bloom in purple light;
The frost-wind soon shall sweep away
That lustre deep from glen and brae;
Yet Nora, ere its bloom be gone,
May blithely wed the Earlie's son."

"The swan," she said, "the lake's clear breast
May barter for the eagle's nest;
The Awe's fierce stream may backward turn,
Ben-Cruaichan fall, and crush Kilchurn;

Our kilted clans, when blood is high,
Before their foes may turn and fly;
But I, were all these marvels done,
Would never wed the Earlie's son."

Still in the water-lily's shade
Her wonted nest the wild-swan made;
Ben-Cruaichan stands fast as ever,
Still downward foams the Awe's fierce river;
To shun the clash of foeman's steel,
No highland brogue has turned the heel;
But Nora's heart is lost and won,
She's wedded to the Earlie's son!

["*The Betrothed.*" 1825.]

SONG.

Woman's faith, and woman's trust,
Write the characters in dust;
Stamp them on the running stream,
Print them on the moon's pale beam,
And each evanescent letter,
Shall be clearer, firmer, better,
And more permanent, I ween,
Than the things those letters mean.

I have strained the spider's thread
'Gainst the promise of a maid;
I have weighed a grain of sand
'Gainst her plight of heart and hand;
I told my true love of the token,
How her faith proved light, and her word was broken;
Again her word and truth she plight,
And I believed them again ere night.

LEIGH HUNT.

1784—1859.

TO MY WIFE—ON MODELLING MY BUST.

Ah, Marian mine, the face you look on now
Is not exactly like my wedding day's:
Sunk is its cheek, deeper-retired its gaze,
Less white and smooth it's temple-flattened brow.
Sorrow has been there with his silent plough,
And straight, stern hand. No matter, if it raise
Aught that affection fancies, it may praise,
Or make me worthier of Apollo's bough.
Loss, after all, such loss especially,
Is transfer, change, but not extinction, no;
Part in our children's apple cheeks I see;
And, for the rest, while you look at me so,
Take care you do not smile it back to me,
And miss the copied furrows as you go.

Jenny kissed me when we met,
  Jumping from the chair she sat in;
Time, you thief, who love to get
  Sweets into your list, put that in:
Say I'm weary, say I'm sad,
  Say that health and wealth have missed me,
Say I'm growing old, but add,
  Jenny kissed me.

JOHN KEATS.

1795—1821.

The last two or three years of the life of Keats were embittered by a hopeless passion. Not that it was not returned, for we are assured it was, but that his circumstances at first, and afterwards his fatal illness, forbade him to think of marriage. The lady of his love is still living, or was in 1848, when Monckton Milnes edited his "Remains," but her name is withheld from the world. Nothing is known of her, here in America, at least, beyond what Keats himself tells us. He met her in the autumn of 1818, shortly after his return from a tour in the Highlands, and probably at Hampstead, whither he retired with his brother Tom, who was dying with consumption. The earliest mention of her in his correspondence is in a letter to his brother George, in America, dated on the 29th of October, 1818. "The Misses ——," he wrote, "are very kind to me, but they have lately displeased me very much, and in this way: now I am coming the Richardson! On my return, the first day I called, they were in a sort of taking or bustle about a cousin of theirs, who, having fallen out with her grandpapa in a serious manner, was invited by Mrs. —— to take asylum in her house. She is an East Indian, and ought to be her grandfather's heir. At the time I called, Mrs. —— was in conference with her upstairs, and the young ladies were warm in her praise downstairs, calling her genteel, interesting, and a thousand pretty things, to which I gave no heed, not being partial to nine days' wonders. Now all is completely changed: they hate her, and, from what I hear, she is not without faults of a real kind; but she has others, which are more apt to make women of inferior claims hate her. She is not a Cleopatra, but is, at least, a Charmian: she has a rich Eastern look; she has fine eyes, and fine manners. When she comes into the room, she makes the same impression as the beauty of a leopardess. She is too fine, and too conscious of herself, to repulse any man who may address her: from habit she thinks that *nothing particular*. I always find myself at ease with such a woman: the picture before me always gives me a life and animation which I cannot possibly feel with anything inferior. I am, at such times, too much occupied in admiring to be awkward or in a tremble: I forget myself entirely, because I live in her. You will, by this time, think I am in love with her, so, before I go any further, I will tell you I am not. She kept me awake one night, as a tune of Mozart's might do. I speak of the thing as a pastime and an amusement, than which I can feel none deeper than a conversation with an imperial woman, the very 'Yes' and 'No' of whose life is to me a banquet. I don't cry to take the moon home with me in my pocket, nor do I fret to leave her behind me. I like her, and her like, because one has no *sensation:* what we both are is taken for granted. You will suppose I have, by this, had much talk with her—no such thing; there are the Misses —— on the lookout. They think I don't admire her because I don't stare at her; they call her a flirt to me—what a want of knowledge! She walks across a room in such a manner, that a man is drawn towards her with magnetic power; this they call flirting! They do not know things; they do not know what a woman is. I believe, though, she has faults, the same as Charmian and Cleopatra might have had." If Keats was not in love when he drew this magnificent portrait, he was certainly on the highway to it, as any person of penetration could have seen. Perhaps he saw it himself, and was struggling to overcome it, knowing it could not lead to his happiness. Be this as it may, the time soon came when he *knew* that he loved, and a terrible knowledge it was—to a dying man! "Seeing him once change countenance," says Hunt, "in a manner more alarming than usual, as he stood silently eying the country out of window, I pressed him to let me know how he felt, in order that he might enable me to do what I could for him; upon which he said, that his feelings were almost more than he could bear, and that he feared for his senses. I proposed that we should take a coach, and ride about the country together, to vary, if possible, the immediate impression, which was sometimes all that was formidable, and would come to nothing. He acquiesced, and was restored to himself. It was, nevertheless, on the same day, that sitting on the bench in Well Walk, at Hampstead, nearest the Heath, that he told me, with unaccustomed tears in his eyes, that 'his heart was breaking.' A doubt, however, was upon him at that time, which he afterwards had reason to know was groundless; and during his residence at the last house which he occupied before he went abroad, he was at times more than tranquil. At length, he was persuaded by his friends to try the milder climate of Italy." He started from England in September, 1820, in company with Severn, the artist, and arrived at Naples in the latter part of October. On the 1st of November he wrote thus to his friend, Charles Armitage Brown: "The persuasion that I shall see her no more will kill me. My dear Brown, I should have had her when I was in health, and I should have remained well. I can bear to die—I cannot bear to leave her. Oh, God! God! God! Everything I have in my trunks that reminds me of her goes through me like a spear. The silk lining she put in my travelling cap scalds my head. My imagination is horribly vivid about her—I see her—I hear her. There is nothing in the world of sufficient interest to divert me from her a moment. This was the case when I was in England; I cannot recollect, without shuddering, the time that I was a prisoner at Hunt's, and used to keep my eyes fixed on Hampstead all day. Then there was a good hope of seeing her again. Now—O that I could be buried near where she lives! I am afraid to write to her—to receive a letter from her; to see her handwriting would break my heart—even to hear of her anyhow, to see her name written, would be more than I could bear. My dear Brown, what am I to do? Where can I look for consolation or ease? If I had any chance of recovery, this passion would kill me. Indeed, through the whole of my illness, both at your house and at Kentish Town, this fever has never ceased wearing me out. When you write to me, which you will do immediately, write to Rome (*poste restante*)—if she is well and happy, put a mark thus +; if ——."

He reached Rome in a terrible state of exhaustion, worn out in body and soul. "When he first came here," his friend Severn wrote to England, on the 14th of February, 1821, "he purchased a copy of 'Alfieri,' but put it down at the second page, being much affected at the lines,

> "'Misera me! sollievo a me non resta,
> Altro che il pianto *ed il pianto è delitto!*'

Now that I know so much of his grief, I do not wonder at it.

"Such a letter has come! I gave it to Keats, supposing it to be one of yours, but it proved sadly otherwise. The glance at that letter tore him to pieces; the effects were on him for many days. He did not read it—he could not—but requested me to place it in his coffin, together with a purse and a letter (unopened) of his sister's; since then he has told me *not* to place that letter in his coffin, only his sister's purse and letter and some hair. I however, persuaded him to think otherwise on this point."

"*Feb. 27th.*—He is gone; he died with the most perfect ease—he seemed to go to sleep. On the twenty-third, about four, the approaches of death came on. 'Severn—I—lift me up—I am dying—I shall die easy; don't be frightened—be firm, and thank God it has come.' I lifted him up in my arms. The phlegm seemed boiling in his throat, and increased until eleven, when he gradually sunk into death, so quiet, that I still thought he slept. I cannot say more now. I am broken down by four nights' watching, no sleep since, and my poor Keats gone. Three days since the body was opened; the lungs were completely gone. The doctors could not imagine how he had lived these two months. I followed his dear body to the grave on Monday, with many English."

> "O Love, what is it in this world of ours
> Which makes it fatal to be loved? Ah why
> With cypress branches hast thou wreathed thy bowers,
> And made thy best interpreter a sigh?"

As Hermes once took to his feathers light,
When lullèd Argus, baffled, swooned and slept,
So on a Delphic reed, my idle spright,
So played, so charmed, so conquered, so bereft
The dragon-world of all its hundred eyes,
And seeing it asleep, so fled away,
Not to pure Ida with its snow-cold skies,
Nor unto Tempe, where Jove grieved a day,

But to that second circle of sad Hell,
    Where in the gust, the whirlwind, and the flaw
Of rain and hail-stones, lovers need not tell
    Their sorrows,—pale were the sweet lips I saw,
Pale were the lips I kissed, and fair the form
I floated with, about that melancholy storm.

1819.

The day is gone, and all its sweets are gone!
    Sweet voice, sweet lips, soft hand, and softer breast,
Warm breath, light whisper, tender semi-tone,
    Bright eyes, accomplished shape, and langourous waist!
Faded the flower and all its budded charms,
    Faded the sight of beauty from my eyes,
Faded the shape of beauty from my arms,
    Faded the voice, warmth, whiteness, paradise;
Vanished unseasonably at shut of eve,
    When the dusk holiday, or holinight,
Of fragrant-curtained love begins to weave
    The woof of darkness thick, for hid delight;
But, as I've read Love's missal through to-day,
He'll let me sleep, seeing I fast and pray

1819.

I cry you mercy, pity, love, aye love!
    Merciful love that tantalizes not,
One-thoughted, never-wandering, guileless love,
    Unmasked, and, being seen, without a blot!
O let me have thee whole, all, all be mine!
    That shape, that fairness, that sweet minor zest
Of love, your kiss; those hands, those eyes divine,
    That warm, white, lucent, million-pleasured breast;
Yourself, your soul, in pity give me all,
    Withhold no atom's atom, or I die,
Or living on perhaps, your wretched thrall,
    Forget, in the mist of idle misery,
Life's purposes—the palate of my mind
Losing its gust, and my ambition blind!

1820.

TO ———

What can I do to drive away
Remembrance from my eyes? for they have seen,
Aye, an hour ago, my brilliant Queen!
Touch has a memory. O say, love, say,
What can I do to kill it, and be free
In my old liberty?
When every fair one that I saw was fair,
Enough to catch me in but half a snare,
Not keep me there:
When, howe'er poor or particoloured things,
My muse had wings,
And ever ready was to take her course
Whither I bent her force,
Unintellectual, yet divine to me;
Divine, I say! What sea-bird o'er the sea
Is a philosopher the while he goes
Winging along where the great water throes?

How shall I do
To get anew
Those moulted feathers, and so mount once more
Above, above
The reach of fluttering Love,
And make him cower lowly while I soar?
Shall I gulp wine? No, that is vulgarism,
A heresy and schism
Foisted into the canon law of love;
No, wine is only sweet to happy men;
More dismal cares
Seize on me unawares;
Where shall I learn to get my peace again?
To banish thoughts of that most hateful land,
Dungeoner of my friends, that wicked strand
Where they were wrecked, and live a wreckéd life;
That monstrous region, whose dull rivers pour,

Ever from their sordid urns unto the shore,
Unowned of any weedy-haired gods;
Whose winds, all zephyrless, hold scourging rods,
Iced in the great lakes, to afflict mankind;
Whose rank-grown forests, frosted, black, and blind,
Would fright a Dryad; whose harsh-herbaged meads
Make lean and lank the starved ox while he feeds;
There bad flowers have no scent, birds no sweet song,
And great unerring Nature once seems wrong.

O for some sunny spell
To dissipate the shadows of this hell!
Say they are gone,—with the new dawning light
Steps forth my lady bright!
O, let me once more rest
My soul upon that dazzling breast!
Let once again these aching arms be placed,
The tender gaolers of thy waist!
And let me feel that warm breath here and there,
To spread a rapture in my very hair;
O the sweetness of the pain!
Give me those lips again!
Enough! Enough! it is enough for me
To dream of thee!

1819.

JOHN CLARE.

1793–

["*Poems, Descriptive of Rural Life and Scenery.*" 1820.]

THE FIRST OF MAY.

A BALLAD.

Fair blooms the rose upon the green,
    Pretending to excel;
But who another rose has seen,
    A different tale can tell.
The morning smiles, the lark's begun
    To welcome in the May:
Be cloudless, skies! look out, bright sun,
    And haste my love away.

Though graceful round the maidens move,
    That join the rural ball,
Soon shall they own my absent love
    The rival of them all.
Go, wake your shepherdess, ye lambs!
    And murmur her delay;
Chide her neglect, ye hoarser dams!
    And call my love away.

Ye happy swains, with each a bride,
    Were but the angel there,

While slighted maids despaired and sighed,
    You'd court th' unequalled fair.
Dry up, ye dews! nor threatening hing,
    To soil her best array:
Ye birds! with double vigour sing,
    And urge my love away.

Welcome, sun! the dews are fled,
    The lark has raised his song;
The daisy nauntles up its head,
    Why waits my love so long?
As flowrets fade, the pleasures bloom,
    All hastening to decay:
The day steals on, and showers may come:
    This instant haste away.

What now, ye fearful, cringing sheep!
    What meets your wondering eyes?
What makes you 'neath the maples creep,
    In homaging surprise?
No ladies tread our humble green:
    Ah! welcome wonders, hail!
I witness your mistaken queen
    Is Patty of the Vale.

CHARLES WOLFE.

1791—1823.

SONG.

If I had thought thou could'st have died,
I might not weep for thee;
But I forgot, when by thy side,
That thou could'st mortal be:
It never through my mind had past
The time would e'er be o'er,
And I on thee should look my last,
And thou should'st smile no more.

And still upon that face I look,
And think 'twill smile again;
And still the thought I will not brook,
That I must look in vain!
But when I speak, thou dost not say
What thou ne'er left'st unsaid;
And now I feel, as well I may,
Sweet Mary, thou art dead!

If thou would'st stay e'en as thou art,
All cold and all serene,
I still might press thy silent heart,
And where thy smiles have been!
While e'en thy chill bleak corse I have,
Thou seemest still mine own;

But there, I lay thee in thy grave,
  And I am now alone!

I do not think, where'er thou art,
  Thou hast forgotten me;
And I, perhaps, may soothe this heart
  In thinking too of thee:
Yet there was round thee such a dawn
  Of light ne'er seen before,
As fancy never could have drawn,
  And never can restore!

REGINALD HEBER.

1783—1826.

LINES

ADDRESSED TO MRS. HEBER.

If thou wert by my side, my love,
How fast would evening fail
In green Bengala's balmy grove,
Listening the nightingale.

If thou, my love, wert by my side,
My babies at my knee,
How gaily would our pinnace glide
O'er Gunga's mimic sea!

I miss thee at the dawning gray,
When, on our deck reclined,
In careless ease my limbs I lay
And woo the cooler wind.

I miss thee when by Gunga's stream
My twilight steps I guide,
But most beneath the lamp's pale beam,
I miss thee from my side.

I spread my books, my pencil try,
The lingering noon to cheer,

But miss thy kind approving eye,
Thy meek attentive ear.

But when of morn or eve the star
Beholds me on my knee,
I feel, though thou art distant far,
Thy prayers ascend for me.

Then on! then on! where duty leads,
My course be onward still;
O'er broad Hindostan's sultry meads,
O'er bleak Almorah's hill.

That course, nor Delhi's kingly gates
Nor wild Malwah detain;
For sweet the bliss us both awaits
By yonder western main.

Thy towers, Bombay, gleam bright, they say,
Across the dark-blue sea;
But ne'er were hearts so light and gay
As then shall meet in thee!

1824.

WILLIAM CULLEN BRYANT.

1794.

O FAIREST of the rural maids!
Thy birth was in the forest shades;
Green boughs, and glimpses of the sky,
Were all that met thine infant eye.

Thy sports, thy wanderings, when a child,
Were ever in the sylvan wild;
And all the beauty of the place
Is in thy heart and on thy face.

The twilight of the trees and rocks
Is in the light shade of thy locks;
Thy step is as the wind, that weaves
Its playful way among the leaves.

Thine eyes are springs, in whose serene
And silent waters heaven is seen;
Their lashes are the herbs that look
On their young figures in the brook.

The forest depths, by foot unpressed,
Are not more sinless than thy breast:
The holy peace, that fills the air
Of those calm solitudes, is there.

1825.

THE FUTURE LIFE.

How shall I know thee in the sphere which keeps
The disembodied spirits of the dead,
When all of thee that time could wither sleeps
And perishes among the dust we tread?

For I shall feel the sting of ceaseless pain
If there I meet thy gentle presence not;
Nor hear the voice I love, nor read again
In thy serenest eyes the tender thought.

Will not thy own meek heart demand me there?
That heart whose fondest throbs to me were given;
My name on earth was ever in thy prayer,
And wilt thou never utter it in heaven?

In meadows fanned by heaven's life-breathing wind,
In the resplendence of that glorious sphere,
And larger movements of the unfettered mind,
Wilt thou forget the love that joined us here?

The love that lived through all the stormy past,
And meekly with my harsher nature bore,
And deeper grew, and tenderer to the last,
Shall it expire with life, and be no more?

A happier lot than mine, and larger light,
Await thee there; for thou hast bowed thy will
In cheerful homage to the rule of right,
And lovest all, and renderest good for ill.

For me, the sordid cares in which I dwell,
Shrink and consume my heart, as heat the scroll;
And wrath has left its scar—that fire of hell
Has left its frightful scar upon my soul.

Yet though thou wear'st the glory of the sky,
    Wilt thou not keep the same belovéd name,
The same fair thoughtful brow, and gentle eye,
    Lovelier in heaven's sweet climate, yet the same?

Shalt thou not teach me, in that calmer home,
    The wisdom that I learned so ill in this,
The wisdom which is love, till I become
    Thy fit companion in that land of bliss?

1837.

EDWARD COATES PINKNEY.

1802—1828.

A HEALTH.

I FILL this cup to one made up
    Of loveliness alone,
A woman, of her gentle sex
    The seeming paragon;
To whom the better elements
    And kindly stars have given
A form so fair, that, like the air,
    'Tis less of earth than heaven.

Her every tone is music's own,
    Like those of morning birds,
And something more than melody
    Dwells ever in her words;
The coinage of her heart are they,
    And from her lips each flows
As one may see the burdened bee
    Forth issue from the rose.

Affections are as thoughts to her,
    The measures of her hours;
Her feelings have the fragrancy,
    The freshness of young flowers;
And lovely passions, changing oft,
    So fill her, she appears

The image of themselves by turns,
 The idol of past years!

Of her bright face one glance will trace
 A picture on the brain,
And of her voice in echoing hearts
 A sound must long remain;
But memory, such as mine of her,
 So very much endears,
When death is nigh my latest sigh
 Will not be life's, but hers.

I fill this cup to one made up
 Of loveliness alone,
A woman, of her gentle sex
 The seeming paragon;
Her health! and would on earth there stood
 Some more of such a frame,
That life might be all poetry,
 And weariness a name.

GEORGE DARLEY.

1785—1849.

Sweet in her green dell the flower of beauty slumbers,
Lulled by the faint breezes sighing through her hair;
Sleeps she, and hears not the melancholy numbers
Breathed to my sad lute amid the lonely air!

Down from the high cliffs the rivulet is teeming
To wind round the willow banks that lure him from above;
O that, in tears, from my rocky prison streaming,
I, too, could glide to the bower of my love!

Ah! where the woodbines, with sleepy arms, have wound her,
Opes she eyelids at the dream of my lay,
Listening, like the dove, while the fountains echo round her,
To her lost mate's call in the forests far away!

Come, then, my bird! for the peace thou ever bearest,
Still heaven's messenger of comfort to me;
Come! this fond bosom, my faithfullest, my fairest,
Bleeds with its death-wound—but deeper yet for thee!

ALFRED TENNYSON.

1810.

["*Poems.*" 1832.]

LADY CLARA VERE DE VERE.

LADY Clara Vere de Vere,
    Of me you shall not win renown;
You thought to break a country heart
    For pastime, ere you went to town.
At me you smiled, but unbeguiled
    I saw the snare, and I retired:
The daughter of a hundred Earls,
    You are not one to be desired.

Lady Clara Vere de Vere,
    I know you proud to bear your name;
Your pride is yet no mate for mine,
    Too proud to care from whence I came.
Nor would I break for your sweet sake
    A heart that dotes on truer charms.
A simple maiden in her flower
    Is worth a hundred coats-of-arms.

Lady Clara Vere de Vere,
    Some meeker pupil you must find,
For were you queen of all that is,
    I could not stoop to such a mind.

You sought to prove how I could love,
    And my disdain is my reply.
The lion on your old stone gates
    Is not more cold to you than I.

Lady Clara Vere de Vere,
    You put strange memories in my head.
Not thrice your branching limes have blown,
    Since I beheld young Laurence dead.
O your sweet eyes, your low replies:
    A great enchantress you may be;
But there was that across his throat
    Which you had hardly cared to see.

Lady Clara Vere de Vere,
    When thus he met his mother's view,
She had the passions of her kind,
    She spake some certain truths of you.
Indeed, I heard one bitter word
    That scarce is fit for you to hear;
Her manners had not that repose
    Which stamps the caste of Vere de Vere.

Lady Clara Vere de Vere,
    There stands a spectre in your hall:
The guilt of blood is at your door:
    You changed a wholesome heart to gall.
You held your course without remorse,
    To make him trust his modest worth,
And, last, you fixed a vacant stare,
    And slew him with your noble birth.

Trust me, Clara Vere de Vere,
    From yon blue heavens above us bent,
The grand old gardener and his wife
    Smile at the claims of long descent
Howe'er it be, it seems to me,
    'T is only noble to be good.

Kind hearts are more than coronets,
    And simple faith than Norman blood.

I know you, Clara Vere de Vere:
    You pine among your halls and towers,
The languid light of your proud eyes
    Is wearied of the rolling hours.
In glowing health, with boundless wealth,
    But sickening of a vague disease,
You know so ill to deal with time,
    You needs must play such pranks as these.

Clara, Clara Vere de Vere,
    If time be heavy on your hands,
Are there no beggars at your gate,
    Nor any poor about your lands?
O, teach the orphan-boy to read,
    Or teach the orphan-girl to sew,
Pray Heaven for a human heart,
    And let the foolish yeoman go.

["*Maud.*" 1855.]

Come into the garden, Maud,
    For the black bat, night, has flown,
Come into the garden, Maud,
    I am here at the gate alone;
And the woodbine spices are wafted abroad,
    And the musk of the roses blown.

For a breeze of the morning moves,
    And the planet of Love is on high,
Beginning to faint in the light that she loves,
    On a bed of daffodil sky,
To faint in the light of the sun she loves,
    To faint in his light, and to die.

Maud.

New York: [illegible]

All night have the roses heard
    The flute, violin, bassoon;
All night has the casement jessamine stirred
    To the dancers dancing in tune:
Till a silence fell with the waking bird,
    And a hush with the setting moon.

I said to the lily, "There is but one
    With whom she has heart to be gay.
When will the dancers leave her alone?
    She is weary of dance and play."
Now half to the setting moon are gone,
    And half to the rising day;
Low on the sand and loud on the stone
    The last wheel echoes away.

I said to the rose, "The brief night goes
    In babble and revel and wine.
O young lord-lover, what sighs are those,
    For one that will never be thine?
But mine, but mine," so I sware to the rosė,
    "Forever and ever, mine."

And the soul of the rose went into my blood,
    As the music clashed in the hall;
And long by the garden lake I stood,
    For I heard your rivulet fall
From the lake to the meadow, and on to the wood,
    Our wood, that is dearer than all;

From the meadow your walks have left so sweet,
    That whenever a March-wind sighs
He sets the jewel-print of your feet
    In violets blue as your eyes,
To the woody hollows in which we meet
    And the valleys of Paradise.

The slender acacia would not shake
    One long milk-bloom on the tree;
The white lake-blossom fell into the lake,
    As the pimpernel dozed on the lea;
But the rose was awake all night for your sake,
    Knowing your promise to me;
The lilies and roses were all awake,
    They sighed for the dawn and thee.

Queen rose of the rosebud garden of girls,
    Come hither, the dances are done,
In gloss of satin and glimmer of pearls,
    Queen lily and rose in one;
Shine out, little head, sunning over with curls,
    To the flowers, and be their sun.

There has fallen a splendid tear
    From the passion-flower at the gate.
She is coming, my dove, my dear;
    She is coming, my life, my fate;
The red rose cries, "She is near, she is near;"
    And the white rose weeps, "She is late;"
The larkspur listens, "I hear, I hear;"
    And the lily whispers, "I wait."

She is coming, my own, my sweet;
    Were it ever so airy a tread,
My heart would hear her and beat,
    Were it earth in an earthy bed;
My dust would hear her and beat,
    Had I lain for a century dead;
Would start and tremble under her feet,
    And blossom in purple and red.

BRYAN WALLER PROCTOR.

"BARRY CORNWALL."

1787.

["*English Songs.*" 1832.]

THE POET'S SONG TO HIS WIFE.

How many Summers, love,
    Have I been thine?
How many days, thou dove,
    Hast thou been mine?
Time, like the wingéd wind
    When 't bends the flowers,
Hath left no mark behind,
    To count the hours!

Some weight of thought, though loth,
    On thee he leaves;
Some lines of care round both
    Perhaps he weaves;
Some fears, a soft regret,
    For joys scarce known;
Sweet looks we half forget;
    All else is flown!

Ah! with what thankless heart
    I mourn and sing!

Look, where our children start,
    Like sudden Spring!
With tongues all sweet and low,
    Like a pleasant rhyme,
They tell how much I owe
    To thee and Time!

GOLDEN TRESSED ADELAIDE.

A SONG FOR A CHILD.

Sing, I pray, a little song,
    Mother dear!
Neither sad nor very long:
It is for a little maid,
Golden tressèd Adelaide!
Therefore let it suit a merry, merry ear,
    Mother dear!

Let it be a merry strain,
    Mother dear!
Shunning e'en the thought of pain:
For our gentle child will weep,
If the theme be dark and deep;
And *We* will not draw a single, single tear,
    Mother dear!

Childhood should be all divine,
    Mother dear!
And like endless summer shine;
Gay as Edward's shouts and cries,
Bright as Agnes' azure eyes:
Therefore, bid thy song be merry: dost thou hear,
    Mother dear?

1831.

HERMIONE.

Thou hast beauty bright and fair,
Manner noble, aspect free,
Eyes that are untouched by care:
What then do we ask from thee?
Hermione, Hermione?

Thou hast reason quick and strong,
Wit that envious men admire,
And a voice, itself a song!
What then can we still desire?
Hermione, Hermione?

Something thou dost want, O Queen!
(As the gold doth ask alloy,)
Tears, amidst thy laughter seen,
Pity, mingling with thy joy.
This is all we ask, from thee,
Hermione, Hermione!

MARIAN.

Spirit of the summer breeze!
Wherefore sleep'st thou in the trees?
Come, and kiss the maiden rose,
That on Marian's bosom blows!

Come, and fawn about her hair!
Kiss the fringes of her eyes!
Ask her why she looks so fair,
When she heedeth not my sighs?

Tell her, murmuring summer air,
That her beauty 's all untrue;
Tell her, she should not seem fair,
Unless she be gentle too!

WILLIAM MOTHERWELL.

1797—1835.

JEANIE MORRISON.

Motherwell entered the school of Mr. William Lennie, No. 8 Crichton street, Edinburgh, on the 24th of April, 1805, and left it for the High School, on the 1st of October, 1808. While at the former, he met and fell in love with Jeanie Morrison. "Jane (Jeanie) Morrison," says Mr. Lennie, writing to Motherwell's biographer, (1846,) "was the daughter of one of the most respectable brewers and corn-factors then in Alloa. She came to Edinburgh to finish her education, and was in my school with William Motherwell during the last year of his course. She was about the same age with himself, a pretty girl, and of good capacity. Her hair was of a lightish brown, approaching to fair; her eyes were dark, and had a sweet and gentle expression; her temper was mild, and her manners unassuming. Her dress was also neat and tidy. In winter, she wore a pale-blue pelisse, then the fashionable colour, and a light-coloured beaver with a feather. She made a great impression on young Motherwell, and that it was permanent his beautiful ballad shows. At the end of the season she returned to her parents at Alloa, with whom she resided till the time of her marriage. She is now a widow, with a family of three children, all of whom are grown up, and, I believe, doing well." "I had the pleasure," the biographer adds in a note, "of a slight acquaintance with this lady in after life, as Mrs. Murdoch. Her husband was a respectable merchant in this city, (Glasgow?) and died about the year 1828. She was, when I knew her, a very elegant woman in her personal appearance, and seemed to have preserved those gentle and agreeable manners for which she had been distinguished in girlhood; but it is proper to remark, that she was wholly unconscious of the ardent interest which she had excited in the mind of her boyish admirer."

Motherwell is said to have made the first draught of "Jeanie Morrison," in his fourteenth year. The poem as it now stands was published in 1832, in an Edinburgh magazine—Tait's, I believe. The sum paid for it was indeed munificent—Thirty Shillings!

JEANIE MORRISON.

I 've wandered east, I've wandered west,
Through mony a weary way;
But never, never can forget
The luve o' life's young day!
The fire that's blawn on Beltane e'en
May weel be black gin Yule;
But blacker fa' awaits the heart
Where first fond luve grows cule.

O dear, dear Jeanie Morrison,
The thochts o' bygane years
Still fling their shadows ower my path,
And blind my een wi' tears:
They blind my een wi' saut, saut tears,
And sair and sick I pine,
As memory idly summons up
The blithe blinks o' langsyne.

'T was then we luvit ilk ither weel,
'T was then we twa did part;
Sweet time, sad time! twa bairns at scule,
Twa bairns, and but ae heart!
'T was then we sat on ae laigh bink,
To leir ilk ither lear;
And tones and looks and smiles were shed,
Remembered evermair.

I wonder, Jeanie, aften yet,
When sitting on that bink,
Cheek touchin' cheek, loof locked in loof,
What our wee heads could think.
When baith bent down ower ae braid page,
Wi' ae buik on our knee,
Thy lips were on thy lesson, but
My lesson was in thee.

O, mind ye how we hung our heads,
    How cheeks brent red wi' shame,
Whene'er the scule-weans laughin' said,
    We cleeked thegither hame?
And mind ye o' the Saturdays,
    (The scule then skail't at noon)
When we ran off to speel the braes,
    The broomy braes o' June?

My head rins round and round about,
    My heart flows like a sea,
As ane by ane the thochts rush back
    O' scule-time and o' thee.
O mornin' life! O mornin' luve!
    O lichtsome days and lang,
When hinnied hopes around our hearts
    Like simmer blossoms sprang!

O, mind ye, luve, how aft we left
    The deavin' dinsome toun,
To wander by the green burnside,
    And hear its waters croon?
The simmer leaves hung ower our heads
    The flowers burst round our feet,
And in the gloamin o' the wood
    The throssil whusslit sweet;

The throssil whusslit in the wood,
    The burn sang to the trees,
And we with Nature's heart in tune
    Concerted harmonies;
And on the knowe abune the burn,
    For hours thegither sat,
In the silentness o' joy, till baith
    Wi' very gladness grat

Ay, ay, dear Jeanie Morrison,
    Tears trickled doun your cheek

Like dew-beads on a rose, yet nane
 Had ony power to speak!
That was a time, a blessèd time,
 When hearts were fresh and young,
When freely gushed all feelings forth,
 Unsyllabled, unsung!

I marvel, Jeanie Morrison,
 Gin I hae been to thee
As closely twined wi' earliest thochts
 As ye hae been to me?
O, tell me gin their music fills
 Thine ear as it does mine!
O, say gin e'er your heart grows grit
 Wi' dreamings o' langsyne?

I've wandered east, I've wandered west,
 I've borne a weary lot;
But in my wanderings, far or near,
 Ye never were forgot.
The fount that first burst frae this heart
 Still travels on its way,
And channels deeper, as it rins,
 The luve o' life's young day.

O dear, dear Jeanie Morrison,
 Since we were sindered young,
I've never seen your face, nor heard
 The music o' your tongue;
But I could hug all wretchedness,
 And happy could I die,
Did I but ken your heart still dreamed
 O' bygane days and me!

THOMAS HOOD.

1798—1845.

FAIR INES.

O saw ye not fair Ines?
She's gone into the West,
To dazzle when the sun is down,
And rob the world of rest:
She took our daylight with her,
The smiles that we love best,
With morning blushes on her cheek,
And pearls upon her breast.

O turn again, fair Ines,
Before the fall of night,
For fear the Moon should shine alone,
And stars unrivalled bright;
And blessèd will the lover be
That walks beneath their light,
And breathes the love against thy cheek
I dare not even write!

Would I had been, fair Ines,
That gallant cavalier,
Who rode so gaily by thy side,
And whispered thee so near!
Were there no bonny dames at home,
Or no true lovers here,

That he should cross the seas to win
The dearest of the dear?

I saw thee, lovely Ines,
Descend along the shore,
With bands of noble gentlemen,
And banners waved before;
And gentle youth and maidens gay,
And snowy plumes they wore;
It would have been a beauteous dream
—If it had been no more!

Alas, alas, fair Ines,
She went away with song,
With Music waiting on her steps,
And shoutings of the throng;
But some were sad, and felt no mirth,
But only Music's wrong,
In sounds that sang, Farewell, Farewell,
To her you've loved so long.

LINES

ON SEEING MY WIFE AND TWO CHILDREN SLEEPING IN THE SAME CHAMBER.

And has the earth lost its so spacious round,
The sky its blue circumference above,
That in this little chamber there is found
Both earth and heaven—my universe of love!
All that my God can give me, or remove,
Here sleeping, save myself, in mimic death.
Sweet that in this small compass I behove
To live their living and to breathe their breath!
Almost I wish that with one common sigh
We might resign all mundane care and strife,
And seek together that transcendent sky,
Where Father, Mother, Children, Husband, Wife,
Together pant in everlasting life!

COBLENTZ, *November*, 1835.

NATHANIEL PARKER WILLIS.

1807.

TO HER WHO HAS HOPES FOR ME.

O STERN, yet lovely monitress,
Thine eye should be of colder hue,
And on thy neck a paler tress
Should toy among those veins of blue!
For thou art to thy mission true,
An angel clad in human guise;
But sinners sometimes have such eyes,
And braid for love such tresses too;
And, while thou talk'st to me of heaven,
I sigh that thou hast not a sin to be forgiven!

Night comes, with love upon the breeze,
And the calm clock strikes, stilly, "*Ten.*"
I start to hear it beat, for then
I know that thou art on thy knees,
And, at that hour, where'er thou be,
Ascends to heaven a prayer for me!
My heart drops to its bended knee,
The mirth upon my lip is dumb;
Yet, as a thought of heaven would come,
There glides, before it, one of thee:
Thou, in thy white dress, kneeling there!
I fear I could leave heaven to see thee at thy prayer!

I follow up the sacred aisle,
Thy light step on the Sabbath day,
And, as perhaps thou pray'st the while,
My light thoughts pass away!
As swells in air the holy hymn,
My breath comes quick, my eyes are dim,
And through my tears I pray!
I do not think my heart is stone;
But, while for heaven it beats alone,
In heaven would willing stay,
One rustle of thy snow-white gown
Sends all my thoughts astray!
The preaching dies upon my ear;
What is the better world—when thy dark eyes are here!

Yet pray! my years have been but few;
And many a wile the tempter weaves,
And many a saint the sinner grieves,
Ere Mercy brings him through!
But O, when Mercy sits serene,
And strives to bend to me,
Pray, that the cloud which comes between
May less resemble thee!
The world, that would my soul beguile,
Tints all its roses with thy smile!
In heaven 't were well to be!
But to desire that blessèd shore—
O Lady! thy dark eyes must first have gone before!

PHILIP PENDLETON COOKE.

1816—1850.

FLORENCE VANE.

I LOVED thee long and dearly,
    Florence Vane;
My life's bright dream and early
    Hath come again;
I renew, in my fond vision,
    My heart's dear pain,
My hopes, and thy derision,
    Florence Vane.

The ruin, lone and hoary,
    The ruin old,
Where thou didst hark my story,
    At even told;
That spot—the hues Elysian
    Of sky and plain—
I treasure in my vision,
    Florence Vane.

Thou wast lovelier than the roses
    In their prime;
Thy voice excelled the closes
    Of sweetest rhyme;
Thy heart was as a river
    Without a main.

Would I had loved thee never,
    Florence Vane!

But, fairest, coldest, wonder!
    Thy glorious clay
Lieth the green sod under,
    Alas, the day!
And it boots not to remember
    Thy disdain;
To quicken love's pale ember,
    Florence Vane.

The lilies of the valley
    By young graves weep,
The daisies love to dally
    Where maidens sleep;
May their bloom, in beauty vying,
    Never wane
Where thine earthly part is lying,
    Florence Vane!

OLIVER WENDELL HOLMES.

1809.

LA GRISETTE.

Ah, Clemence! when I saw thee last
    Trip down the Rue de Seine,
And turning, when thy form had passed,
    I said, "We meet again,"
I dreamed not in that idle glance
    Thy latest image came,
And only left to memory's trance
    A shadow and a name.

The few, strange words my lips had taught
    Thy timid voice to speak;
Their gentler sighs, which often brought
    Fresh roses to thy cheek;
The trailing of thy long, loose hair
    Bent o'er my couch of pain,
All, all returned, more sweet, more fair;
    O, had we met again!

I walked where saint and virgin keep
    The vigil lights of Heaven,
I knew that thou hadst woes to weep,
    And sins to be forgiven;
I watched where Genevieve was laid,
    I knelt by Mary's shrine,

Beside me low, soft voices prayed;
    Alas! but where was thine?

And when the morning sun was bright,
    When wind and wave were calm,
And flamed, in thousand-tinted light,
    The rose of Notre Dame,
I wandered through the haunts of men,
    From Boulevard to Quai,
Till, frowning o'er Saint Etienne,
    The Pantheon's shadow lay.

In vain, in vain; we meet no more,
    Nor dream what fates befall;
And long upon the stranger's shore
    My voice on thee may call,
When years have clothed the line in moss
    That tells thy name and days,
And withered, on thy simple cross,
    The wreaths of Père-la-Chaise!

WINTHROP MACKWORTH PRAED.

1802—1839.

JOSEPHINE.

We did not meet in courtly hall,
    Where Birth and Beauty throng,
Where Luxury holds festival,
    And Wit awakes the song;
We met where darker spirits meet,
    In the home of Sin and Shame,
Where Satan shows his cloven feet,
    And hides his titled name;
And she knew she could not be, Love,
    What once she might have been,
But she was kind to me, Love,
    My pretty Josephine.

We did not part beneath the sky,
    As warmer lovers part,
Where Night conceals the glistening eye,
    But not the throbbing heart;
We parted on that spot of ground
    Where first we laughed at love,
And ever the jests were loud around,
    And the lamps were bright above:
"The heaven is very dark, Love,
    The blast is very keen,
But merrily rides my bark, Love,
    Good night, my Josephine!"

She did not speak of ring or vow,
    But filled the cup with wine,
And took the roses from her brow
    To make a wreath for mine;
And bade me, when the gale should lift
    My light skiff on the wave,
To think as little of the gift,
    As of the hand that gave:
"Go gaily o'er the sea, Love,
    And find your own heart's queen;
And look not back to me, Love,
    Your humble Josephine!"

That garland breathes and blooms no more,
    Past are those idle hours;
I would not, could I choose, restore
    The fondness or the flowers;
Yet oft their withered witchery
    Revives its wonted thrill,
Remembered, not with Passion's sigh,
    But O, remembered still:
And even from your side, Love,
    And even from this scene,
One look is o'er the tide, Love,
    One thought with Josephine!

Alas! your lips are rosier,
    Your eyes of softer blue,
And I have never felt for her,
    As I have felt for you;
Our love was like the snow-flakes,
    Which melt before you pass,
Or the bubble on the wine, which breaks
    Before you lip the glass.
You saw these eyelids wet, Love,
    Which she has never seen;
But let me not forget, Love,
    My poor, poor Josephine!

JAMES RUSSELL LOWELL.

1819.

My Love, I have no fear that thou shouldst die;
Albeit I ask no fairer life than this,
Whose numbering-clock is still thy gentle kiss,
While Time and Peace with hands enlockéd fly;
Yet care I not where in Eternity
We live and love, well knowing that there is
No backward step for those who feel the bliss
Of Faith as their most lofty yearnings high:
Love hath so purified my being's core,
Meseems I scarcely should be startled, even,
To find, some morn, that thou hadst gone before;
Since, with thy love, this knowledge too was given,
Which each calm day doth strengthen more and more,
That they who love are but one step from Heaven.

1841.

I cannot think that thou shouldst pass away,
Whose life to mine is an eternal law,
A piece of nature that can have no flaw,
A new and certain sunrise every day;
But, if thou art to be another ray
About the Sun of Life, and art to live
Free from all of thee that was fugitive,
The debt of love I will more fully pay,
Not downcast with the thought of thee so high,
But rather raised to be a nobler man,

And more divine in my humanity,
As knowing that the waiting eyes which scan
My life are lighted by a purer being,
And ask meek, calm-browed deeds, with it agreeing.

IN ABSENCE.

These rugged, wintry days I scarce could bear,
Did I not know, that, in the early spring,
When wild March winds upon their errands sing,
Thou wouldst return, bursting on this still air,
Like those same winds, when, startled from their lair,
They hunt up violets, and free swift brooks
From icy cares, even as thy clear looks
Bid my heart bloom, and sing, and break all care:
When drops with welcome rain the April day,
My flowers shall find their April in thine eyes,
Save there the rain in dreamy clouds doth stay,
As loath to fall out of those happy skies;
Yet sure, my love, thou art most like to May,
That comes with steady sun when April dies.

I thought our love at full, but I did err;
Joy's wreath drooped o'er mine eyes; I could not see
That sorrow in our happy world must be
Love's deepest spokesman and interpreter;
But, as a mother feels her child first stir
Under her heart, so felt I instantly
Deep in my soul another bond to thee
Thrill with that life we saw depart from her;
O mother of our angel-child! twice dear!
Death knits as well as parts, and still, I wis,
Her tender radiance shall enfold us here,
Even as the light, borne up by inward bliss,
Threads the void glooms of space without a fear,
To print on farthest stars her pitying kiss.

ROBERT BROWNING.

1812.

["*Bells and Pomegranates.*" 1845.]

THE LOST MISTRESS.

All's over, then; does truth sound bitter
    As one at first believes?
Hark! 't is the sparrow's good-night twitter
    About your cottage eaves.

And the leaf-buds on the vine are woolly,
    I noticed that to-day;
One day more bursts them open fully,
    You know the red turns gray.

To-morrow we meet the same then, dearest?
    May I take your hand in mine?
Mere friends are we; well, friends the merest
    Keep much that I'll resign:

For each glance of that eye so bright and black,
    Though I keep with heart's endeavour,
Your voice, when you wish the snowdrops back,
    Though it stays in my soul forever!

Yet I will but say what mere friends say,
    Or only a thought stronger;

I will hold your hand but as long as all may,
    Or so very little longer!

["*Men and Women.*" 1856.]

EVELYN HOPE.

Beautiful Evelyn Hope is dead!
    Sit and watch by her side an hour.
That is her book-shelf, this her bed;
    She plucked that piece of geranium-flower,
Beginning to die, too, in the glass.
    Little has yet been changed, I think:
The shutters are shut, no light may pass,
    Save two long rays through the hinge's chink.

Sixteen years old when she died!
    Perhaps she had scarcely heard my name;
It was not her time to love: beside,
    Her life had many a hope and aim,
Duties enough and little cares;
    And now was quiet, now astir;
Till God's hand beckoned unawares,
    And the sweet white brow is all of her.

Is it too late, then, Evelyn Hope?
    What! your soul was pure and true;
The good stars met in your horoscope,
    Made you of spirit, fire and dew;
And just because I was thrice as old,
    And our paths in the world diverged so wide,
Each was naught to each, must I be told?
    We were fellow mortals, naught beside?

No, indeed! for God above
    Is great to grant, as mighty to make,

And creates the love to reward the love;
    I claim you still, for my own love's sake!
Delayed, it may be, for more lives yet,
    Through worlds I shall traverse, not a few;
Much is to learn and much to forget
    Ere the time be come for taking you.

But the time will come, at last it will,
    When, Evelyn Hope, what meant, I shall say,
In the lower earth, in the years long still,
    That body and soul so pure and gay?
Why your hair was amber, I shall divine,
    And your mouth of your own geranium's red,
And what you would do with me, in fine,
    In the new life come in the old one's stead.

I have lived, I shall say, so much since then,
    Given up myself so many times,
Gained me the gains of various men,
    Ransacked the ages, spoiled the climes;
Yet one thing, one, in my soul's full scope,
    Either I missed or itself missed me;
And I want and find you, Evelyn Hope!
    What is the issue? Let us see!

I loved you, Evelyn, all the while;
    My heart seemed full as it could hold;
There was place and to spare for the frank young smile,
    And the red young mouth and the hair's young gold.
So, hush, I will give you this leaf to keep,
    See, I shut it inside the sweet cold hand.
There, that is our secret! go to sleep;
    You will wake, and remember, and understand.

WALTER SAVAGE LANDOR.

1775.

[" *Works.*" 1846.]

One year ago my path was green,
My footstep light, my brow serene;
Alas! and could it have been so
One year ago?

There is a love that is to last
When the hot days of youth are past:
Such love did a sweet maid bestow
One year ago.

I took a leaflet from her braid
And gave it to another maid.
Love! broken should have been thy bow
One year ago.

I love to hear that men are bound
By your enchanting links of sound:
I love to hear that none rebel
Against your beauty's silent spell.
I know not whether I may bear
To see it all, as well as hear;
And never shall I clearly know
Unless you nod and tell me so.

Have I, this moment, led thee from the beach
Into the boat? now far beyond my reach!
Stand there a little while, and wave once more
That 'kerchief; but may none upon the shore
Dare think the fond salute was meant for him!
Dizzily on the plashing water swim
My heavy eyes, and sometimes can attain
Thy lovely form, which tears bear off again.
In vain have they now ceased; it now is gone
Too far for sight, and leaves me here alone.
O could I hear the creaking of the mast!
I curse it present, I regret it past.

Here, ever since you went abroad,
    If there be change, no change I see,
I only walk our wonted road,
    The road is only walked by me.

Yes; I forgot; a change there is;
    Was it of *that* you bade me tell?
I catch at times, at times I miss,
    The sight, the tone, I know so well.

Only two months since you stood here!
    Two shortest months! then tell me why
Voices are harsher than they were,
    And tears are longer ere they dry.

Little it interests me how
Some insolent usurper now
    Divides your narrow chair;
Little heed I whose hand is placed
(No, nor how far) around your waist,
    Or paddles in your hair.
A time, a time there may have been
(Ah! and there was) when every scene

    Was brightened by your eyes.
And dare you ask what you have done?
My answer, take it, is but one;
    The weak have taught the wise.

The maid I love ne'er thought of me
Amid the scenes of gaiety;
But when her heart or mine sank low,
Ah, then it was no longer so.
From the slant palm she raised her head,
And kissed the cheek whence youth had fled.
Angels! some future day, for this,
Give her as sweet and pure a kiss.

Often I have heard it said
That her lips are ruby-red.
Little heed I what they say,
I have seen as red as they.
Ere she smiled on other men,
Real rubies were they then.

When she kissed me once in play,
Rubies were less bright than they,
And less bright were those which shone
In the palace of the sun.
Will they be as bright again?
Not if kissed by other men.

RICHARD MONCKTON MILNES.

1809.

["*Poems of Many Years.*" 1846.]

The words that trembled on your lips
Were uttered not—I know it well;
The tears that would your eyes eclipse
Were checked and smothered, ere they fell:
The looks and smiles I gained from you
Were little more than others won,
And yet you are not wholly true,
Nor wholly just what you have done.

You know, at least you might have known,
That every little grace you gave,
Your voice's somewhat lowered tone,
Your hand's faint shake, or parting wave,
Your every sympathetic look
At words that chanced your soul to touch,
While reading from some favourite book,
Were much to me—alas, how much!

You might have seen, perhaps you saw,
How all of these were steps of hope
On which I rose, in joy and awe,
Up to my passion's lofty scope;
How after each, a firmer tread
I planted on the slippery ground,

And higher raised my venturous head,
And ever new assurance found.

May be, without a further thought,
It only pleased you thus to please,
And thus to kindly feelings wrought
You measured not the sweet degrees;
Yet, though you hardly understood
Where I was following at your call,
You might—I dare to say you should—
Have thought how far I had to fall.

And thus when fallen, faint, and bruised,
I see another's glad success,
I may have wrongfully accused
Your heart of vulgar fickleness:
But even now, in calm review
Of all I lost, and all I won,
I cannot deem you wholly true,
Nor wholly just what you have done.

EDGAR ALLAN POE.

1811—1849.

TO HELEN.

I SAW thee once, once only, years ago:
I must not say *how* many, but *not* many.
It was a July midnight, and from out
A full-orbed moon, that, like thine own soul, soaring,
Sought a precipitate pathway up through heaven,
There fell a silvery-silken veil of light,
With quietude, and sultriness, and slumber,
Upon the upturned faces of a thousand
Roses that grew in an enchanted garden,
Where no wind dared to stir, unless on tiptoe;
Fell on the upturned faces of these roses,
That gave out, in return for the love-light,
Their odorous souls in an ecstatic death:
Fell on the upturned faces of these roses
That smiled and died in this parterre, enchanted
By thee, and by the poetry of thy presence.
  Clad all in white, upon a violet bank
I saw thee half reclining; while the moon
Fell on the upturned faces of the roses,
And on thine own, upturned, alas, in sorrow!
  Was it not Fate, that, on this July midnight,
Was it not Fate, (whose name is also Sorrow,)
That bade me pause before that garden-gate,
To breathe the incense of those slumbering roses?

No footstep stirred: the hated world all slept,
Save only thee and me. (O, Heaven! O, God!
How my heart beats in coupling those two words!)
Save only thee and me. I paused, I looked,
And in an instant all things disappeared.
(Ah, bear in mind this garden was enchanted!)
The pearly lustre of the moon went out:
The mossy banks and the meandering paths,
The happy flowers and the repining trees,
Were seen no more: the very roses' odours
Died in the arms of the adoring airs.
All, all expired save thee, save less than thou:
Save only the divine light in thine eyes,
Save but the soul in thine uplifted eyes.
I saw but them—they were the world to me.
I saw but them, saw only them for hours,
Saw only them until the moon went down.
What wild heart-histories seemed to lie enwritten
Upon those crystalline, celestial spheres!
How dark a woe! yet how sublime a hope!
How silently serene a sea of pride
How daring an ambition! yet how deep,
How fathomless a capacity for love!
  But now, at length, dear Dian sank from sight,
Into a western couch of thunder-cloud;
And thou, a ghost, amid the entombing trees
Didst glide away. *Only thine eyes remained.*
They *would not* go—they never yet have gone.
Lighting my lonely pathway home that night,
They have not left me (as my hopes have) since.
They follow me—they lead me through the years.
They are my ministers, yet I their slave.
Their office is to illumine and enkindle,
My duty, *to be saved* by their bright light,
And purified in their electric fire,
And sanctified in their elysian fire.
They fill my soul with Beauty (which is Hope,)
And are far up in Heaven the stars I kneel to

In the sad, silent watches of my night;
While even in the meridian glare of day
I see them still—two sweetly scintillant
Venuses, unextinguished by the sun!

TO ONE IN PARADISE.

Thou wast all that to me, love,
For which my soul did pine;
A green isle in the sea, love,
A fountain and a shrine,
All wreathed with fairy fruits and flowers,
And all the flowers were mine.

Ah, dream too bright to last!
Ah, starry Hope! that didst arise
But to be overcast!
A voice from out the Future cries,
"On! On!" but o'er the Past
(Dim gulf!) my spirit hovering lies,
Mute, motionless, aghast!

For, alas! alas! with me
The light of Life is o'er!
"No more—no more—no more"—
(Such language holds the solemn sea
To the sands upon the shore)
Shall bloom the thunder-blasted tree,
Or the stricken eagle soar!

And all my days are trances,
And all my nightly dreams
Are where thy dark eye glances,
And where thy footstep gleams,
In what ethereal dances,
By what eternal streams.

GEORGE MEREDITH.

[*"Poems."* 1851.]

LOVE IN THE VALLEY.

UNDER yonder beech-tree standing on the green sward,
    Couched with her arms behind her little head,
Her knees folded up, and her tresses on her bosom,
    Lies my young love sleeping in the shade.
Had I the heart to slide one arm beneath her!
    Press her dreaming lips as her waist I folded slow,
Waking on the instant she could not but embrace me—
    Ah! would she hold me, and never let me go?

Shy as the squirrel, and wayward as the swallow;
    Swift as the swallow when athwart the western flood
Circleting the surface he meets his mirrored winglets,
    Is that dear one in her maiden bud.
Shy as the squirrel whose nest is in the pine tops;
    Gentle—ah! that she were jealous as the dove!
Full of all the wildness of the woodland creatures,
    Happy in herself is the maiden that I love!

What can have taught her distrust of all I tell her?
    Can she truly doubt me when looking on my brows?
Nature never teaches distrust of tender love-tales,
    What can have taught her distrust of all my vows?
No, she does not doubt me! on a dewy eve-tide
    Whispering together beneath the listening moon,

I prayed till her cheek flushed, implored till she faltered,
Fluttered to my bosom—ah! to fly away so soon!

When her mother tends her before the laughing mirror,
Tying up her laces, looping up her hair,
Often she thinks, "Were this wild thing wedded,
I should have more love, and much less care."
When her mother tends her before the bashful mirror,
Loosening her laces, combing down her curls,
Often she thinks, "Were this wild thing wedded,
I should lose but one for so many boys and girls."

Clambering roses peep into her chamber,
Jasmine and woodbine, breathe sweet, sweet,
White-necked swallows twittering of summer,
Fill her with balm and nested peace from head to feet.
Ah! will the rose-bough see her lying lonely,
When the petals fall, and fierce bloom is on the leaves?
Will the Autumn garners see her still ungathered,
When the fickle swallows forsake the weeping eaves?

Comes a sudden question—Should a strange hand pluck her!
O! what an anguish smites me at the thought,
Should some idle lordling bribe her mind with jewels!
Can such beauty ever thus be bought?
Sometimes the huntsmen prancing down the valley
Eye the village lasses, full of sprightly mirth;
They see as I see, mine is the fairest!
Would she were older, and could read my worth!

Are there not sweet maidens if she still deny me?
Show the bridal Heavens but one bright star?
Wherefore thus then do I chase a shadow,
Clattering one note like a brown eve-jar?
So I rhyme and reason till she darts before me,
Through the milky meadows from flower to flower she flies,
Sunning her sweet palms to shade her dazzled eyelids
From the golden love that looks too eager in her eyes.

When at dawn she wakens, and her fair face gazes
Out on the weather through the window panes,
Beauteous she looks! like a white water lily
Bursting out of bud on the rippled river plains.
When from bed she rises clothed from neck to ankle
In her long nightgown, sweet as boughs of May,
Beauteous she looks! like a tall garden lily,
Pure from the night, and perfect for the day!

Happy, happy time, when the gray star twinkles
Over the fields all fresh with blooming dew;
When the cold-cheeked dawn grows ruddy up the twilight,
And the gold sun wakes and weds her in the blue.
Then when my darling tempts the early breezes,
She the only star that dies not with the dark!
Powerless to speak all the ardour of my passion,
I catch her little hand as we listen to the lark.

Shall the birds in vain then valentine their sweethearts,
Season after season tell a fruitless tale?
Will not the virgin listen to their voices,
Take the honied meaning, wear the bridal veil?
Fears she frosts of winter, fears she the bare branches?
Waits she the garlands of spring for her dower?
Is she a nightingale that will not be nested
Till the April woodland has built her bridal bower?

Then come merry April with all thy birds and beauties!
With thy crescent brows and thy flowery, showery glee;
With thy budding leafage and fresh green pastures;
And may thy lustrous crescent grow a honeymoon for me!
Come merry month of the cuckoo and the violet!
Come weeping Loveliness in all thy blue delight!
Lo! the nest is ready, let me not languish longer!
Bring her to my arms on the first May night.

THOMAS BUCHANAN READ.

1822.

["*Poems.*" 1853.]

A GLIMPSE OF LOVE.

SHE came as comes the summer wind,
A gust of beauty to my heart;
Then swept away, but left behind
Emotions which shall not depart.

Unheralded she came and went,
Like music in the silent night;
Which, when the burthened air is spent
Bequeaths to memory its delight.

Or, like the sudden April bow,
That spans the violet-waking rain:
She bade those blessèd flowers to grow,
Which may not fall or fade again.

Far sweeter than all things most sweet,
And fairer than all things most fair,
She came and passed with footsteps fleet,
A shining wonder in the air!

MATTHEW ARNOLD.

["*Poems.*" 1854.]

EXCUSE.

I TOO have suffered: yet I know
She is not cold, though she seems so:
She is not cold, she is not light;
But our ignoble souls lack might.

She smiles and smiles, and will not sigh,
While we for hopeless passion die;
Yet she could love, those eyes declare,
Were but men nobler than they are.

Eagerly once her gracious ken
Was turned upon the sons of men.
But light the serious visage grew;
She looked, and smiled, and saw them through.

Our petty souls, our struggling wits,
Our laboured puny passion-fits—
Ah! may she scorn them still, till we
Scorn them as bitterly as she!

Yet O, that Fate would let her see
One of some worthier race than we;
One for whose sake she once might prove
How deeply she who scorns can love.

His eyes be like the starry lights,
His voice like sounds of summer nights;
In all his lovely mien let pierce
The magic of the universe.

And she to him will reach her hand,
And gazing in his eyes will stand,
And know her friend, and weep for glee,
And cry—*Long, long I've looked for thee.*

Then she will weep—with smiles, till then,
Coldly she marks the sons of men,
Till then her lovely eyes maintain
Their gay, unwavering, deep disdain.

ROBERT BULWER LYTTON.

"OWEN MEREDITH."

["*Clytemnestra.*" 1854.]

SONG.

IN the warm, black mill-pool winking,
    The first doubtful star shines blue:
And alone here I lie thinking,
    O such happy thoughts of you!

Up the porch the roses clamber,
    And the flowers we sowed last June;
And the casement of your chamber
    Shines between them to the moon.

Look out, love! fling wide your lattice:
    Wind the red rose in your hair,
And the little white clematis
    Which I plucked for you to wear:

Or come down, and let me hear you
    Singing in the scented grass,
Through tall cowslips, nodding near you,
    Just to touch you as you pass.

For, where you pass, the air
    With warm hints of love grows wise:

You—the dew on your dim hair,
    And the smile in your soft eyes!

From the hayfield comes your brother;
    There, your sisters stand together,
Singing clear to one another,
    Through the dark blue summer weather;

And the maid the latch is clinking,
    As she lets her lover through:
But alone, love, I lie thinking
    O such tender thoughts of you!

WILLIAM ALLINGHAM.

[*"The Music Master."* 1855.]

LOVELY MARY DONNELLY.

O, LOVELY Mary Donnelly, it's you I love the best!
If fifty girls were round you I'd hardly see the rest.
Be what it may the time of day, the place be where it will,
Sweet looks of Mary Donnelly, they bloom before me still.

Her eyes like mountain water that's flowing on a rock,
How clear they are, how dark they are! and they give me many a shock.
Red rowans warm in sunshine and wetted with a shower,
Could ne'er express the charming lip that has me in its power.

Her nose is straight and handsome, her eyebrows lifted up,
Her chin is very neat and pert, and smooth like a china cup,
Her hair's the brag of Ireland, so weighty and so fine;
It's rolling down upon her neck, and gathered in a twine.

The dance o' last Whit-Monday night exceeded all before,
No pretty girl for miles about was missing from the floor;
But Mary kept the belt of love, and O but she was gay!
She danced a jig, she sung a song, that took my heart away!

When she stood up for dancing, her steps were so complete,
The music nearly killed itself to listen to her feet;
The fiddler moaned his blindness, he heard her so much praised,
But blessed himself he was n't deaf when once her voice she raised.

And evermore I'm whistling or lilting what you sung,
Your smile is always in my heart, your name beside my tongue;
But you've as many sweethearts as you'd count on both your hands,
And for myself there's not a thumb or little finger stands.

O, you're the flower o' womankind in country or in town;
The higher I exalt you, the lower I'm cast down.
If some great lord should come this way, and see your beauty bright,
And you to be his lady, I'd own it was but right.

O might we live together in a lofty palace hall,
Where joyful music rises, and where scarlet curtains fall!
O might we live together in a cottage mean and small,
With sods of grass the only roof, and mud the only wall!

O lovely Mary Donnelly, your beauty's my distress.
It's far too beauteous to be mine, but I'll never wish it less.
The proudest place would fit your face, and I'm too poor and low;
But blessings be about you, dear, wherever you may go!

Minnehaha.

New York: Derby & Jac[illegible]

HENRY WADSWORTH LONGFELLOW.

1807.

[" *The Song of Hiawatha.*" 1855.]

HIAWATHA'S WOOING.

At the doorway of his wigwam
Sat the ancient Arrow-maker,
In the land of the Dacotahs,
Making arrow-heads of jasper,
Arrow-heads of chalcedony.
At his side, in all her beauty,
Sat the lovely Minnehaha,
Sat his daughter, Laughing Water,
Plaiting mats of flags and rushes;
Of the past the old man's thoughts were,
And the maiden's of the future.
He was thinking, as he sat there,
Of the days when with such arrows
He had struck the deer and bison,
On the Muskoday, the meadow;
Shot the wild goose, flying southward,
On the wing, the clamorous Wawa;
Thinking of the great war-parties,
How they came to buy his arrows,
Could not fight without his arrows.
Ah, no more such noble warriors
Could be found on earth as they were;

Now the men were all like women,
Only used their tongues for weapons!
  She was thinking of a hunter,
From another tribe and country,
Young and tall and very handsome,
Who, one morning, in the Spring-time,
Came to buy her father's arrows,
Sat and rested in the wigwam,
Lingered long about the doorway,
Looking back as he departed.
She had heard her father praise him,
Praise his courage and his wisdom;
Would he come again for arrows
To the Falls of Minnehaha?
On the mat her hands lay idle,
And her eyes were very dreamy.
  Through their thoughts they heard a footstep,
Heard a rustling in the branches,
And with glowing cheek and forehead,
With the deer upon his shoulders,
Suddenly from out the woodlands
Hiawatha stood before them.
  Straight the ancient Arrow-maker
Looked up gravely from his labor,
Laid aside the unfinished arrow,
Bade him enter at the doorway,
Saying, as he rose to meet him,
"Hiawatha, you are welcome!"
  At the feet of Laughing Water
Hiawatha laid his burden,
Threw the red deer from his shoulders;
And the maiden looked up at him,
Looked up from her mat of rushes,
Said with gentle look and accent,
"You are welcome, Hiawatha!"
  Very spacious was the wigwam,
Made of deer-skin dressed and whitened,
With the Gods of the Dacotahs

Drawn and painted on its curtains,
And so tall the doorway, hardly
Hiawatha stooped to enter,
Hardly touched his eagle-feathers
As he entered at the doorway.
  Then uprose the Laughing Water,
From the ground fair Minnehaha,
Laid aside her mat unfinished,
Brought forth food and set before them,
Water brought them from the brooklet,
Gave them food in earthen vessels,
Gave them drink in bowls of bass-wood,
Listened while the guest was speaking,
Listened while her father answered,
But not once her lips she opened,
Not a single word she uttered.
  Yes, as in a dream she listened
To the words of Hiawatha,
As he talked of old Nokomis,
Who had nursed him in his childhood,
As he told of his companions,
Chibiabos, the musician,
And the very strong man, Kwasind,
And of happiness and plenty
In the land of the Ojibways,
In the pleasant land and peaceful.
  "After many years of warfare,
Many years of strife and bloodshed,
There is peace between the Ojibways
And the tribe of the Dacotahs."
Thus continued Hiawatha,
And then added, speaking slowly,
"That this peace may last for ever,
And our hands be clasped more closely,
And our hearts be more united,
Give me as my wife this maiden,
Minnehaha, Laughing Water,
Loveliest of Dacotah women!"

And the ancient Arrow-maker
Paused a moment ere he answered,
Smoked a little while in silence,
Looked at Hiawatha proudly,
Fondly looked at Laughing Water,
And made answer very gravely:
"Yes, if Minnehaha wishes;
Let your heart speak, Minnehaha!"
And the lovely Laughing Water
Seemed more lovely, as she stood there,
Neither willing nor reluctant,
As she went to Hiawatha,
Softly took the seat beside him,
While she said, and blushed to say it,
"I will follow you, my husband!"
This was Hiawatha's wooing!
Thus it was he won the daughter
Of the ancient Arrow-maker,
In the land of the Dacotahs!
From the wigwam he departed,
Leading with him Laughing Water;
Hand in hand they went together,
Through the woodland and the meadow,
Left the old man standing lonely
At the doorway of his wigwam,
Heard the Falls of Minnehaha
Calling to them from the distance,
Crying to them from afar off,
"Fare thee well, O Minnehaha!"

BAYARD TAYLOR.

1825.

—•◆•—

[*"Poems of the Orient."* 1855.]

THE MYSTERY.

Thou art not dead; thou art not gone to dust;
No line of all thy loveliness shall fall
To formless ruin, smote by Time, and thrust
Into the solemn gulf that covers all.

Thou canst not wholly perish, though the sod
Sink with its violets closer to thy breast;
Though by the feet of generations trod,
The head-stone crumbles from thy place of rest.

The marvel of thy beauty cannot die;
The sweetness of thy presence shall not fade;
Earth gave not all the glory of thine eye;
Death may not keep what Death has never made.

It was not thine, that forehead strange and cold,
Nor those dumb lips, they hid beneath the snow;
Thy heart would throb beneath that passive fold,
Thy hands for me that stony clasp forego.

But thou hadst gone—gone from the dreary land,
Gone from the storms let loose on every hill,

Lured by the sweet persuasion of a hand
    Which leads thee somewhere in the distance still.

Where'er thou art, I know thou wearest yet
    The same bewildering beauty, sanctified
By calmer joy, and touched with soft regret
    For him who seeks, but cannot reach thy side.

I keep for thee the living love of old,
    And seek thy place in Nature, as a child
Whose hand is parted from his playmate's hold,
    Wanders and cries along a lonesome wild.

When, in the watches of my heart, I hear
    The messages of purer life, and know
The footsteps of thy spirit lingering near,
    The darkness hides the way that I should go.

Canst thou not bid the empty realms restore
    That form, the symbol of thy heavenly part?
Or on the fields of barren silence pour
    That voice, the perfect music of thy heart?

O once, once bending to these widowed lips,
    Take back the tender warmth of life from me;
Or let thy kisses cloud with swift eclipse
    The light of mine, and give me death with thee!

GEORGE HENRY BOKER.

1823.

[" *Plays and Poems.*" 1856.]

NAY, not to thee, to nature will I tie
The gathered blame of every pettish mood;
And when thou frown'st, I'll frown upon the wood,
Saying, "How wide its gloomy shadows lie!"
Or, gazing straight into the day's bright eye,
Predict ere night a fatal second flood;
Or vow the poet's sullen solitude
Has changed my vision to a darksome dye.
But when thou smil'st, I will not look above,
To wood or sky; my hand I will not lay
Upon the temple of my sacred love,
To blame its living fires with base decay;
But whisper to thee, as I nearer move,
"Love, thou dost add another light to day!"

Where lags my mistress while the drowsy year
Wakes into Spring? Lo! Winter sweeps away
His snowy skirts, and leaves the landscape gay
With early verdure; and there's merry cheer
Among the violets, where the sun lies clear
On the south hill-sides; and at break of day
I heard the blue-bird busy at my ear;
And swallows shape their nests of matted clay

Along the eaves, or dip their narrow wings
Into the mists of evening. All the earth
Stirs with the wonder of a coming birth,
And all the air with feathery music rings.
Spring, it would crown thee with transcendent worth,
To bring my love among thy beauteous things.

Your love to me appears in doubtful signs,
Vague words, shy looks, that never touch the heart;
But to the brain a scanty hint impart
As to whose side your dear regard inclines:
Thence, forced by reason through the narrow lines
That mark and limit the logician's art,
Catching from thought to thought, my mind combines
In one idea the mystic things you start,
And coldly utters to my heart, that swells
With tardy rapture, "It is thee she loves!"
Alas! alas! that reason only proves
A fact your cautious action never tells,
That I must reach my joy by slow removes,
And guess at love as at the oracles.

I do assure thee, love, each kiss of thine
Adds to my stature, makes me more a man,
Lightens my care, and draws the bitter wine
That I was drugged with, while my nature ran
Its slavish course. For didst thou not untwine
My cunning fetters? break the odious ban,
That quite debased me? free this heart of mine
And deck my chains with roses? While I can
I'll chant thy praises, till the world shall ring
With thy great glory; and the heaping store
Of future honours, for the songs I sing,
Shall miss thy poet, at thy feet to pour
A juster tribute, as the gracious spring
Of my abundance. Kiss me, then, once more.

I will not blazon forth thy sacred name,
Holding thee up for wonder to the mood
Of those poor fools whose darts of malice strewed
Thy path of life, and might thy grave defame;
I will but hint it dimly. Love's pure flame
Will shine as brightly, though the spicy wood
Whereon it feeds be little understood;
For, to all light man's reverence is the same.
And if, in coming time, some lover weep
Over the sorrows of my mournful line,
Some wretch whose fortune has been sad as mine,
Wondering, meanwhile, what gentle name may sleep
Under my phrase, the homage shall be thine,
Though my sealed lips thy mystic title keep.

All the world's malice, all the spite of fate,
Cannot undo the rapture of the past.
I, like a victor, hold these glories fast;
And here defy the envious powers, that wait
Upon the crumbling fortunes of our state,
To snatch this myrtle chaplet, or to blast
Its smallest leaf. Thus to the wind I cast
The poet's laurel, and before their date
Summon the direst terrors of my doom.
For, with this myrtle symbol of my love,
I reign exultant, and am fixed above
The petty fates that other joys consume.
As on a flowery path, through life I'll move,
As through an arch of triumph, pass the tomb.

JOHN GREENLEAF WHITTIER.

1808.

["*The Panorama, and other Poems.*" 1856.]

MAUD MULLER.

Maud Muller, on a summer's day,
Raked the meadow sweet with hay.

Beneath her torn hat glowed the wealth
Of simple beauty and rustic health.

Singing, she wrought, and her merry glee
The mock-bird echoed from his tree.

But, when she glanced to the far-off town,
White from its hill-slope looking down,

The sweet song died, and a vague unrest
And a nameless longing filled her breast;

A wish, that she hardly dared to own,
For something better than she had known.

The Judge rode slowly down the lane,
Smoothing his horse's chestnut mane.

He drew his bridle in the shade
Of the apple-trees, to greet the maid,

And ask a draught from the spring that flowed
Through the meadow across the road.

She stooped where the cool spring bubbled up,
And filled for him her small tin cup,

And blushed as she gave it, looking down
On her feet so bare, and her tattered gown.

"Thanks!" said the Judge, "a sweeter draught
From a fairer hand was never quaffed."

He spoke of the grass and flowers and trees,
Of the singing birds and the humming bees;

Then talked of the haying, and wondered whether
The cloud in the west would bring foul weather.

And Maud forgot her brier-torn gown,
And her graceful ankles bare and brown;

And listened, while a pleased surprise
Looked from her long-lashed hazel eyes.

At last, like one who for delay
Seeks a vain excuse, he rode away.

Maud Muller looked and sighed: "Ah, me!
That I the Judge's bride might be!

"He would dress me up in silks so fine,
And praise and toast me at his wine.

"My father should wear a broadcloth coat;
My brother should sail a painted boat.

"I'd dress my mother so grand and gay,
And the baby should have a new toy each day.

"And I'd feed the hungry and clothe the poor,
And all should bless me who left our door."

The Judge looked back as he climbed the hill,
And saw Maud Muller standing still.

"A form more fair, a face more sweet
Ne'er hath it been my lot to meet.

"And her modest answer and graceful air
Show her wise and good as she is fair.

"Would she were mine, and I to-day,
Like her, a harvester of hay:

"No doubtful balance of rights and wrongs,
Nor weary lawyers with endless tongues,

"But low of cattle and song of birds,
And health and quiet and loving words."

But he thought of his sisters proud and cold,
And his mother vain of her rank and gold.

So, closing his heart, the Judge rode on,
And Maud was left in the field alone.

But the lawyers smiled that afternoon,
When he hummed in court an old love-tune;

And the young girl mused beside the well,
Till the rain on the unraked clover fell.

He wedded a wife of richest dower,
Who lived for fashion, as he for power.

Yet oft, in his marble hearth's bright glow,
He watched a picture come and go:

And sweet Maud Muller's hazel eyes
Looked out in their innocent surprise.

Oft, when the wine in his glass was red,
He longed for the wayside well instead;

And closed his eyes on his garnished rooms,
To dream of meadows and clover-blooms.

And the proud man sighed, with a secret pain:
"Ah, that I were free again!

"Free as when I rode that day,
Where the barefoot maiden raked her hay."

She wedded a man unlearned and poor,
And many children played round her door.

But care and sorrow, and childbirth pain,
Left their traces on heart and brain.

And oft, when the summer sun shone hot
On the new-mown hay in the meadow lot,

And she heard the little spring brook fall
Over the roadside, through the wall,

In the shade of the apple-tree again
She saw a rider draw his rein.

And, gazing down with timid grace,
She felt his pleased eyes read her face.

Sometimes her narrow kitchen walls
Stretched away into stately halls;

The weary wheel to a spinnet turned,
The tallow candle an astral burned,

And for him who sat by the chimney lug,
Dozing and grumbling o'er pipe and mug,

A manly form at her side she saw,
And joy was duty and love was law.

Then she took up her burden of life again,
Saying only, "It might have been."

Alas for maiden, alas for Judge,
For rich repiner and household drudge!

God pity them both! and pity us all,
Who vainly the dreams of youth recall.

For of all sad words of tongue or pen,
The saddest are these: "It might have been!"

Ah, well! for us all some sweet hope lies
Deeply buried from human eyes;

And, in the hereafter, angels may
Roll the stone from its grave away!

COVENTRY PATMORE.

["*The Angel in the House.*" 1856.]

THE ESPOUSALS.

BY THE SEA.

I, WHILE the shop-girl fitted on
The sand-shoes, looked where, down the bay,
The sea glowed with a shrouded sun.
"I'm ready, Felix; will you pay?"
That was my first expense for this
Sweet stranger whom I called my Wife:
How light the touches are that kiss
The music from the chords of life!

Her feet, by half a mile of sea,
In spotless sand, left shapely prints;
Then, from the beach, she loaded me
With agate-stones, which turned out flints;
And, after that, we took a boat:
She wished to see the ships-of-war,
At anchor, each a lazy mote
Dotting the brilliance, miles from shore.

A vigorous breeze the canvas filled,
Lifting us o'er the bright-ridged gulf,
And every lurch my darling thrilled
With light fear smiling at itself:

And, dashing past the Arrogant,
    Asleep upon the restless wave
After its cruise in the Levant,
    We reached the Wolf; and signal gave
For help to board: with caution meet,
    My bride was placed within the chair,
The red flag wrapped about her feet,
    And so swung laughing through the air.

"Look, Love," she said, "there's Frederick Graham,
    My Cousin, whom you met, you know."
And, seeing us, the brave man came,
    And made his frank and courteous bow,
And gave my hand a sailor's shake,
    And said, "You asked me to the Hurst:
I never thought my luck would make
    You and your wife my guests the first."
And Honor, cruel, "Nor did we:
    Have you not lately changed your ship?"
"Yes: I'm commander, now," said he,
    With a slight quiver of the lip.

We saw the vessel, shown with pride;
    Took luncheon; I must eat his salt!
Parting he said, (I think my bride
    Found him unselfish to a fault,)
His wish he saw had come to pass,
    (And so, indeed, her face expressed,)
That that should be, whate'er it was,
    Which made his Cousin happiest.
We left him looking from above,
    Rich bankrupt! for he could afford
To say most proudly that his love
    Was virtue and its own reward.
But others loved as well as he,
    (Thought I, half-angered,) and, if fate,
Unfair, had only fashioned me
    As hapless, I had been as great.

As souls, ambitious, but low-born,
If greatly raised by luck or wit,
All pride of place will proudly scorn,
And live as they 'd been used to it,
So we two wore our strange estate:
Familiar, unaffected, free,
We talked, until the dusk grew late,
Of this and that; but, after tea,
As doubtful if a lot so sweet
As our's was our's in very sooth,
Like children, to promote conceit,
We feigned that it was not the truth;
And she assumed the maiden coy,
And I adored remorseless charms,
And then we clapped our hands for joy,
And ran into each other's arms.

THOMAS BAILEY ALDRICH.

1836.

["*The Ballad of Babie Bell.*" 1859.]

PALABRAS CARIÑOSAS.

Good night! I have to say good night
To such a host of peerless things!
Good night unto that snowy hand,
All queenly with its weight of rings!
Good night to fond delicious eyes,
Good night to chestnut braids of hair,
Good night unto the perfect mouth,
And all the sweetness nestled there!
    The snowy hand detains me, then
    I'll have to say good night again!

But there will come a time, my love,
When, if I read our stars aright,
I shall not linger by this porch
With my adieus. Till then, good night!
You wish the time were now? and I.
You do not blush to wish it so?
You would have blushed yourself to death
To own so much a year ago!
    What, both these snowy hands! ah, then
    I'll have to say good night again!

www.ingramcontent.com/pod-product-compliance
Lightning Source LLC
LaVergne TN
LVHW021313110826
845150LV00003B/560